PODBORSKI!

Podborski!

STEVE PODBORSKI WITH GERALD DONALDSON

Foreword by John Ritchie

M&S

Canadian Cataloguing in Publication Data

Podborski, Steve, 1957–
Podborski

ISBN 0-7710-7025-X

1. Podborski, Steve, 1957–   . 2. Skiers –
Canada – Biography. I. Donaldson, Gerald.
II. Title.

GV854.2.P63A3 1987   796.93′092′4
C87-094534-3

Printed and bound in Canada

McClelland and Stewart
The Canadian Publishers
481 University Avenue
Toronto, Ontario
M5G 2E9

Contents

Foreword 7

Acknowledgements 8

1. Downhill Racer 9

2. Ski Weekends 14

3. Born to Ski 26

4. The Crazy Canucks 41

5. Ski Bums 56

6. Eating My Liver 67

7. Uphill All the Way 88

8. On the Loud Pedal 101

9. Skiing My Buns Off 120

10. On Top of the World 137

11. Fringe Benefits 154

12. Peaks and Valleys 163

13. Après Ski 176

14. Pod's Perspective 189

15. Statistics 202

*For my family
and for the Crazy Canucks*

Foreword

When you reach the top of the mountain, as the Zen saying goes, keep on climbing.

I coached Steve Podborski for seven years. And for seven years I marvelled as Steve stood on the top of mountains around the world, pushed out of the starting gate, and kept on climbing.

He put his soul into his sport. He wanted to win. Badly. He would *will* it to happen. You could see it when he put on his game face. The face of mastery.

We all know that success takes character, discipline, and mental toughness. What we all don't know about success is that it takes *attitude*. The right attitude. The "Pod" in Podborski.

He had to surrender. To his coach and to the demands of his discipline. He had to surrender to competence. Steve would renounce his level of proficiency and go through the pain that comes when one keeps on learning.

I remember Pod once told me that losing hurt most. He knew the pain of injury; he'd been there. But in the starting gate he was more afraid of losing than falling.

Steve taught himself to handle fear. Yet he realized that fearlessness did not mean giving up his own intelligence – or his ability to question what the hell he was doing as he went under the knife for a knee operation . . . one more time.

Pod had trouble coping with his superstar status at times. He taught me what a superstar is: someone who spends much less time thinking about us than we do about them. He taught me many things and made me wonder sometimes, as did the other Crazy Canucks, who was coaching whom.

7

Enjoy his book . . . the life of this outstanding Canadian and World Champion.

JOHN RITCHIE
Former Head Coach of the men's Canadian National Alpine Ski Team.

Acknowledgements

It would fill another book to pay tribute to all the people who helped me in my career. But I would like to mention some of them collectively, beginning with my coaches who contributed so much more than people generally realize. Thanks to the Canadian Ski Association for providing the system for my sport and thanks also to everyone I skied with over the years, rivals included, for their companionship and/or competition. I am grateful to the doctors, surgeons, nurses, chiropractors, and physiotherapy people who helped put me together again when I fell apart. Thanks to everybody at the Craigleith Ski Club where it all started. Their support was inspirational as was that of the thousands of ski-racing fans, in Canada and abroad, who encouraged me over the years. A special thanks to all my good friends who were always there whether I won or lost . . . and finally, I would like to thank Gerald Donaldson for helping me with this book.

STEVE PODBORSKI

1. Downhill Racer

I stand in the darkness of the start hut perched on top of a mountain in Austria. Outside, in brilliant sunshine, two miles of treacherous ice and snow plummet spectacularly down into the picturesque Tyrolean village far below. In just a few minutes I'll be down there – in Kitzbühel – if I survive the Hahnenkamm, the most difficult and dangerous Downhill race in the world.

My heart pounds. I feel the blood surging through my veins. I breathe deeply and rhythmically. Gripping my poles to keep my hands from shaking, I stand in a line of ski racers in brightly coloured skintight suits. Barely restrained chaos surrounds us in the hut. Walkie-talkie radios hiss and crackle between bursts of excited voices babbling in several languages. Equipment technicians fuss over last-minute adjustments to boots, bindings, and skis. Team masseurs scramble among us, slapping thigh and leg muscles into readiness. Harassed race officials gesticulate and scurry about, trying to keep us on schedule.

Suddenly, the racer in front of me leaps from the shadows of the hut into the brightness of space and disappears. About a minute and a half to go!

My pulse quickens. Inside my helmet I can hear my heart thumping at nearly three times its normal rate. I shift my weight as Toulouse, my masseur, moves to my other leg. He chatters about something, but I don't reply and he falls silent. Hans, my ski rep, stands up from my skis, grips my arm, mutters "Good Luck," and moves away. I nod, but continue looking straight ahead out over the Alpine valley. Now I'm just a ski length away from the timing wand that separates me from the course . . . from the rest of my life.

"One minute." The Starter turns and announces the remaining time to me in German. I nod acknowledgement.

Toulouse rubs my lower back and mumbles something in my ear. The radios blare out reports of another racer crossing the finish line . . . or crashing off the course. I hear only the pounding of my blood. In my mind I'm running down the hill, feeling the tensions of muscles and ligaments as I plunge onward, making every turn perfectly. I *will* my body to do it now – to win! – not to fall. I've won Kitzbühel before. I've also been badly hurt. But I can win again today. I force away the awful memories, the sickening feeling of tearing ligaments, the gut-wrenching pain, and the terrible hopelessness and despair. Not this time. Never again. I finish my perfect mental run and start over, repeating a single phrase: "Gotta go for it – Gotta go for it – Gotta go for it" . . . .

"Thirty seconds."

Toulouse gives me a final pat on the butt and says, "Good Luck." I nod and try to swallow. My mouth is dry. I slide forward into the gate. "Good Luck." The Starter says it too, a tradition between him and me. No one else. I blink in the dazzling sunlight. My pupils contract as I see the course for the first time today. The TV camera swings around and zooms in on my bright gold suit and black helmet with the red maple leaf on it.

The huge crowd below the start area focuses on me, screaming, yelling, and jumping up and down in anticipation. I shut out the wall of noise and movement. A girl standing behind the start clock weeps with emotion. I ignore her. I concentrate hard with every fibre of my being, analysing and assessing the conditions. In my mind's eye I see only the snow, feel the cold air, hear the wind. "Gotta go for it – Gotta go for it – Gotta go for it" . . . .

"Ten seconds."

Carefully, methodically, I lift my poles over the timing wand in the starting gate and plant them in the snow. They can't stick or slip when I push off. My heart slams in my chest. My body is awash in adrenalin. My mind is stripped of all conscious thought. The last sound I hear is the final countdown of the electronic beeper: *beep – beep – beep –*

I spring forward, out of the darkness of the hut and into the light of the day – my boots snapping open the timing wand to start the seconds ticking off my race time. Nothing matters now but speed – and survival. "*Gotta go for it! – Gotta go for it!* – GO!"

I explode down the hill, accelerating wildly. My wood-and-fibreglass skis bang and clatter crazily over the rock-hard ice through the first two gates. Right – left and I'm airborne over Mausfalle. One hundred feet later, I smack down onto the course again and readjust my line instinctively. It's a screamer today! The sun has warmed the snow and Hans has really nailed the wax!

I rocket through the compression at the bottom of Mausfalle at 75 miles an hour. My thighs burn from absorbing the tremendous G-forces. The wind howls in my helmet as I carve around the sweeping left-hand turn. I dig in the razor-sharp edges of my skis . . . just enough, not too much, or I'll slow down. "Go for it – Go for it – Go for it!"

I shoot up onto the bank on the left, then plunge into the 180-degree right-hand fallaway. My skis send up a roostertail of snow and ice chips as I hurtle toward the dreaded Steilhang, the toughest turn in ski racing. "Go! – Go! – Go!"

Over a hump at 70 miles an hour. Dive onto the Steilhang. The gate whips past on my left. My skis rattle and slap violently across the glare ice that clings to the sheer rock face. The vibration blurs my vision. I slam on the edge of my inside ski for the fallaway right. I *will* my skis to change direction: "Turn!"

I curse and yell. It's steep – too steep! "Turn! – Harder! – *Turn!!*" Over the first roller and my skis go light. Drop lower. Bounce off the last roller. Thump down onto the road heading for the safety net in front of the Bamboo Curtain at 55 miles an hour. I've hit it before and it hurts. "*Turn!*"

I dig in, turning as hard as possible. The net looms closer. My projected line heads straight for it. I *think* I can make it safely by. Fight against centrifugal force. Must not panic or I'll lose control and hit the Curtain for sure. I struggle for more grip. Violent contact with the net seems inevitable. *I will not give up!* – "TURN!!!"

My ski runs over the edge of the net! I pull it in and drop into my tuck. I crouch down as low as possible to regain momentum. Nothing counts but speed. I'm down to 50 miles an hour. My average has to be nearly 70 miles an hour to win. There are other slow sections to come. Tuck – Tuck – Tuck. Faster – Faster – *Faster!*

11

I slash through the shadowy forest, along the road, only 30 feet wide and bordered by threatening fences. Clearings are momentary flashes of light in my consciousness. My world is the track. I focus on the crystals of snow. I feel the ruts beneath me. I concentrate on keeping my skis as flat as possible.

I hit the Alte Schneise at 80 miles an hour. I careen over the very rough sidehill. My legs judder up and down like a jackhammer. The wind wails like a banshee in my ears. The sunlight flickers in my eyes like a berserk strobe light. I blitz through the Larchenschuss and tuck harder as the Hahnenkamm tries to shake me off. I bear down. My whole body aches with effort. I'm just over half way down the hill . . . .

Left – right, over the Hausbergkante cliff and into the air, soaring like a ski jumper. In mid-air, I switch edges to prepare for landing on the sidehill swinging left. I crash down at 60 miles an hour, turning. I'm close enough to the fence to hit it with my pole. Involuntarily, I growl deep in my throat. I don't think about the day I blew my knee here in 1976. Just "Go for it – Go for it – *Go for it!*"

I rocket across the sidehill approaching the fastest part of the run. The course bucks like a wild mustang beneath me. The ice tries to knock my skis off. The edge of the Zeilhang flies toward me at 75 miles an hour. I'm exhausted but must concentrate on hitting the right spot on the launching pad. I take off into orbit. My air speed accelerates as I fly for over 130 feet, bang down, and ram through the compression at the bottom.

I hold my tuck and skip and dance over the frozen terrain – a human projectile now travelling at 90 miles an hour. The snow is sucked up in the turbulence of my wake like the contrail of a jet aircraft. My velocity is such that I steer with my helmet, turning my head a fraction to make adjustments in my line. Only a few hundred feet to go – a handful of seconds. I tuck even harder, willing another hundredth of a second off my time. "*Go – Go!*"

My mind and body are numb. Instinct and reflexes still work. I reach out at the finish line to cut the electronic beam with my hand. I've worked it out and know it will save .05 of a second. People have won Kitzbühel by that margin . . . . I flash under the banners and stand up. The wind tears at me, slowing me down. With my last dregs of energy I throw my skis sideways. I skid to a halt in a shower of snow.

My body sags and I support myself on my poles. Panting, I lift up my goggles, hang my head, and take deep gulps of the fresh Alpine air. It seems I've spent a lifetime racing down Kitzbühel. And I have. But this time it has taken me less than two minutes.

Gradually, the sensations of my run fade. My heartbeat recedes. I feel the chill of the air on my skin. I smell the stale saliva on my face mask. The noise of the wind is gone, replaced by an ear-splitting roar as the finish-line crowd goes mad. I look up at the scoreboard . . . .

2. Ski Weekends

The idea of using skis to travel over snow is as old as the hills, though making a sport of it is relatively recent. The first competitive events, ski jumping and cross-country racing, were popular in Scandinavia in the late 19th century. About the same time, adventurous travellers began to see the European Alps as a potential source of challenge and pleasure. They clambered around on the peaks, conquered the Matterhorn and Mont Blanc, admired the spectacular scenery for a while, then looked for further amusement.

They discovered it was quite thrilling to whiz down a mountainside on a toboggan or bob sled, and even more so when somebody tried it on barrel staves strapped to his feet. Competitive natures came to the fore, stopwatches came into play, and Alpine ski racing began to take shape. In 1905, a Downhill ski race was first organized at the village of Kitzbühel in the Austrian Tyrol. In 1922, some British tourists invented the Slalom, a slower and safer variation on the Downhill theme with more gates for the skier to negotiate.

Winter resorts like Wengen in Switzerland began to stage races to attract crowds and, in 1930, Alpine ski-racing competition became an officially recognized form of sport under the International Ski Federation (FIS). In 1938, when the annual World Championships were first held, in Engelberg, Switzerland, teams represented their countries and international rivalries began. The addition of ski racing to the Winter Olympics drew more attention to the sport and the first skiing heroes came from Austria, Switzerland, France, Italy, Germany, and, to a lesser extent, the Scandanavian countries. Giant Slalom races began (enlarged versions of the

Slalom), but the glamour event was still plunging down the mountain as fast as possible in the Downhill.

By the 1960s, television had created opportunities to make Alpine ski racing an international spectator sport like Formula One motor racing for the World Championship of drivers. The World Cup of ski racing began in the 1966-67 season, master-minded by French sports journalist Serge Lang who patterned it after the Formula One series. Each year, a number of FIS-sanctioned races in different countries counted for World Cup points and international champions were declared. A separate series was held for men and women and Jean Claude Killy of France and Nancy Greene of Canada became the first World Cup Champions, both winning their titles again in 1967-68.

Nancy Greene and Killy scored points in the three Alpine disciplines of Slalom, Grand Slalom, and Downhill, to become overall World Cup Champions. But, increasingly, skiers became specialists, concentrating on one type of racing, either the Slalom events or the Downhill, and World Cup Champions were declared in each category. There is still an overall World Cup Champion and a new event, Super GS, has been added to the disciplines. And there are two separate World Cup tours for devotees of each faction. While all the various forms of ski racing have their exponents and enthusiasts, Downhill is still tops in terms of thrills, spills, chills . . . and popular appeal.

Since 1967, the World Cup tour, or White Circus as it's sometimes called, has visited over 120 ski resorts in about 15 countries. From Europe, the series expanded to North America, South America, and Japan. Ski racing is hugely popular in many countries and the most popular of all in Alpine Europe, where the front-runners are treated as superstars. At Kitzbühel, the most famous Downhill race, over 35,000 spectators crowd the Hahnenkamm hill, 25 television networks cover the event, and over 500 journalists send the news around the world.

Various point-scoring formulae were used over the years, with points being awarded to finishers as far down in the results as 25th. Since 1980, the fastest 15 skiers are allocated points on the basis of 25 for finishing first, 20 points for second, 15 for third, 12 for fourth, and so on down to one point for the 15th placed skier in a race. In the Downhill, up to a dozen races are held in a season, but the World Cup is awarded to the skier who accumulates the highest point total in five races.

Less than 50 skiers were world-ranked when the World Cup began in 1967; nowadays there are about 120. Skiers are ranked, or seeded, according to their previous season's finishing position in the points standings. The winners usually come from the first seed, the top 15 racers who enjoy a position of privilege, and they start before the rank and file in each race, and earn more prestige and more money.

The money in ski racing comes mainly from equipment manufacturers who sponsor teams and individual racers to cash in on the publicity. Ski companies, in particular, invest heavily in the sport and supply representatives (or "reps") who travel with the teams and look after the equipment. Governments, and the tourist bureaus of some Alpine nations, help support their national teams financially. To comply with the "amateur" rules of the International Olympic Committee, money earned by skiers is placed in trust funds. Working within the framework of the FIS, the various national federations look after the administration of the teams, and take a percentage of the skiers' earnings.

In Canada, the National Alpine Ski Team is organized by the Canadian Ski Association. The CSA operates a farm system for younger skiers who come up through the ranks, the best of them eventually making it to the World Cup level as members of Canadian teams competing in the various ski disciplines. After Nancy Greene's brilliant achievements in the first two years of the World Cup, no Canadians won for nearly ten years. It was a long uphill struggle until the "Crazy Canucks" era. Then, for several seasons, we were among the best ski racers in the world, and I was fortunate enough to become the World Cup Downhill Champion.

I took part in over 80 World Cup Downhill races and, while the routine was similar for each one, every race was a new adventure. The race ritual began with setting up camp in the hotel room, our home for the week in whichever country we found ourselves. We'd unpack our bags, and it looked as if a clothing bomb had gone off. Then we tended to sneak a peak at the hill. There was always a certain amount of underlying apprehension in the air, particularly at a place like Kitzbühel. There were worries about course conditions: was it going to be soft, or icy, easier or harder than before?

16

And so on. But you didn't want to seem overly intimidated, so you just sidled over to the window and glanced casually over your shoulder when you thought no one was looking. It was important not to show chinks in your macho male armour.

The first night would end with a team meeting where the schedules were presented and we'd plan our moves for the days prior to race day – which was always Saturday, unless there was a double-header or bad weather forced a postponement. We sorted out the logistics of where to do our free skiing or private practice, how to get our various pairs of skis (usually three per person) up and down the hills, which lifts to use, and so on. Then we focused on Wednesday, Thursday, and Friday, which were set aside by the organizers for official inspection and training.

Besichtigun, inspection in German, usually began at 10 o'clock in the morning and lasted for an hour. Before that, we did our daily exercises and maybe some free skiing, then joined the crowd at the start area to wait for the hill to open up. There would be 60 to 80 racers, three to five coaches and other personnel per team, assorted equipment reps and officials – all milling around, laughing, joking, and chattering away. We might kick around the previous race with rival skiers, congratulate or commiserate as the situation warranted, and talk about the weather and likely course conditions. Then, inspection began and suddenly it was all business.

We'd all jump onto the hill en masse, coaches included, and sideslip down the course. Moving very slowly sideways and stopping frequently, we tried to commit every significant factor to memory. You'd take mental photo images of the turns, sizing up their angles, and trying to find the fastest line through them. You'd visualize your approach and plan how to handle an abrupt fallaway or terrain change that will alter your line depending on whether it's curved, scooped, or dished. You'd bore into the snow with your eyes because, under close observation, you can see snow conditions change with every foot. You'd feel the snow under your skis and try to imprint that impression on your brain. The Inuit are supposed to have over 40 words for snow, each of them describing a different type. There must be 40 kinds of snow in ski racing and we used words like grippy or slidy and tried to decide what kind of traction and balance it would translate into on a run.

Every little thing matters on a Downhill run and you not only have to see it during inspection, you have to memorize two miles of it in one hour. In many ways, races are won during inspection and the training runs, so doing your homework is vital – with the proviso that your final exam, the race, will be conducted at 70 to 80 miles an hour. So the practical application of the lessons learned at a snail's pace during inspection are a major obstacle to overcome in ski racing. There are distractions at speed and your memory tends to get a bit fuzzy when you're whipping down the hill with the wind howling in your ears. Your skis rattle, your teeth shake, your brain vibrates, and your vision blurs. But you still watch the snow and you can see it coming at you like a freight train. You know it's changing under your skis and you can feel it and you make continual minute adjustments to maintain balance and momentum. The race is brain and muscle power working in tandem and you have to plan for this during inspection.

Having a clear image in your mind of the muscular requirements of the hill is a key to solving the puzzle. You have to be able to envision the muscular tensions involved on various parts of the course and imagine how you will have to lean forward, back, or to either side to counteract centrifugal force, depending on the steepness and sharpness of the turns. You ask yourself how much is this going to push me off line and if it pushes me off line this much what are the implications farther down the hill? You weigh this over in your mind and you have to plan for screw-ups so that if you blow a turn near the top you have an escape hatch, the fastest way to get back on line to make up the lost time. You can't be so completely precise in your inspection calculations that you don't leave room to maneuver in the race. You have to plan to be able to readjust and adapt instantly. The great racers are not the guys who can always get the right line, but the guys who can blow their line and recover quickly. Very seldom do you have an absolutely perfect run with no mistakes. The winners are those who can correct the mistakes the fastest.

By the time you've done your inspection of the hill, your mind is a very crowded place, but you have to be able to separate the wheat from the chaff to create the whole picture. Everybody stands around the finish area leaning on their poles with their minds in high gear in preparation for the first training run, when all the theorizing is put to the test. Often, things aren't as you imagined.

In some ways you have to be a bit of a pilot because flight is a big part of the business of Downhill racing and the faster you go the bigger role it plays. You're airborne a great deal of the time on a course like Kitzbühel and this tends to poke holes in your calculations – unless you can think like our feathered friends. Experience helps, but it's hard to enjoy flying through the air when you're really at the mercy of the gods: you're literally out of control and you just hope you'll come down fairly soon because that fence or net is approaching at a rapid rate and you'd prefer not to eat it and wind up with unbecoming hatch marks all over the only face you have. You want to have more say in the matter of take-offs and landings, so the first training run tends to be taken at less than full throttle as you test the wind around the jumps.

On the first run, we usually experimented, gunning it full speed through certain sections to feel how it was, cruising for a bit, then letting her rip again. There were synchronized timing machines set up at five or six intervals and the information was fed into computers, which would spit out a list of the interval times of the top 15 or 20 guys. If you were a fraction of a second slower in a 30-second section, you were in trouble, and so you'd talk to the coaches, watch what the faster guys were doing, and try to play catch up as best you could. We set up video cameras in the most difficult sections and spent hours pouring over the tapes, watching people in slow motion, and trying to figure out why some were faster than others. You'd watch superstars like Peter Mueller from Switzerland or the great Austrian Franz Klammer and analyse their runs, then compare them to yours to try and establish where the differences were. Skiing becomes a very cerebral thing at this stage as you apply a metaphorical magnifying glass to your technique and form, and tax your brain like Sherlock Holmes to try and solve the mystery of the missing milliseconds.

The three training runs before each race meant you had about six minutes of on-hill experience at speed to file away under your helmet. Then you talked to the coaches and equipment reps some more and worked on your ego. There's a blurry area between ego and confidence. You need a fairly large ego to be able to come to grips with the task at hand. At a place like Kitzbühel, there are very clear reasons why you should not be confident and, if you let your imagination run away with you, it's very easy to wish you were back home in Don Mills lying in bed with a blanket over your head. But you're not, you're lying in bed at Kitzbühel the night before the race and you may feel a bit restless. When this happened, I flipped up the race in my brain and took an imaginary run down the course. Sometimes, as I was running it through my head, I'd make a mistake, catch an edge or goof up in some way. Then I'd just back it up and repeat that section properly, so I always ended up with a perfect run. Instead of counting sheep, I ticked off the seconds down the Hahnenkamm, and I could doze off peacefully after a perfect run. I never fell in my dreams.

At Kitzbühel when I woke up, the first thing I saw when I looked out my window was the place near the bottom of the hill where I got hurt in 1976, so I tended not to let my gaze linger there. Before 7 o'clock on Saturday morning, you could see hordes of spectators on foot heading up the hill to get a good vantage point, an indication of the stature of ski racing in Europe. The race didn't start until 12:00 or 12:30, yet these people were willing to claw their way up a steep hill and hang around in the cold for several hours.

Meanwhile, the racers are beginning their pre-race ritual: coach John Ritchie always had us locked into a race-day routine that began with a run and warm-up exercises. Then we'd cruise downstairs for breakfast: the waitresses and waiters are whizzing around like mad and everybody seems to be flipping out because it's the biggest day of the year in Kitzbühel. There'd be more adrenalin in the air than caffeine in your coffee, but we had to keep a steady hand on our psyches at this stage – which was hard to do when you're surrounded by people who are going off the deep end.

I whip downstairs to confer with my "rep" Hans Ramelmuller who's been slaving over my skis for several hours. He's worrying about the snow conditions and has a coach up on the hill already taking the snow temperatures. They've been doing this for several days to monitor the wax requirements, and if the weather has changed everybody's anxiety level goes up several notches. The guy up on the hill with the thermometer talks to us on the radio and poor old Hans is trying hard to keep relaxed. He sits there with his little babies, the skis, in front of him and sips away at his ritual bottle of beer. He only drinks it on race-day morning, partly as a good luck charm, but mainly to try and calm his nerves.

It becomes increasingly harder to remain blasé as the witching

20

hour approaches. We give our ski suits to our masseur/factotum "Toulouse" Spence – you don't put them on until race time because they might get stretched and let air in. Toulouse is also weighed down with a big bag of helmets. Firmly, persuasively, without actually knocking people down, but using a certain amount of physical effort, we make our way to the lift. This scrimmage was always worst at Kitzbühel where race fans were willing to sell their souls for lift passes (and a brisk trade in forged tickets flourished). We nudge, push, and wedge our way through the milling throng and by 9:30 we're up at the top. For the next hour or 90 minutes, we free ski around the easy slopes near the start area, getting the feel of our skis, and generally dialling ourselves in.

Around 11:00 o'clock, one hour before the race, we converge on the restaurant near the start where Toulouse and the reps have commandeered a corner for the team. We proceed to disrobe in front of a mixed audience, always good for a few laughs as we parade around in our jockey shorts (which is all we wear under our skintight Downhill suits). Then we squirm and wiggle into our suits and tug up the zipper – which starts at the belly button – don our helmets, and wander outside. We've gone to the bathroom several times before this, but it seldom fails that you feel the urge again as soon as you're nicely stuffed into the confines of your racing suit. Relief requires some complicated maneuvering and no sense of modesty. You struggle out of your warm-up gear, lower the zipper of your racing suit, bend over from the waist, and let fly – taking care to aim away from your helmet while directing the stream at gaps in the surrounding crowd . . . .

I was always at the start area at 11:30, bopping around killing time and pondering the possibilities of my starting position. Start numbers for the 15 top-seeded racers were chosen at random by pulling numbered pingpong balls out of two hats. The rest of the field ran according to their world ranking. In my later years, the top seeds started at 90-second intervals to give them more time on television, while the others went every minute. Depending on the weather, that extra 30 seconds could be an advantage or disadvantage. If it was snowing, the skiers who started after the first seed might have a clearer course because the closer intervals kept the snow plowed. But then changing course conditions might mean the first runners had the fastest track, so it usually balanced out.

At this point, as Foster Hewitt used to say about a Stanley Cup final, "the tension is electric." Just recalling it makes me nervous. As the minutes tick off, I start moving into the crowd looking for familiar faces. I feel like I'm in a goldfish bowl as everyone stares at me. Somewhere nearby Hans has my skis laid flat on the ground so they'll cool to the same temperature as the snow and run properly. I'm beginning to sweat and feel the chill from standing around with the cold and clammy nylon suit next to my skin, despite having thrown on several layers of warm-up gear. I'm very excited, but not shaking like some of the others. The policemen and officials trying to keep order around the start hut are just as jittery as everybody else. You have to prove your identity to make it into the inner circle and when they see me they try to grab a last-minute autograph. There's no time for that and I push through to Hans and the little knot of people who await me.

When I get nervous I tend to withdraw and try to remain peaceful within, but it's hard to keep your head when those around you are losing theirs. There's a veritable army of service people and reps up in the start area, every one of them intent on doing their best on this, one of the most important days of their life. They tend to run around flapping their wings, fussing over their skiers like mother hens. I report to Hans, check in with Toulouse, and hand my Carrera goggles to their company rep for a final checkover of the new lens I get for each race. The boot man makes sure I'm buckled in properly, as I chat with John Ritchie on the radio. He's stationed himself somewhere down the hill and we shoot the breeze a bit about course conditions and the weather. There's no joking around now and, exactly 15 minutes before my scheduled take-off, I give Hans the nod.

He picks up my skis and we head over to Peter Ess, the Tyrolia binding man. I stand there patiently like a horse being shod as Peter does his thing. He's dug a hole in the snow so the bindings are at eye level when he kneels. Hans has positioned my skis beside the hole. Peter picks up one foot, carefully knocks the snow off the boot, sets it into the binding, clicks it closed, and adjusts the forward tension and the up-and-down tension at the toe and heel. He repeats this on the other foot, pokes around, and examines everything one last time. Then he slaps me twice on the back of the leg, looks up at me, and says good luck.

With five minutes to go, I'm standing in the line-up of racers with several officious organizer types jumping up and down and yelling as they try to keep us in starting order. Toulouse is beside me and gives me the latest radio news bulletins as I start unzipping my warm-up gear. There are a lot of zippers and it's a fact of zipping life that they become contrary when the zippee is tense. Sometimes I'd get stuck and Toulouse would have to pitch in: if tugging, pulling, jerking, and yanking failed to do the trick, I'd say, "Toulouse, rip them off!" Toulouse does whatever is necessary to peel off my outer layers and make me look like a Downhill racer. Then he rubs my leg muscles and I make last-minute mental reviews of my run.

I'm in an advanced state of hyperness now and don't want to hear anything, probably couldn't hear anything, from the radio via Toulouse. Rival radios are blaring in several languages. The assembly line of racers gets shorter as those in front drop off on their runs. I ignore their departures as I move forward into the start hut. I'm thinking only of myself and don't want to even look at another skier. Nothing else matters except obeying the timing beeper that clicks off the last six seconds prior to my departure.

The rules require that you leave the gate within three seconds either side of the one-minute-and-thirty-second interval. I always went right after the first couple of beeps because I was ready and didn't want to prolong the agony of waiting. My last contact with humanity is the Omega timing guy, the official Starter on the tour. He's in all the Downhill racing movies standing beside the skier in the gate and each time he would wish me good luck. I stick my poles over the wand of the electronic beam, dig them in, and think: "Gotta go for it! *Gotta Go For It!!* GO FOR IT!!!"

In the race, there's very little sense of self-awareness as in "Here I am running the Downhill." You have very basic thought patterns as you react intuitively to the rapid sequence of events. It's really quite primitive, but also sophisticated, involving muscle and mind power. The various parts of your body work in concert as they've been programmed to do, moving in response to the constant input of data that you feel, see, and hear. It's two minutes of total sensory involvement and all that information your senses receive is absolutely critical. One time in my early racing days in Canada, a guy on the Quebec team named Bobby David decided to put cotton in his ears to block out the sound of the wind. He went cruising down the hill at Mont Ste-Anne and crashed head-on into the trees. He had no idea how fast he was going because he couldn't hear, and thus couldn't gauge his speed properly. The wind screaming in your ears and your skis banging and clattering over the snow are vital signs necessary for control over your destiny.

It's possible to intellectualize yourself into neutral if you don't trust your body to do the things it's been trained to do for so many years. It's like hitting a serve in tennis. You don't think about bringing the racket back, then throwing it forward, angling it just so to put a spin on the ball and bringing your arm back in a proper follow-through. You think it through beforehand, visualize it, then forget it. When you serve, you just hit the ball: wham! If you stand back and think about your form, you're likely to get smacked between the eyes with the ball. You react, and a ski race is two minutes of sustained action and reaction. There's no holding back for the next run. It's like the charge of the Light Brigade the whole way down.

Only once in a race did I manage to pull off a mind-over-matter stunt and actually think my way out of a problem. At Schladming one year, I was whipping around a right-hand turn which has a bump or up-shoot in the middle. Just at take-off, I thought: "I'm not going to make it!" My body went bloop and I sat right back as I flew into the air. There are pictures of me flying along at about 70 miles an hour with my feet in front and my ski tips way back over my head. One hundredth of a second into this potential disaster, I said to myself: "THERE'S NO WAY I'M GOING TO FALL HERE!" I dug the tails of my skis into the snow, leaned on them, and hauled myself upright by sheer force of will. Those who saw it on television and in the photos couldn't believe I'd recovered. I couldn't either. The only reason I did was because I consciously commanded myself to do it. When I finally got straightened out, I could hardly stand up, because I'd put so much energy into surviving – and I had a very slow run to the finish. I knew then I could make the turn in future and didn't have to think about it any more. To have to think is to slow down.

The only things that matter are the line and the snow and the terrain. I shut out the two miles of wildly cheering people, the waving banners, the din of the cowbells, and the blur of the fences.

I just race and see the light shining off the snow crystals and the shadows marking the undulations. At 60, 70, 80, 90 miles an hour, the gates fly by at a terrific rate, but it sometimes seems surreal . . . like slow motion: almost leisurely, I feel the snow beneath my skis and get a reading on it: as slippery snow touches the tips, I gradually edge a little harder to hold my line; in softer snow, I ease off the edge slightly . . . it seems I've got lots of time . . . .

My concentration is so intense that the finish is often a surprise. I try to think back and recall the run, but all I get are fleeting impressions. Only later do the details come back. Gradually, the madhouse at the finish area comes into focus with screaming people, blaring loudspeakers, and the general mayhem penetrating my consciousness. I see my time on the scoreboard and force myself into the here and now. I have to hold up my skis for the cameras to give the manufacturer that vital exposure, and speak into the microphones thrust into my face. Performing in this après-ski mode is hard after the high of the race. If I say something banal to an interviewer, it's because I haven't yet tuned out the euphoria of the Downhill. I'm exhausted, physically and mentally, but the supreme pleasure of having skied as fast as you possibly can leaves a void that's hard to fill. I've just had the experience of a lifetime and been more truly alive than I can ever be . . . until the next race.

3. Born to Ski

I was born on the 25th of July, 1957, and about two and a half years later I first skied down a two-foot slope in the front yard of our house in Don Mills, Ontario. Not long after that my mother held me between her legs and we snowplowed slowly down a larger hill nearby. All I remember from my very early days of skiing was the damn cold. That and often having to go to the bathroom so bad I could hardly stand it. After several hours on the hills I would have to walk home with my legs crossed. Fortunately, our chalet at Craigleith is right near the bottom of the hill and I usually made it on time.

My dad and mom and my brother Craig and I built our chalet at the Craigleith Ski Club, near Collingwood on Georgian Bay, working on it mainly during the weekends in the summer. One day, we were hammering away and a raging rain storm came along, followed by a howling, drumming noise. Sure enough, it was a twister, a small tornado, and it blew everything to bits. We ran to our car about 30 feet away and my mom barely made it in time after my dad yelled to her. I remember looking out the car window and seeing pieces of plywood flying down the street and everything going WHOOSH. It was just incredible and I was scared stiff. My brother, who's a year younger than me, didn't like storms for quite a while after that. It was a major trauma.

My dad was the keen skier in those days. He discovered it first and really loved it; then my mother started skiing to be with him and she began to enjoy it too. Since they had neither time nor money for any other sport, they put everything they had into skiing

26

and Craig and I followed their lead. Before we had the chalet, I remember waking up really early on pitch-black mornings in Don Mills and having to drive an hour and a half or longer up north. We'd ski all day, drive back home at night, then go back up the next morning. We did that every weekend throughout the winter. Thank goodness the chalet cut down the driving.

At first, it was a chore for me to get up in the morning and go skiing. I didn't have the motivation. I liked to ski, but when I was sleepy I wanted to sleep. I was there so I skied. But the older I got, the more I wanted to do it and we made a game of it. On our last runs before lunch or at the end of the day, my brother and I would try to glide to our front door. We'd barrel down the hill from as high as possible, trying to maintain a straight line, and see how far we could make it along the flats. A lot of the time we'd actually make it all the way back to the chalet. Gliding that far was a real challenge and we'd create challenges to make skiing more fun.

The hills in Southern Ontario don't exactly boggle the mind and just going up and down them is boring. So a gang of us, about 15 kids, would create havoc on the hill. We'd do crazy things like going down between each other's legs or racing down the "Back Stairs" which is really an access road. It's a long flat run and we'd all be hunkered down in our tucks trying to pass each other like in a car race. We'd sneak up behind the other guy to get in his slipstream, then pull out and pass him. We'd hardly stop for lunch: just cruise back to the chalet, grab a sandwich or something, then hit the hills again and resume our terrorist activities.

What a great way to learn how to ski. And scare yourself to death! We'd go whipping down through the trees or leap off jumps. I remember rocketing into the "Birches" where there was a jump that was a real kicker. A kicker is a kind of jump that just hits you – Pow! – and shoots you straight up in the air and you can only hope you're going to be in the right place when you launch yourself. Sure enough, one time I went off that baby too far forward and the first three points that landed were the tips of my skis and my head. Another time, when my brother and I were doing our tuck trick and trying to glide back to the chalet, I fell very hard on some crusty snow and broke a ski. My dad came running out and said, "Look at that! You've broken a ski. How could you do such a stupid thing?" I was kind of disappointed at his apparent lack of concern for his son but I guess he figured a kid was cheaper to fix than a broken ski.

After episodes like that my parents probably thought it would be safer for me to go into organized racing, but there were economic reasons too. They wanted to ski themselves and not have to look after my brother and me, but they also wanted us to improve. Racing was less expensive than taking ski lessons. So we raced and it was fun because it was really a good way of testing yourself. There were new challenges in the Nancy Greene League where I started racing when I was ten years old. In those days, organized skiing for kids was very simply structured, starting with Grand Slalom events in the Nancy Greene League and progressing up to more serious racing in the Southern Ontario Ski Zone.

When I look back now, I can see important milestones and signposts that guided me on the route I was to eventually take in life but, at the time, growing up in the Podborski household in Don Mills, Ontario, seemed normal in an all-Canadian way. My father worked as a mechanical engineer, my mother was a housewife, and my brother and I went to school. It was your classic average family . . . at least it seemed that way to me. I watched *Star Trek* after school and I read a lot. If I hadn't started skiing I might have turned into a blimpish bookworm. I read voraciously and I'd often be so absorbed I wouldn't hear people who were trying to talk to me. When friends would come over and ask me to go and play road hockey or something, it was always a struggle for me to decide whether to drop my book or not. A lot of times reading won over games.

When I was about ten, I read the classic book *Dune* and I've been hooked on science fiction ever since. It's a chance to fantasize and escape reality if your existence happens to be humdrum, though mine seldom was. And all those hours spent immersed in the other worlds of science fiction may have helped me in the real world of ski racing because science fiction requires the reader to use imagination and fill in the blanks with a bit of creativity.

In ski racing you're dealing with the cold, hard facts of snow-covered terra firma and gravity but, just as in Sci-Fi, you've got to make a leap of faith beyond the limitations of your own experience. When you examine a Downhill course, you evaluate the bumps, terrain changes, different gate combinations, snow conditions, and so on, and you have to imagine how they'll all affect your run. I find it very easy to do this with a minimum of effort, while others haven't a clue. They just don't have the ability to memorize and visualize and apply the realities of the course in a creative way to their run. When you're going down the hill, there are any number of lines to take: a good line, a better line, and maybe another line that will end in disaster, and so on. They're all there and you have to choose them, weave them together, and pull them apart instantaneously. Reality and experience enter into the equation too but you have to be able to read between the lines with some inventiveness. If you look at a ski hill and can only see the obvious you're very limited in what you can do. While the basics of Downhill racing are rooted in science, you can't win until you go beyond conventional perceptions.

Back in the reality of my boyhood I went to Overland Public School, then Don Mills Junior High, and found schoolbooks to be mainly uninspiring and the lessons tedious. As usual, skiing rescued me from the monotony. One time we had a winter sports activity day in the Don Valley near the school and I won the ski events. I was Joe Hotshot and one of the teachers came up to me and said, "Steve, I had no idea you were such a good skier." He was amazed. People knew I skied on weekends, but nobody could really comprehend how good I was. Only other skiers can know and it's still that way. It's not conceit but a fact of life that I'm a better skier than most people can ever imagine. All of us Crazy Canucks were. We did stuff over in Europe that most Canadians can't appreciate, through no fault of their own. They tend to know hockey or baseball inside out, but ski racing remains somewhere out in left field in the public consciousness. It's sad in a way and I must admit I feel strange when people come up to me and say, "Steve, you're really a great skier." I'll look at them and say, "Thank you very much," but I'll think, "You don't know the half of it." I'm pleased to hear their accolades, but if another racer compliments me it means a lot more.

In Junior High I discovered I have a rather vicious temper, at least others discovered it. I have a fairly high boiling point, but when I'm provoked and have to let off steam people can get scalded. One day I was coming home from school and one of the guys from my neighbourhood winged a snowball at me when I wasn't looking and got me right in the eye. He wasn't trying to hurt me but it really pissed me off. I ran over and jumped him. I was really mad, kind of irrational, and crunched him a few times.

I didn't have many fights but I always won them, no matter what the odds were. One summer our street played baseball against a team from the street above ours and we beat them. One of their guys, he was older and a lot bigger than me, started hassling us and thumbing his nose. Then he grabbed my brother's glove and I went into a blind rage. I was around ten or 11 at the time and I threw him on the ground and got my arm around his throat and was choking him. He went limp and I said WHOA! – get a grip here Steve. Of course I hadn't really hurt him and he jumped up and threatened to get a lawyer. But I had scared the bejeebers out of him and his friends so we didn't have any trouble with them after that.

He learned a lesson, but so did I. It worried me that I could go berserk like that and have no idea what was going on until my mind kicked back into gear and I had the sense to ease up. I never really fought after that and I never want to hurt anybody, but I realized I have this ability to go for it, forget my inhibitions, pull out all the stops, and concentrate completely on bringing the task at hand to a successful conclusion. Fortunately my tasks involved going down hills fast and not punching people out, but I've overcome serious odds in many cases by using the same principle: quickly marshalling all my resources to overcome adversity.

In ski racing this didn't necessarily mean unleashing all my aggression on my opponents. I didn't say to myself, "I'm going out there to slash them up, rip them to shreds and beat them until they're on their knees." It was more a letting go of inhibitions on the hill as opposed to an attack against a bully after a baseball game. Standing at the starting gate, you're concentrating intensely on the task at hand. Your brain goes click and it drops all those extra doodads that are always floating around in there. It's just BANG! – you've got to make it down. All you've got to do is ski. It's very similar to that fighting fury or berserk rage, but if you get too flipped out you just can't function. There are fancy words for it these days like "excitation phase," but really it's a supreme state of readiness. It's very primitive, but also sophisticated in many ways.

When I was about 12 and in my second year on the Nancy Greene team at Craigleith, I started falling in nearly every race. Our coach Leo Vogrin chose the running order for the start according to how well each person was skiing, the best starting first and the worst last. Until then I'd started somewhere in the middle, but Leo moved me back in the starting order because I was falling so much. I was devastated. Skiing was the thing I enjoyed most in life. It was tremendously distressing that I was getting worse instead of better.

I told my mother I was going to quit. She said, "You're going to finish what you started. I've been driving you around to all these races and you've got the whole team to think about. If you're going to quit do it at the end of the season." She threw all this responsibility at me, saying I owed it to her and the team, and especially myself, to keep on skiing.

I went to the next Grand Slalom at Devil's Glen and won! What a feeling, I'll never forget it. I came whipping through to the finish, came to a stop, and Leo Vogrin's wife Lotte grabbed me and hugged me. She's a beautiful person, just a lovely lady, and she whirled me around yelling, "Yay Steve! You won!" I thought, "If this is what winning is like, wow! It's great!" I'd been really down in the dumps, with a bad start number and everything going against me, yet I had triumphed. The old cliché about persevering to succeed worked, and from then on it was built in: you can never just quit.

Absolute stubbornness and stick-to-it-iveness, to the point of never giving up, came from both my parents. For example, I remember being impressed by the way my father played badminton at our chalet. There he was in a pair of shorts diving after this stupid bird, even though it was way out of reach, with no concern for decorum. If he was going to play the game, it was all out with no holding back. I thought, "Here's my dad, an engineer in a dignified profession, and yet he plays hard." That's the way it should be.

One year at Kitzbühel, when I was one of the best in the world, I won all the timed runs and the odds against me winning were something like two to one. I was almost a sure thing. Then I came through the top part of the course and went wide and just missed a fence. I thought, "Steve, this is a disaster. Your time will be dead slow. You should just STOP! Just pull over now and it will be less humiliating at the finish line." It's the only time I ever felt that way, but I kept going. It turned out that the top of the course was so rough everybody else had a worse time than mine and I won the race by half a second – only because I talked myself out of stopping. NEVER stop.

My parents were very much straight-arrow types: work hard and don't fool around was their credo. My father's parents came over from the Ukraine and lived the work ethic to the hilt. My grandfather worked on the railway and in the mines in Sudbury until his lungs gave out, so my grandparents then moved to a farm near Burlington which they worked to put my father through university. The idea of going to school so you wouldn't have to do manual labour was firmly implanted in us. This presented a problem when I left high school to devote my life to a sport with seemingly no future – nobody from Canada had ever made a living in ski racing. But my dad never objected to it and he supported me, even monetarily. I'll be eternally grateful for that. It wasn't easy for him.

My mother was a Morris. Her father was a Cockney, a real character who came to Canada from England with his wife who was from a wealthy family and was disowned for marrying him. They lived under the Burlington Skyway near Hamilton which in those days was the wrong side of the tracks. They were very strict and authoritarian and my mother left home when she was 17. Her sense of independence must be in my genes.

We didn't display much affection in our family, but it was always there. I did more hugging and kissing after I'd lived in Europe where it was de rigueur. Our parents showed their love for Craig and me by respecting us and letting us do what we thought was right, but only after they had imprinted certain values. They were strict in many ways. Not swearing was one example: I had a major confrontation with my dad about that when all my playmates were swearing and I started too. He spanked me then, I think for the last time, when I was about 12. But they're both still parenting in some ways. My dad sometimes thinks of me as his child and my mom is hilarious, still telling me how to do things: "Steve you should phone this person, do this, do that . . . ."

Mostly, they led by example. At income-tax time, my dad would be sweating to get it all right on the tax forms. There was never any question that he was going to fudge anything. Lies were taboo, and to this day I find it incredibly difficult to pretend I'm not in when somebody telephones me. In our house you never tried to scam anybody and the Podborskis never tried to impress the Joneses.

Most of our neighbours were WASPS, but our parents never thought in those terms. People were just Fred or Ralph, never poor or rich or Jewish or Catholic, and that was that.

Our family was probably closer to poor than rich, though we never really wanted for anything and home was a comfortable place to be. Don Mills was the original version of suburbia and most kids hung around the shopping plaza. That never appealed to me and I never ran with the pack; only our ski gang at Craigleith. I hung around home and hardly even ventured downtown to the bright lights of Toronto. We seldom even went to movies. The first ones I saw were *Born Free* and *Mary Poppins*, only because my aunt Gwynn took us. We never went out for meals, my dad doesn't like it. Maybe it was because of his Ukrainian heritage: you just don't pay other people for food. You make it yourself (at least your wife does; though my dad does make a great omelette).

We watched sports on TV and I remember the amazing emotion when Canada beat Russia in hockey in 1972. We were let out of school early to see that last game of the series and Paul Henderson's winning goal really impressed me as a great individual effort. I had this image of one guy going against the odds, skating around three Russians and dumping it in the net. Another player might have said, I'll never make it, and passed the puck to somebody else. I wasn't a hero-worshipper, but I did admire the top skiers, particularly Nancy Greene, the all-Canadian girl. I read her autobiography and Jean Claude Killy's. I saw the world's best skiers on TV in the 1968 Olympics and in my mind's eye I can still see Killy rocketing down the hill at Grenoble. To me it was the ultimate.

My school marks were always in the 75% range, but I never put nearly as much effort into them as I did with other things in my life. I procrastinated like mad and always had projects to do at the last minute. I would slave away in one night and do what we were supposed to do over a whole semester. The pressure made it interesting and I always managed to pull it off, though my mother would be really angry with me. But later on this highwire method of studying was the only way I could operate.

After I joined the National Team, my cramming technique got me through several years at Don Mills Collegiate Institute, but eventually I had to choose either school or the slopes. I was away from school from September to March, then I'd try to catch up from April to June. I worked 12 hours a day on my lessons at home and checked in with the teachers once or twice a week. Some of the teachers objected to all the extra tutoring they had to give me and I was literally driving myself into exhaustion. Finally, when I checked into a skiing camp one summer, the doctor looked at the blue circles under my eyes and said I was killing myself. He really shocked me and I quit school after completing Grade 11. I took some grade 12 and 13 courses the next year, but a low mark in geology, 60%, was the last straw for me and I quit school.

My coach Leo Vogrin made skiing in the Nancy Greene Little League a ball. He loved the sport and was so enthusiastic and full of energy that he made everything fun for us. We'd do anything for Leo who was a weekend coach at Craigleith, but as devoted a coach as I've ever had. One year, he awarded me the Red Devil Hat, patterned after one they give at Kitzbühel, as the most improved kid. I still treasure it as the first thing I won in skiing. It's just a little red cone thing with a ball on the end like a dunce cap. Later on, we got red team jackets and hats and if we won a race we got a little snowflake. I have all this stuff at the chalet now and they would probably fall apart if I took them down from the wall.

The emphasis was on team performance and we won the regional title in 1967-68, the same season Nancy Greene won her second overall World Cup title and a gold medal in the Giant Slalom at the Olympics in Grenoble, France. There was a big parade for Nancy in Toronto and our team of 13 kids was in it. We piled into convertible limousines with our names on the side, my brother and I, our friends Rob and Al Safrata, Tony Camisso and all the others, many of whom I'm still in contact with. (In fact, many of these ten-year-old kids went on to prominence in the sport and are still involved in the sales end of skiing: Craig and I, the Safrata brothers, and Tony Camisso in particular.) Bobby Gimby was in the parade and we toured up Bay Street with everybody singing his Centennial song about Canada: bands were playing and tickertape was flying through the air. Nancy made a speech at city hall and I was awestruck with my eyes bugged out and my mouth open. It was my first exposure to public acclaim, even though it wasn't for me, and I was overwhelmed. I had no conception that later on in my career I could ever generate that kind of enthusiasm.

To this point I was never brilliant in racing but I was an adequate team player, despite using inferior skis. Many of the Craigleith members were fairly affluent and most kids had the latest Rossignols with metal edges on them, while I was using ordinary skis with screw-in edges. Whenever I hit a rock and damaged them, I would have to play around with putty and work on them in the lodge while the others kept skiing. That's when I realized my dad's income was less than most of the others at Craigleith. Maybe my screw-in-edge handicap made me try harder.

From the Nancy Greene Little League I went into the Southern Ontario Ski Zone division of Juvenile racing as an independent. I really was a juvenile on and off the hills. I started to improve through the class structure from D to C to B and at the age of 13 I was an A-level racer. At first, we travelled to nearby events at Beaver Valley and Devil's Glen where I knew everybody. Then I made the division team and started going on road trips to Quebec. We'd leave on Friday night and drive like crazy at 80 and 90 miles an hour in vans and cars. We raced Saturday and Sunday, then barrelled back home. I'd be constipated for the whole weekend. I couldn't wait to get back home to go to the bathroom. It was very uncomfortable and probably a reaction to these strange new circumstances.

At 13 I was the youngest guy there and didn't know any of the others. I was a babe in the woods, ignorant and inexperienced. One time at Mont Ste-Anne in Quebec some of the 17- and 18-year-old guys brought an obscene photo of a hooker into our room at the camp and I was shocked. I couldn't believe that these things happened to real people! I stuck strictly to skiing which paid off later when two or three people who were better than me were kicked off the team for smoking or drinking. Their departure meant I was moved up the ladder and suddenly yours truly was invited to go to the 1970 National Juvenile Championships in Fernie, B.C.

I got the trip to Fernie through the back door, but I came out in front when I won a gold medal in the Slalom and a bronze in the Downhill. This was my first time on a big mountain and it was thrilling when Nancy Greene presented me with my medals and kissed me on the cheek. I did well the next year too, but I began to find out that skiing can be a pretty miserable existence. In fact, the whole life of a racer is frequently just a grunt, and not only when the weather is cold.

We often ate in greasy spoons on the road. On one trip to Mont

Tremblant we ate some yogurt that had obviously gone bad and everybody got food poisoning. There was a whole van full of kids puking their guts out. We would try to stop but seldom made it in time during that eight-hour trip home and the floor of our van was covered with vomit. Eventually I learned how to throw up out of a moving vehicle. You stick your head out the window, face backward, and tilt your head to one side – if you don't, the wind blows it up over your face and into your ears. Despite the stomach disorders, I enjoyed the adventure and discovery of travelling to new places and I always loved the skiing part of it.

During those winters we raced somewhere in Ontario or Quebec nearly every weekend. My parents sent us to summer camps for one or two weeks out west where, instead of fooling around with birch bark, my brother and I went skiing. It cost about $300 for each of us, and we had to watch our money carefully, so the family usually drove out to the Rockies and mom and dad stayed in a campground while we skied. Their sacrifices paid off later on because Craig made it to the World-Cup level too, but several serious knee injuries forced him into early retirement.

In 1973, just prior to my 16th birthday, I went to a summer camp at Whistler, B.C. where the overall winner would be given a chance to attend a National Ski Team Selection Camp that fall for some exposure to the "big guys." I was just blithering along happily, learning to ski better, and the National Team was the furthest thing from my mind. Conditions at the Whistler camp were rather primitive: there were no showers and accommodation was in tents in the snow near the top of the mountain. We'd get up at something like 3:00 am before the sun came up, have breakfast in the Round House, and hike up the hill in the freezing cold to our lift, which was a big rope dragged by an old Volkswagen engine. Often it wouldn't start, so we'd all grab the rope and haul away in unison until it fired up.

We skied up and down that hill for four or five hours each day until the sun came up over the peaks and softened the snow. Then we just hung around the tents and got bored stiff. My friend Rob Safrata won the Slalom and I won the Giant Slalom. But Rob won the combined while I finished second overall. So Rob was invited to the Selection Camp, but I didn't care because my prize for winning my race was a pair of skis while Rob only won poles. The guy with the screw-in edges was ecstatic about winning skis with real edges. Then came an unexpected bonus. A couple of weeks later, I got a letter at home saying sorry, we made a little mistake and the winner of each race at Whistler is invited to the Selection Camp. Obviously the selection committee had decided both of these kids were good and deserved the top prize.

Though I didn't think I had a hope in heck of making the big team, I trained hard for the next couple of months with my brother and a friend, Andy Bryce. I rode my bike, lifted weights in our basement, and did sit-ups and stuff every day. Then Rob and I went to Kimberley where we were raw rookies compared to the 18- and 19-year-old guys, some of whom had been on the team before. We trained for a few days, then went under the gun in timed runs in Downhill, GS, and Slalom. Points were awarded in a scoring system similar to the World Cup: 25 for first and so on down the line. Remarkably, I won all the Downhill time trials and was in the top three in the other two categories while Rob did very well too.

I felt quietly confident at the selection announcement, hoping they *had* to put me on the team even though I was so young. It was very hard emotionally waiting for the good word. We were all crowded into a little hotel room in Kimberley, all the would-be heroes and the coaches. One of the latter, Butch Boutry, stood up and read out the names, including Rob Safrata and Steve Podborski. I just gulped. I wanted to yell, "Yay, I made it!" but I knew you needed more than basic ski talent to fit in with the team, otherwise they'd just crucify you for being a jerk. My philosophy was shut up and listen, but there wasn't a happier kid in Canada that day. Still, I had no idea what had begun. I didn't even have a passport!

While I was on the "Talent Squad," the lowest category of the Canadian National Alpine Ski Team, it seemed like a miracle. I had no concept of what I was getting myself into, but it was a really neat feeling when they sent me team jackets, shells, and equipment. For seasoning Rob and I competed in the Can Am circuit, a series of North American races for World Cup Team asipirants, during that winter of 1973-74. I got off to a flying start by winning the first event, at Whistler, after finishing second in the Canadian National Championship Downhill the day before. I had been very unsure of myself when I arrived at Whistler and blurted out to the coach Butch Boutry that I might be in over my head. I said, "I don't know if I can do it." He said, "Sure you can," and those three words gave me confidence. I was really good at being brainwashed. I don't know if the coaches always believed what they said, but I believed them.

Most of the Can Am guys were 18 or over and when you're 16 that seems a tremendous difference. Rob and I stuck together. Ken Read was there too but the age gap kept us apart until later. I was the youngest on the team, but only two weeks younger than Rob, which pissed him off for years because the media always focused on my age. Podborski and Safrata seemed unusual names to the Anglo Saxon-oriented press and we became known as Smith and Jones, the aliases used by Butch Cassidy and the Sundance Kid.

So Smith and Jones and the rest of the Can Am crew, about ten of us, bombed all over North America that season in high-powered station wagons. I didn't win any more races but had good results and learned things like how to exist on six or seven bucks a day food allowance: you decide whether to have lunch or dinner. It was still costing me money to buy ski equipment, but at least the team had enough travel money from the Canadian Ski Association to stay in fairly decent motels and Holiday Inns. We raced on weekends in B.C., Utah, Colorado, California, Minnesota, New York, Ontario, and Quebec. Though it was run on a shoestring budget, the team had all the trimmings: coaches, a bunch of bamboo poles for gates to train with, and a stopwatch or two. Some of the guys had real stretch suits from Europe, but I was still racing in a homemade Downhill suit my mom cobbled up for me with zippers all over the place to make it fit tightly.

The whole thing is a blur of highways, motels, and ski hills now, but I remember a fall in the last downhill at Aspen, Colorado, where I broke my best pair of skis in a big wipeout. I fell frequently, it's inevitable in the sport and especially in your rookie days, but this one sticks in my memory because it meant I had to fork out more of my dad's hard earned cash for new skis. Our ski technology was primitive then and we didn't really know there were faster and slower skis even though they looked identical. Anyway, I was sure these were "fast" skis and they were destroyed in this comprehensive crash where I slewed around a corner and lost it in a huge, spinning, egg beater-type fall. This generated tremendous force and one ski chopped right through the other, including the steel edges. It was as if somebody had taken an axe to it. I was glad my leg hadn't been in the way, but the wrecked ski seemed more important.

Despite the inevitable falls, my forward progress continued in Slalom, GS, and particularly Downhill races. Our team developed well as a cohesive unit and Gary Aiken won the overall Can Am series, which was quite amazing considering the Americans, as usual, were much better funded and had ten times the talent pool to draw from. Gary, Ken Read, myself, and a couple of others who had good results were invited to train with the Canadian World Cup squad in South America that summer of '74, which proved to be bad news and good news for me. The camp was in Portillo, Chile, where I caught the world's worst case of dysentery and felt so horrible I just wanted to lie down and die.

It must have been from the local water or from eating unwashed fruit and The Kid, that's what they were calling me now, was green around the gills, which gave me a technicolour face. It was sunny all the time and I was tanned dark brown between my goggles and my chin strap and lily white elsewhere. The hills in the Andes are something like 12,000 feet high above sea level at the bottom and even turning over in bed makes you gasp for air, though the snow was terrific and the skiing conditions the best I'd ever had.

But I was feeling so weak and miserable most of the time that I scarcely noticed my surroundings and gave little thought to any likelihood of joining guys like Dave Murray, Jim Hunter, and Dave Irwin who were already on the World Cup Team. Instead, I was forced to focus on the source of pain and embarrassment in my guts. By the end of the camp, it seemed I had spent more time in the bathroom than on the hills, but I somehow managed to show quite well.

I got the good news on camera from a National Film Board interviewer. The NFB was doing a documentary on the Canadian team and, unknown to me, they decided to capture my big moment on film. I was really very ill at the time and certainly didn't give an Academy Award performance, but they showed no mercy. There I was with the camera whirring and the sound man hovering and this guy shoves the mike in my face and says, "Well Steve, you've made it, you're going to Europe to race on the World Cup tour."

I managed a bit of a grin and mumbled some "Aw shucks" stuff but there was no jumping up and down and screaming on camera.

I just wanted to get off-screen and to the nearest bathroom. While I was pleasantly surprised at my promotion to the World Cup team, I wasn't shocked or scared. I should have been. But I hardly knew where Europe was on the map, let alone what was in the script for me over there.

4. *The Crazy Canucks*

When I first joined the World Cup tour for the 1974-75 season, there were no stars on the Canadian team yet, though Jim Hunter was close to the top in GS races. The Daves, Murray and Irwin, were also veterans on the team while Ken Read, Gary Aiken, and I were the main rookies, although Rob Safrata and others raced with us a few times that year. Over time, I came to be intimately acquainted with my teammates and they certainly were a fascinating bunch of characters. It would be hard to find a more disparate collection of personalities.

Jim Hunter was a character and a half and one of the great personalities of the World Cup tour until he retired after the 1976-77 season. The Europeans loved him for his Jungle Jim antics, like breaking off tree branches with his bare hands. But Jim could also ski like crazy and served as a kind of benchmark for the rest of us. While the team reached its zenith after he was gone, Jungle Jim was the prototypical Crazy Canuck.

Before we concentrated exclusively on the Downhill, Jim cut quite a swathe in the Giant Slalom, in and out of the races. During inspection and training runs, Jim would often decide to put on a show for the thousands of fans looking on. He'd take his skis off and whip down the hill on his boots, making turns and spinning around, with the crowd going wild. It was totally at odds with the serious nature of the sport, but Jim was an entertainer. When we were on the road, he was the kind of guy who would climb up on the roof of the van and hang onto the equipment rack, howling into the wind as we tore down a mountain pass in a blinding snowstorm.

Blond and as big as an ox, hard as nails, yet very emotional, Jim was in many ways a contradiction in terms and at odds with himself – often because we put him in a quandary with our teasing. I'm afraid we sometimes made sport of his religious evangelism, particularly when he tried to convert us. When he threw it on the table and reprimanded us for taking the Lord's name in vain, we'd give him the gears. We tried not to deliberately provoke him, but our language was frequently salty and he suspected us of having loose morals. We tested his convictions by asking him that if he really loved a girl and was going to marry her, wouldn't he go to bed with her? Not until they were married, he was adamant about that. One time in South America, somebody had the book *The Joy of Sex* and we suspected Jim badly wanted to read it. We left it around to see if he would give in to temptation and sneak a peak. I don't know if he ever did read it, but it was an example of the kind of thing that went on with the team.

Everybody got their fair share of jibes and ribbing, but Jim took it more seriously. At one point it was reported that Jim quoted biblical scriptures in the starting gate before a race. He may have done that earlier in his career, but by the time he left he had changed a lot. When he came back each season after a summer at home, where his family was very religious, his convictions were stronger. Being away from them and exposed to us heathens tended to blunt his zeal and near the end of his career he was less obvious about it, probably in self defense.

Jim was very intense and wanted to win so badly it may have interfered with his results. He sometimes went too far and it would rub off on the rest of us. One time, after Jim was fastest in the first of two GS races, he was very nervous and anxious about the next race, running around and wringing his hands. We all felt his pressure, including the coach who over-sharpened Jim's edges for the second run, making them too grabby and he fared poorly. Had he skied as well in that second race, Jim might easily have been the first Canadian male to win a World Cup event. He came that close several times, but was never quite able to put it all together for a win. But his free skiing was superb, beautiful to watch, and he could handle powder or crud equally well.

Jim could be very warm and generous and a very nice guy, but I don't think he felt secure enough within to be totally giving of himself. I think he suffered a lot of inner conflict. After five years on the team, he decided he deserved to have a good car to drive. So he bought his famous yellow Porsche, not the best choice for winter driving in the Alps with the engine hanging out over the back, big fat tires and so on. It also lacked cargo space for the 16 pairs of skis, five pairs of boots, two or three ski outfits, helmet, ordinary clothes, stereo, and all the junk you need for six months on the road. There was no room to carry a buddy and the impracticality and selfishness was not lost on Jim. We knew he wasn't sure about the car and rode him about it, calling it the "Yellow Volkswagen." We asked him if the Lord would approve of such an ostentatious mode of transport. He always said he was sure it was ok with the Almighty, but our bugging him and his own doubts probably interfered with his driving pleasure. But he was always a colourful personality and well-liked by the public and continues to be. After he left the team, Jim went into promotional work and he helped organize the cross-Canada torch relay for the Winter Olympics.

Dave Murray was my favourite guy on the Crazy Canucks. In the early years, he truly enjoyed travelling with the team and being on the road. Sometimes he would go over to Europe on his own to camps run by the ski-binding companies and, one time, he and Ken took a holiday and travelled through Greece together. But Dave was an enigmatic fellow, more reserved than the rest of us, and more of a loner. His personal baggage included a guitar which he plunked away on for his own amusement. He never played for anyone else, which in a way sums up Mur, he tended to perform for himself. We used to make jokes about getting him a pair of gloves to keep his hands warm when the rest of us were unloading our equipment. He always unloaded his own stuff, then just stood around and watched us share the work. We never did get him the gloves and he remained insular and aloof. Mur wanted to have a single room, a difficult thing to have on the tour but he managed it frequently. I think in some ways it was hard for him to become involved in the team spirit.

He wasn't naturally gregarious or out-going but, when he put his mind to it, he handled himself beautifully in public situations. Like the rest of us, he learned a lot on the team and he's done well since retiring. He's Director of Skiing at Whistler now and does a super job, and I work closely with him on the Molson Canadian

Master's Alpine Series. I have great respect for his ability to work with people. On the team Mur could always see the forest when we were floundering around in the trees, if not hitting them head on. He had the ability to step back, take an overview, and isolate the problem. He got to the root of the matter by taking a different perspective. He was our resident philosopher.

Dave Murray's unique vision of the world had people as a certain kind of virus infesting the planet. We were actually tubes, he said, with an opening at either end. You stuffed food in one aperture and it came out the other as food for the land. That appealed to my science fiction interests and we had a lot of fun playing on the tube theory. He lived at Whistler for several years when it was a hippy haven of rebel squatters. In the late 70's, he wore his hair down to his shoulders, its reddish colour contrasting with his long golden beard. He was quite an amazing spectacle on skis and when he really went for it in the turns he looked like the Maharishi Yogi Mur. He tended to be airborne a lot on the hills, a family trait since his father and brothers were all pilots. He was a particularly good slider, and a good all-round skier, though he never managed to win . . . a great tragedy really, because he undoubtedly had the ability.

Mur always knew exactly what his priorities were and remained cool under fire. One time, he was in the passenger's seat in a Saab I was driving on a snow-covered autoroute in France. I was cruising at about 80 miles an hour when a warning sign, one of those pictographs showing skid marks going all over the place, loomed into view and the road narrowed into a donkey track about a meter wide. The situation was further complicated by the fact that we were now negotiating a 90-degree turn with a guard rail threatening to attack the Saab, which had assumed the attitude of a classic four-wheel slide. As I hung on like Gilles Villeneuve, the Saab edged over to the rail which was covered with a few inches of snow. Poof! We dusted the snow, but missed the guard rail, and continued on our way. I apologized to the guys in the back and Mur, who had remained calm throughout, said philosophically, "Maybe you should drive a bit slower." I did.

The year I won the World Cup, Mur was my room-mate at Whistler when the demands being made on me by the public and the media got out of hand. His natural state of calm was beneficial to me and, as we were talking in our hotel room, Mur said, "Pod, you know I never really understood what it was like for you until now. It must be really hard to deal with." I appreciated his realization, but I also found it shocking that someone who'd been so closely involved with me for years and years didn't know what I was going through until this late date. I knew it was partly because he kept himself isolated from the everyday cut and thrust of team life, but it reinforced my belief that no one except myself could fully understand what it was like. Yet I was grateful for Mur's comment because it was very unusual for anyone on the team to commiserate. We may have felt like it, but it was never expressed – part of the whole macho male thing no doubt. I was quite impressed when Mur broke through that barrier. Nowadays, he and I are good friends as well as business associates and go on holidays together with our ladies.

Dave Irwin was the most intense and combative member of the team, and continually engaged the rest of us in various forms of one-on-one competition. At one point early on, when he and Mur were using Head skis, a new shipment arrived for them at Garmisch. They were the latest design of "lead sleds" with lead inlays and soft tips to better absorb the shock, and it was first come, first serve, between Ir and Mur as to choice of skis. The rest of us stood back and watched as they ripped open the box and stacked the skis against a wall. They raced through the lineup flexing the tips to find a preferred pair and Ir, ever aggressive, tore a tip completely off and was forced to keep that pair. I nearly peed my pants laughing.

Though he was quiet and reserved and wore glasses, Ir's super-competitive streak lurking just beneath a benign exterior made him a Clark Kent/Superman kind of guy. His highly developed aggressive nature came into play in everything we did. When we had soccer games, he stormed around bumping into people as if he would rather kick you than the ball. He was very, very physical and never backed down. He was the biggest guy on the team at about 185 pounds and he hurt a lot of people on the soccer field. He played no favourites, belting anybody in sight and eventually, whenever we played soccer, I stationed myself at the opposite end of the field from Ir. He attacked the hills with the same kind of aggression and became the second Canadian male to win a World Cup race, at Schladming in 1975, two weeks after Ken's first win.

Ir also had some incredibly spectacular falls, particularly at Wengen soon after his Schladming victory, and to the European fans he epitomized the Crazy Canucks. His hell-bent-for-leather approach really shook up the ski-racing establishment and the rest of us followed suit. The downside of this is the injury factor and Ir had more than his share of those. At Zermat one year, we were training on a glacier in brilliant sunshine which made visibility difficult. Ir skied full tilt into a rope which was stretched across his path and received a bad rope burn that gave him an artificial, ear-to-ear grin. Poor Ir had to wear makeup for some time to hide his misfortune from the photographers.

I don't think he ever fully recovered from the serious concussion he received at Wengen in the 1975-76 season. He really rang his bell there and the injuries piled up after that: two compression fractures in his back in 1977, calcium deposits from a bad bruise in his thigh, and a huge fall at Schladming in 1978 that gave him another concussion, bad facial cuts, a chipped kneecap, and a severe general body sprain. An Austrian coach who watched this crash said, "Today I saw the end of Dave Irwin." The Austrian was wrong of course and Ir never stopped trying after that and always, even if he was less than fit, he stuck it on the line and pushed himself as hard as he possibly could. He never held back and I learned from his attitude. I watched him succeed because he pushed and I watched him fail because he pushed. I watched others who didn't push and they neither succeeded nor failed. In my pursuit of success I took Ir's route. Ir succeeded in his après ski life as well, and is now Director of Marketing of Sunshine Village in Banff.

On the team it was inevitable that people cooped up together for months at a time would get on each other's nerves. Most of us had few common interests other than skiing and I suppose everybody bugged everybody else, but I singled out Ken Read. At first, he and I didn't get along at all well. He rubbed me the wrong way with small things like turning on the lights in my room when I was asleep and refusing to let anybody else look at the maps when we were on the road. Little things like that built up over a period of time until, for my own piece of mind, I made a list of the things about Ken that really bugged me. It was a *long* list and every once in a while I'd read it to myself and fume privately. After a while, when both of us grew up, I was able to tear it up.

Most of the time I was closest to Ken: we had the same skis, travelled to the factories, worked the ski camps together, and our performance levels were similar. On the hills Ken had a wild, flailing, windmilling style, while his public persona was the opposite – calm, studied, poised. He gave the impression of being very self-assured and confident with a clear idea of where he was going. It was hardest for him when things didn't go the way he wanted; then he could get very upset. He occasionally displayed fits of temper in the finish area if he hadn't had a good run, though mostly he tried to control his emotions.

Sometimes Ken worked so hard at controlling his own situation that he developed a kind of tunnel vision and failed to notice his impact on others. Selfish is too strong a word, it was more like being so wrapped up in himself that he didn't think of the implications. Ken and Ir didn't really get along at all, mainly because Ir would never back down and they shared a competitive intensity that sometimes bordered on the silly. While the rest of us had a big laugh over the furious competitions they had trying to outdo each other in preparing their skis, even to filing the bindings, they were quite serious and "growled" at each other for a long while.

Earlier on, it seemed one of my roles on the team was to act as a mediator and try to iron out differences of opinion. I usually stepped in when tensions developed between Ken and the coaches or others on the team. There were always little undercurrents of friction: when someone felt another was getting too much attention from a coach or rep, or if they resented somebody getting a better room – stupid little things that ruffled feathers. Good old Pod would try to sort it out and soothe fevered brows.

Because he was so inwardly focused Ken could be difficult to live with and he wasn't exactly in demand as a room-mate, except by the groupies. I bunked with him for many years and we compared notes frequently and gave each other advice on matters other than skiing. Though he was wonderfully skilled at handling himself on the hills, he had trouble dealing with aspects of his matinée idol image. It bugged him when we called him Lance Romance and it bothered Ken that women flocked around him and the rest of us joked about making supreme sacrifices and relieving him of his burden – poor Lance, we all have our crosses to bear. Sometimes I helped him get off the hook when girls pestered him with phone calls – by hanging up on them. Over time, I assisted him in developing his skills as a room-mate. To cure him of his unsettling habit of barging into a darkened room and flicking on the lights when I was sleeping, I unscrewed all the light bulbs before he came in. I only had to do it once!

Most of the problems we had with Ken stemmed from the fact that, for several years, he was one giant step ahead of us as a skier. He was more motivated, on a different plateau of intensity, and simply did anything he deemed necessary to improve his performance. He was ruthless and demanding and the rest of us resented it until he demonstrated that it worked. He set the standard and I learned from him that the intensity level is critical to success. Ken literally won Kitzbühel by himself in 1980, skiing with inferior equipment and overcoming all kinds of adversity to beat the best in the world on the toughest course there is.

The guy was a real workhorse in training. He didn't go in for the glitzy, flashy kind of one-armed push-ups that Jim Hunter did, just sheer powerhouse workout stuff. He knew that ski racing is a mental sport too and you've got to have it in your head to win. We were always careful to avoid doing anything to psych each other out at the start where Ken, in particular, would be in a "hands off" mode. In 1982, while waiting for the start at Kitzbühel, I had my helmet on and didn't see his lying in the snow. I tripped and fell, throwing snow onto his specially tinted goggles. It was potentially disastrous because they could easily have been scratched. It was a very tense moment for me: I didn't want to throw him off his run and I worried about him thinking I might have done it on purpose. Then I worried that my being bothered about his goggles might interfere with my own run. I apologized profusely and he assured me I was forgiven, though he must have felt less charitable when I won the race and he was third.

Ken and I went through a period of estrangement after he got hurt and I started winning. The media noticed it and played on it and media exposure had something to do with our drifting apart. Ken had always been the focus of attention, because he was the best skier and because he was so articulate. The press attitude was: if you wanted to talk to a Crazy Canuck Ken Read was the main man. When he came back from being injured, the situation had changed. I had spread my wings and flown from the nest. I was now the one sought out for interviews. It must have been very hard for Ken and when we switched to different ski companies the break was even more pronounced.

We never stopped speaking to each other, but the closeness, the sharing of confidences, was no longer there. After Mur and Ir retired, Ken and I were all that remained of the original Crazy Canucks. The new young guys on the team tended to regard Ken and me as something like living legends and we must have looked the part, each with a retinue of followers, our own reps, and our own cars. These circumstances dictated that we go our separate ways and the mutual support we once shared fell by the wayside on the hills. After a run, we were less likely to call back information by radio to those waiting back at the top of the course. In the old days, you'd cross the line and run for the radio; then, later, with our success, you were waylaid by interview-seekers. The previous "us against the world" attitude had gone and we were skiing more as individuals who happened to be on the Canadian team.

When Ken returned from his bad knee injury, I got the impression that he had lost some of his commitment. He scored some good results, but the reckless abandon didn't seem to be there and I wondered if he had other things on his mind. I think there was probably pressure from his family to quit. His father is a medical professor at the University of Calgary and both he and Ken's mother played a prominent role in his career. While they both skied and were members of the establishment of the sport in Canada, I'm not sure they approved of their son choosing skiing as a profession. When he did leave the team, the year before I did, it threw everybody off for some time. He and I had joined the team on the same day and his departure left a large void.

When I joined Ken as an ex-Crazy Canuck, there was a period of uneasy adjustment concerning the zones of influence in Canada as we staked out our territories. He had been closest to me on a competitive level and the competition continued in our commercial activities. At first, we were reluctant to even mention our business affairs and there was a kind of unspoken struggle over who would get which jobs and so on. Everything gradually settled into place and, as we developed our new identities, our self-confidence as businessmen grew so we were able to re-establish contact and become closer friends. I'm very happy about that because it was tough being at odds with Ken. Our relationship had been something like a marriage, living together for years, working together, playing together, and sharing our hopes, dreams, and fears.

Our new careers are remarkably parallel, yet we bring two completely different personalities to the job so there's no way of getting Ken Read confused with Steve Podborski – even if you're not aware that Ken's the good-looking one. Ken's *Read Report* and his commentaries on CBC TV are first rate and, like me, he works for suppliers to the ski industry and is very active in the Olympic movement.

The team coaches were characters in their own right: they had to be to deal with such a bunch of weirdos. Scott Henderson was a really gung-ho guy with a straightforward philosophy: just train your buns off and go for it. He was a super motivator in the Vince Lombardi mould: winning isn't everything, it's the only thing. Scott was one of the boys, laid back and friendly, and had raced previously on the Canadian team in Europe so he knew the ropes. We had some difficulty adjusting to having his wife Sullie along at first, but she became a valuable contributor as the video person. Scott's methods weren't very sophisticated, but in the early days we had neither the experience nor the budget to get terribly clever. Obviously he was the right coach at the right time because he got us to specialize in Downhill and the Crazy Canucks came into being under his guidance. Scott got us up and flying, then handed over the reins to John Ritchie.

John was also a former member of the Canadian ski team. He had taken psychology in university so he had a more cerebral approach to coaching and was accurately described in the press as being "a mild-mannered psychologist." He wasn't the dictator type and consulted us regularly, asking our opinions about what course of action we might take with respect to training programs and racing strategy.

He joined the team as coach in 1976 and when we started to be successful more and more of his time was spent managing the Crazy Canucks, reducing the hassle factors, and interceding between the racers and the press. This was vitally important because you can get totally overwhelmed in a real hurry without someone to guide and advise you and give you the overall picture. When the ski companies began to invest big bucks in the team they pressured us to perform off the hills in press conferences and publicity functions.

The European teams could arrange this kind of thing more easily as an extracurricular activity, but we were over there to ski and manufacturers' demands could interfere with our training. John worked out scheduling compromises to keep everybody happy.

He wasn't a strict disciplinarian and didn't need to be because we were tougher on ourselves than any coach could be. Team morale was usually good when we were on the way up, but when we got to the top there were occasional problems. After Ken got hurt, John focused most of his attention on me which pissed off the other guys. Obviously he wanted anybody to win who could, but I happened to be the one most likely to win. For the longest time the most likely winner had been Ken and when he came back from his injury he wasn't very pleased with this shift in the balance of power either. It led to a split into two different factions when Ken aligned himself with the assistant coach Heinz Kappeller.

John wasn't showing favouritism, he was doing the only thing he could in the circumstances. We were under tremendous pressure to win, from our suppliers as well as the media. We needed good results to keep the team funding in place and in this sense when I won the team won. John didn't neglect the others, he coached them on the hill as much or more than me, but he did everything he could to help me win and it strained his relationship with the others.

Coaching is a dirty job. When people ask me if I'm ever going to be a coach I say, "Are you kidding?" I'm a Level III coach and instructor and also a Level II examiner for the Canadian Coaching Federation and I help coach adults and kids frequently, but I wouldn't want it as a career, especially at the World Cup level. If things are going well and the racers are happy, the coach is a hero, but when the going gets tough the coach often goes – right out the door. A coach works just as hard as the racers, he's on the road with them, on the hills, looking after their lives 24 hours a day, and planning continually. On the one hand he's serving the team, on the other he's the boss. It's an extremely difficult position to fill and best left to the experts, like John Ritchie.

Joey Lavigne joined the team the year after I did as a racer on the Can Am squad, skied up through the ranks for a while, then went into coaching. He and I went to coaching and instructing clinics to get accreditation from the Canadian Ski Coaches Federation and the Canadian Ski Instructors Alliance and had a ball together. Then Joey came to the National Team, first as an assistant to John, then as head coach of the Downhill team for two years when John took over at the top. John gave the overview and direction, and Joey carried it out. Joey is soft-spoken and really good at handling people. When he took over the Downhill, he said, "Steve, you know I can't tell you what to do. You know more about your skiing needs than I do, so what do you think we should do for you now?" During my last couple of years, I set my own program and Joey took it from there.

One of our earlier coaches, Butch Boutry, was a tough guy, big and hard and mean and likeable. So was Germaine Barrette, another skier who also became a coach, though he was smaller than Butch. Mostly the Canadians were a peaceable lot on the road and confined their physical aggression to the ski hills. One exception was an incident in a bar at Wengen involving a couple of the coaches. Some Scottish fans were into their cups and decided to enliven the place with a punch-up. After it was over everybody kissed and made up and the chief instigator bought drinks for his victims for the rest of the night. We heard about it the next morning at breakfast when the coaches appeared wearing sunglasses and swollen lips. They were embarrassed and one of them laughed it off by saying he'd hit his opponent as hard as he could, applying his mouth to the end of the Scot's fist with considerable force. In deference to his reputation I won't mention his name, but his initials were John Ritchie.

Skis are the most important arrow in a ski racer's quiver of equipment, and probably more vital to performance than the equipment in any sport other than a racing driver's car. A racing driver relies on his chief engineer/mechanic to keep his car in trim and a Downhiller relies on his ski man. When Ken and Ir began winning races on Fischer skis, they had to give our team a service man. After a false start with a bad rep, they increased their budget and brought up a guy from the minor leagues in Europe to look after our skis. He turned out to be brilliant and eventually, in my opinion, he became the best ski man in the world. He also became my friend and was a guest at my wedding. A lot of the credit for my success must go to Hans Ramelmuller.

When Hans, an Austrian living in Austria and working for an Austrian ski manufacturer, joined us, John decided that our first task was to convince him he was a Canadian. We needed him to feel he was on our side and we did win him over. He's a great person, a tall skinny guy with a big nose and very likeable. He worked just as hard for Ken Read and Steve Podborski as he would have for Franz Klammer or Harti Weirather . . . and we beat them. In fact, Hans became so much a part of the Crazy Canucks that it caused some aggravation among the ski companies when he began helping us with the timing during the day, after working half the night on our skis. He put everything he could into the team, above and beyond the call of duty.

In the morning when we woke up, Hans would have our skis ready. We'd do our training and timed runs then come back after lunch for another session. Four of us used two or three pairs each per day, so Hans prepared 16 to 24 skis a day. There was a lot of labour involved, but it was a labour of love for Hans who was an artist at heart. First, he put the ski on a bench and cleaned it off with solvent, taking all the guck off the base. Then he filed the edges and polished them with emery paper, cleaned the ski again, and applied a base coat of wax. He scraped that off and gave it a final coat of wax for the next day. He chose the wax, working in concert with the coaches so they knew what was going on.

My relationship with Hans came to be closer than any other skier/ rep twosome on the tour. He really wanted me to win on his skis and we lived and died together. I knew he put every ounce of his talent and love into preparing them and if the skis, or the skier, didn't perform as expected I would tell him I was sorry. Then, when we went down the hill and just killed the opposition, we rejoiced together. When I rode his skis down the hill at Whistler and came second to clinch the title in 1982, Hans Ramelmuller won too.

Terry "Toulouse" Spence was a great friend to all of us, the kind of guy who just loves life and people. Officially, he was the team masseur but he was a lot more than that. John knew Toulouse and gave him the job because he knew he could trust him and that he could get along with everybody and adjust to life on the tour. Before he joined us we went through a lot of physiotherapists who couldn't take the life or had the wrong personalities for a high-pressure situation. Beyond standing at the start area and warming you up by massaging your leg muscles, Toulouse was the guy who relayed information from down the hill. He helped get you prepared mentally, kept you calm, and massaged edgy nerves like a jockey with a race horse at the starting gate. Later, when you lay on his massage table, he was the guy who listened to your troubles.

Toulouse even did our partying for us. Before a race we couldn't go out and get totally immersed in a good time, so Toulouse did it and came back to tell us what we had missed. It turned out that several times when he staggered back from one of his adventures the weather on race day was perfect, so it became a kind of tradition. Toulouse would greet us with bloodshot eyes in the morning: "Guys, I did it again. I sacrificed my liver for good weather." He got his nickname one time when he attended a strip club, though he wasn't there on our behalf. The joint featured body painting and one of the scantily clad ladies handed Terry a brush and some paints. On the empty canvas of her anatomy he proceeded to create a work of art, just like Toulouse Lautrec.

There was never a master/servant relationship on the team. The Austrian equipment reps, including Hans and people who came from other suppliers, always had trouble with this. They were accustomed to being slaves and hating it. We invited them to become one of the guys and share in the fun as well as the work. It was the Canadian way of doing things and really the only way to work on such a small team.

Over the years, other skiers came along to join and/or replace the original Crazy Canucks and there was always a period of transition for them, to prove themselves on the hill and to adjust to life on the team. The World Cup Squad, or the Downhill "A" Team as it came to be known, had a farm system of teams with names that varied through the years, as in "B" or "C" Team, Can Am Squad, and Talent Squad. The Downhill Backup Team was the least popular name with the guys on it because we used to joke about them backing up the Downhill. Robin McLeish, one of the characters who came up through the system, had a devil-may-care attitude and wild cackle of a laugh to match. He made it up to the A Team for a couple of years while I was there and livened things up with his cackling and joking around. Chris Kent was a very intense and brooding type, but he contributed a lot of words to the team jargon. Gary Athans, who was nicknamed "Harv," had some kind of physiological problem that left him exhausted a lot of the time and which interfered with his racing. Gary "Snake" Aiken was a real hard rock kind of personality, tough as nails, who drove a souped-up Chevy Nova back in Warfield, B.C. But he was also a joker and quick with a quip and always had a smile on his face.

The best of the newcomers in terms of results was Todd Brooker, a good guy, a lot of fun, and very open and joyful in his approach to life. In my opinion his impulsiveness was a weakness as well as a strength. Todd would just go for it, all out at all times, as opposed to my more studied approach. But he won races and I'm all for whatever it takes to win. I had my share of accidents too and can fully appreciate the agonies Todd went through, physical and mental, when he finally crashed out of ski racing after his bad fall in 1987. In fact, it was accidents that finished most of the Crazy Canucks.

5. *Ski Bums*

The Crazy Canucks were just ski bums at heart and that's often what we wrote under "occupation" in hotel registries, sometimes varying it to become unemployed or brain surgeons. On the road, our spare-time pursuits tended to be individual ones. We occasionally went to a movie en masse when we were at our headquarters hotel in Zurich, Switzerland, but, since we ate, slept, and skied together for weeks on end, I preferred to disappear into a book in my private time. My reading was 99 per cent Sci-Fi and Fantasy, although I waded through Homer's *Iliad* and *Odyssey* and some other classics. One of our favourite expressions – "Eating your liver" – came from Greek mythology via coach John Ritchie. When one god pissed off another, he was chained to a rock and every morning a big bird came and ate out his liver. In the Greek version the organ was magically renewed every day so the bird could have his breakfast, and in the Crazy Canuck translation "to eat your liver" meant to wipe out in a grand manner. In either version of the legend it was a very painful experience.

We developed a whole lexicon of Crazy Canuck jargon. You never just fell in a race, you "ate your liver," "maxed out," "got chewed" or "munched" or "eaten" because you did a "faceplant" or a "head-plant" or a "downhill herringbone." The latter involved catching both your inside edges which forced your skis into a snowplow causing you to "chew miserable." A lot of the terms referred to maneuvers necessary to negotiate differing terrain. A "pre-jump" meant to jump before you arrived at the actual bump; "suck" was to pull up your legs in the pre-jump; and "press" was dropping your upper body down as you came to a jump. The suck and the

56

press had different effects. Pulling up your legs in a suck takes you on a longer roll or ride through the air while pressing gives you a really sharp angle change as you fly. When you land, a "fallaway" is when the terrain drops away from the direction you're going in, while an "airplane" turn is banked in the same direction you want to go.

We called those we didn't like (and often each other) ordinary improper names like nerd, jerk, dork, and prick, though "shrub," meaning any or all of those terms, was our own invention. A collection of nerds was called a "shrubbery." Like most red-blooded Canadian boys, we frequently lapsed into popular Anglo-Saxon profanities to describe our adventures – but all of that was usually switched off when we came under the scrutiny of the media. Once, under duress, I forgot myself on television. It was at Garmisch in 1984, after my third win there, and the Swiss TV people interviewed me for their national French network. I was asked how it felt to win Garmisch again. I'd just done English and German interviews and in the confusion I forgot to delete the French expletive referring to a bodily function. My reply of "Merde!" was beamed in living colour all over Switzerland. I apologized immediately and they forgave me, saying I was the only person in the world who could have gotten away with it. If I'd been Swiss I might have been jailed.

"Rude" was a favourite all-purpose adjective for some time. Everything was rude: you had a rude run, that was a rude car, those are rude guys. "Saga" became a synonym for story: what's your saga, that was a long saga. To leave was to "blow," and to go fast was to "step on the loud pedal," and you never just went fast when you stepped on the loud pedal on a Downhill run. You "howled" and you "skied your buns off" and, of course, you frequently, "ate your liver." Franz Klammer was always "Frank Clamp" to us, a literal translation of his name. Another Austrian, Werner Grissmann, was a real character and we christened him "Greaseball."

We could curse fluently and make obscene gestures in three languages. We learned the sphinctre-muscle gesture, closing the thumb and forefinger to emulate the bowel action incurred in fearful situations, from Werner Grissmann. A former chimneysweep in Austria, "Greaseball" Grissmann was fast but never won a race, though his jokes and crazy antics made him famous. He was a huge bear of a man which earned him the nickname of "Grizzly" in Europe,

57

though we stuck to "Greaseball." During his career, he was frequently fastest down the first part of the hill but always seemed to blow it in the final sections. When he retired he had a beautiful bronze trophy made, a sculpture of a grizzly bear looking real mean, and awarded it to skiers who lost races in the last stretch. He was a race commentator and made his presentation in front of the crowd. One year, I finished second at Kitzbühel and Greaseball called me up to the podium to present me with his trophy. He made a speech to the crowd explaining its significance. He pointed out that the front part of the trophy was perfect in every detail, just like the first part of my race. But the last part of my race was also like the trophy, not very good at all. Then he turned it around and demonstrated that the back of the bear was completely unfinished. I nearly fell off the podium laughing and the Grizzly trophy is one of my prized possessions.

We always seemed to be up on some God-forsaken mountain where there were only pinball machines and video games for amusement. I played them until my eyeballs spun. After three weeks in a place like Val d'Isère I must have pumped a ton of francs into Space Invaders. Ken never played, but Mur and Ir sometimes did. True to form, Ir would just stand there and shoot and inevitably got blown up because he would never back off. I was a prime game player and enjoyed the challenge of working out the patterns. But Robin McLeish and especially Todd were the best players. Backgammon was big for a while but we stopped it when the betting got out of hand.

Nobody made specific rules, we just did things that made collective sense to the team. Everybody agreed to a certain code of behaviour because we all had the same goals. And you never did anything to interfere with anybody's performance. You didn't go out partying at night because you didn't want to affect your own performance and, just as importantly, you didn't want to come crashing in late at night and bug the other guys. Anybody who persisted in doing this risked a fall from grace, in the results as well as in popularity, and he would get a free trip home, fast. It seldom ever happened and never to the top skiers.

Racing was an extremely serious business and you couldn't muck about. The more successful you became, the more serious you got.

After you became a winner, you had your own ski man who had his own car and was being highly paid to look after you. You had at least 16 pairs of skis that cost $400 to $500 each, you had three or four Downhill suits that cost $400 each, you had five pairs of custom-made ski boots, a custom-made helmet, and so on. You had video cameras, timing devices, tons of equipment, team cars, and team personnel, and a coaching staff whose whole raison d'être was to make you ski faster. This was not playground stuff. You had to play the game by the rules. And you only got to stay in the game if you got better.

However, we weren't saints and sometimes we broke the rules outside the team. A favourite form of amusement for a while was The Great French Telephone Scam. Because the team operated outside the normal levels of society, it was easier for us to find out about underground activities that respectable people might not know about or, it must be said, wish to engage in. We always knew about the latest anti-establishment games in town and in France we heard about a way to call our loved ones back in Canada without having to bother about formalities like money. You could beat the telephone system by drilling a hole in a French franc, tying a piece of dental floss to it, and dangling it over just the right point in the slot. You could phone anywhere in the world for free and for as long as you wanted.

This happened before we were winners and it was an amazing bonanza to our impoverished crew. It was a riot: "Hi, how're ya doin'? I'm just hangin' around over here in France and I thought I'd give ya a buzz." It was wonderful, you felt like Joe Big Bucks standing there in a telephone booth with his cigar. We phoned everybody we knew and some we didn't know. One guy, who must remain nameless, used to phone Japan just to find out what time it was there. It was a big joke but also a lifeline to us to be able to communicate with our families and friends back home. We all did it and for guys like Dave Irwin it was an alternative to jogging runs. Poor Ir was so bashed up most of the time that running was difficult and not good for his wrecked body. So Ir would pretend he was off on his morning run but he'd sneak into a phone booth and spend two hours calling home. This was at 6:00 am in France so he must have been catching people going to bed in B.C. We used to joke about Ir being so keen for his morning run and as we jogged along we'd see him huddled there in a phone booth, all bundled up and yammering away to the folks back in Canada. It was hilarious.

We eventually told the other teams about it and they did it too, particularly the Americans. It went on for a couple of years until the authorities finally found out and changed the system. We stopped before that when it became just too much. We knew it was a dumb thing to do and we had trouble sneaking around and looking over our shoulders all the time and feeling guilty. Even though loyalty to our families and fellow Canadians was the main motive behind our criminal activities, we worried about getting thrown in the slammer and bringing infamy to our native land. Though I was a mild abuser of the French phone system using the dangling coin trick, I was never up to the skill level of some of the others and I tended to be a law-abiding citizen abroad. Besides, I always look guilty when I've committed a misdemeanour.

Most of our fun and games tended to be of a more innocent variety though we occasionally ran afoul of the local constabulary. Before I joined the team, there was a tradition of borrowing national flags as souvenirs. One time at Schladming, some of the guys decided to stage a heist to capture an Austrian flag from in front of the police station. One car came whipping by to create a diversion on the other side of the street while another van slid up to the station and the guy on the roof slashed off a flag and they took off. They were eventually apprehended and severely reprimanded.

Anti-social behaviour was more dangerous in Switzerland where you're guilty until proven innocent and the population of six million or so is said to consist of six million policemen. However, the normally law-abiding Swiss tended to go berserk at ski races. In the hotels at Wengen the most desirable rooms to us were at the back, away from the view, but also away from the streets which were filled with raging drunks who yodelled and yahooed at the top of their lungs, accompanying themselves by bonging humungous cow bells that vibrated the mountain tops all night long.

We became very familiar with the European postal systems and were mightily impressed. Once when I suffered the ultimate death of leaving my address book in a hotel in Switzerland, it was mailed to me at our next destination and arrived almost as fast as we drove. It looked a bit battered, something like our cars, but it was amazing for someone accustomed to Canada Post. At first, when I got letters in Switzerland that were posted on the same day, regular postage, I was convinced the date on the envelope was wrong. Stuff that I mailed from Austria or Switzerland to Canada arrived within five days. It often takes a week for one of my letters mailed in Toronto to get a couple of miles down the street. But it was nice when I was on the team to hear from the Canadian posties who would recognize my name on envelopes sent from home and scribble messages of encouragement: "Way to go Steve!" "Keep on trucking Steve!" "Go for it Pod!" It might have been a misuse of the mails but I loved it.

Rah, rah, cheerleading stuff from Canada was really inspiring to combat boredom as much as anything else. Training could be a big yawn, particularly at six o'clock in the morning when it was pitch black and you had to face up to beginning each new day with a series of "ups." After you got up and did your 20-minute to half-hour run (though I skipped instead after my knees were rebuilt), you came back to your room and did endless ups. This was a Ritchieism referring to sit-ups, pull-ups, push-ups, and variations on those themes. The usual finale to this routine, after you had pushed yourself particularly hard, was to say you were going to *throw up*. Then we did calisthenics and finished with lots of stretching, the theory being that a supple body would bend instead of break when you ate your liver.

Our first coach Scott Henderson suffered along with us and we banded together for the sake of survival. Scott's approach to coaching was quite simple: Go for it! Push, push, push! We trained incessantly, regardless of the weather conditions. I remember one session in a howling blizzard where we were quaking in our boots, shivering in the freezing cold in our skimpy Downhill suits at the top of a hill. They gave us little blankets while we waited our turn, then we took off. It was snowing like crazy and you could hardly see the tips of your skis. The NFB were there with their cameras and the film shows me whipping through this raging snowstorm past Scott, who's standing halfway down the hill, and I'm yelling "MOTHERRRR!" because it's so ridiculous. I'm going 60 or 70 miles an hour into the teeth of the storm and can't see a darn thing.

Scott's dryland training was just as tough. Hiking in the mountains, bicycling, running – they were torture tests. He'd push us 'til we dropped. But he pushed himself as hard as us and we didn't resent it . . . much. It wasn't a very sophisticated approach, but it was effective. We needed to be in better shape and ski and ski like crazy to catch up to the Europeans and we began to improve.

It was a long time before our diet improved. Breakfast was especially important to fuel our fires on the hills, but it was always a scramble to get eggs or anything more substantial than coffee and a bun, or a croissant if you were in France. We always tried to get "extras" from the hotels, like cereal or fruit, usually to no avail. We got the standard tourist fare which was ok for a week or so, but we had to live on this stuff, and perform on it, and it was nutritionally only several notches up from survival. Ken pioneered the concept of bringing over his own granola creation from home, huge bags of it in his luggage. After a while, most of us brought over our own breakfast on which we'd throw quantities of European pasteurized/demolished milk. Amazingly, we won races on these concoctions and it became the breakfast of champions.

On a typical training day we left the hotel at 8:30 or 9 o'clock and headed for the hills where we used to jump the queues of spectators waiting for the lifts, unless they were relatively short. After all, we were going to work, they were going to watch. We skied until lunch, which was usually from 12:00 to 1:00 pm, and the fare was whatever was on the cheapest fixed price menu. Since ski boots weren't allowed in the dining-room, we often gobbled down our soup, main course, and dessert in the hallway of the hotel. Other times, we might even eat on the hill; then we skied again to 4 o'clock. We skied through sets of gates, making turns, going over jumps and changing terrain, feeling our edges, continually testing the skis and our techniques. We skied in all kinds of conditions, sometimes going off track to find powder, hard-packed snow, and solid ice. We tested ourselves on nerd balls (chunks of snow left by the snowcats), always a challenge because it was like skiing on marbles. We went up and down the hill all day long, non-stop, hardly even noticing the often beautiful scenery. We skied down to the bottom of the lifts, hopped on in one motion, and talked about skiing on the way up. It was assembly-line skiing and, before the lift stopped, we were doing up our buckles, ready to go down again. We skied fast, we skied slow, we skied on the runs, and we skied off the runs, sometimes for miles and miles until we were so far away we had to take a bus back. We just skied. And it was fun.

Back at the hotel, we'd bring our skis to the ski room and talk to the rep: "Hans, next year you're going to get out there on the course"; "Sorry I hit so many rocks today"; "Which skis am I going to use tomorrow?"; "How are things back at the factory?" Then we went upstairs to change for the afternoon workout. We went on really hard 20 or 30 minute "psycho" runs. The object of this exercise was to get your heart rate up around its limit; then we tried to keep it there by doing our "ups" all over again. Near the end of my career I went on 20-minute "psycho" skipping marathons, whipping away with a skipping rope that had a counter on it, always trying to beat yesterday's record. It was great sport. At 6:00 or 6:30, we showered and shaved (we never had time to shave in the morning) to get presentable for dinner at 7:30. After another boring hotel meal, we'd have a team meeting for an hour or an hour and a half to review the videos of our day's runs, outline the next day's schedule, and plan strategy. We fell into bed about 10 o'clock where I'd usually take in a few minutes of science fiction, then dreamland.

That was our daily routine, except for race days. On travel days, we'd leap out of bed, brush our teeth, hop into the cars, drive all day to the next hotel, have a team meeting, then hit the sack. We had to be the most boring individuals in the world. Yet I loved it. It was the most structured, yet freest flowing, existence imaginable. It had a single focus, but within that framework you could do a lot or do a little. It was your choice as to how much you put into it. We put everything into it because it worked. This ritual was arrived at through an evolutionary process. It might seem restricted and boring, but it was really fascinating because we could always see the light at the end of the tunnel. Training was important and we enjoyed it, team meetings were critical and we wanted to attend them, bed was great because we wanted to rest and be ready to run the next day. Everything was significant and had its purpose and place, even shaving at night to save time in the morning. The routine was comforting and exciting at the same time. The goal was running the Downhill faster and there was no greater reward than that. It was a great life.

We pushed ourselves into learning the languages of skiing. Mur was pretty good in French and Italian though Ken was the first real linguist. He had a good basic grounding in French because of the year he'd lived with his family in Switzerland. We used to tease him that he sounded as if he had marbles in his mouth when he spoke French but he was really quite fluent. Ken tended to look farther ahead than most of us and he saw that German was necessary to survive in World Cup circles, especially when he first started winning and was being interviewed in German. It was also the lingua franca of the reps and you needed it to get your skis done properly.

We had problems with the many German dialects and accents from the various regions of Germany, Austria, and Switzerland. Each of us had a German/English dictionary and we dug words out of them and checked meanings with our reps. It was hard with these guys rocketing along in German at dinner, for instance. Sometimes the Fischer manager and two or three of their reps would take me out for a meal and I would sit there in the middle just listening and intercepting words and adding them to my repertoire. Sometimes I went with Hans to his home village, off the beaten track in Austria, where no one could speak English. I would be babbling on in German and they'd correct me when I goofed up on a word or got my grammatical tenses wrong. My vocabulary grew and eventually I came to understand what sounded right. I even started to *dream* in German after being interviewed on TV and radio and in newspapers for days on end. I could talk up a storm on ski-related topics, though the finer shades of meaning escaped me. I survived in French with reasonable comprehension but poor conversational abilities. At least I could communicate so I could hack it.

Life on the road wasn't all work and no play. Sometimes we played rough and resorted to terrorist acts for amusement, like bombing cars with firecrackers. We carried the 24th of May concept a bit too far by arming ourselves with powerful Austrian firecrackers that you lit by striking them on a matchbox. One time, our grenade tactics nearly caused an explosive international incident. Toulouse, Rob McLeish, and I were tooling along in a van with a gross of firecrackers at our feet when we decided to relieve the tedium by lobbing a burst or two at a following car. We were having a riot, igniting the fuse, holding the firecracker for a few seconds, then tossing it into the wind and . . . WHAM! Our target was not amused, he roared past, slammed on the brakes in front of us, and leaped out of his car. We locked the doors and rolled up the windows while he screamed and yelled abuse at us. Eventually his rage subsided and he stalked off, jumped in his car, and took off, shaking his fist at the Crazy Canucks.

It was dumb of us, but very funny at the time. However, we weren't yet cured of our lust for explosions. A few miles further on we decided to blow up the Arlberg tunnel! Rob rolled down the window and lobbed a grenade at the wall. It bounced back into the van and landed spitting fire on the floor at our feet. Suddenly, I was driving with two guys sitting on my shoulders, one hand on the wheel, and the other trying to cover my ears. BOOM! The thing went off, the van was filled with smoke, and we were deaf for some time. That ended our firecracker phase . . . .

For awhile another favourite pursuit, after we became winners, was to go "Hoovering," as we called it, snapping up all the freebies offered by the manufacturers. At first, we sucked the stuff in like Hoover vacuum cleaners, but then we veterans came to realize nothing was free. When companies gave away equipment or clothing there was always a catch and somebody always had to pay somewhere down the line, and it was usually the top skiers. There was a limit to the favours offered by manufacturers and the young "Hooverers" would use them up. Ken and I tended to preach this to the newcomers on the team, telling them they were there because we were winners, but they had to get it out of their systems as we had.

But there was always a great temptation to give in to "Hoover Madness." One time we went on a tour through the factory of a big European sportswear manufacturer. We proceeded in an orderly fashion until somebody heard they were giving away free shirts in another room. There was a wholesale stampede with everybody wading into the stuff, throwing things around, piling it up, and generally behaving like a frenzied school of feeding sharks. I didn't participate and afterward people were a bit sheepish at having run amok. It was ok to Hoover quietly for yourself on occasion, but it was an entirely different kettle of fish to accumulate a ton of stuff that you would never be able to use. Sometimes it signified that a guy was about to leave the team and, it must be said, some had thoughts of selling their booty back in Canada. It was a way to tide them over until they got a job.

Another reason for frowning on extracurricular Hoovering was a mercenary one. It upset the applecart when somebody wore clothes or used equipment that came from outside the equipment pool of the team. We were quite happy to accumulate the gear given to us by the manufacturers who supplied the team. They did it because we were mobile billboards for them, millions of potential consumers would see us and, if they were suitably impressed, they bought the products. Both skier and manufacturer knew which side their bread was buttered on. The companies got free advertising, we got free clothing and equipment, and both factions collected from the revenues earned through the exposure we gave the clothing and equipment. Some of this revenue was also pumped into the team by the manufacturers who paid the CSA tens of thousands of dollars to be associated with us. It was simply bad for business to go outside the equipment pool, but it took a while for new guys to realize this.

One time at Zermat, I was rooming with Todd Brooker and Robin McLeish came in and said, "Look Todd, we've got a couple of days off. Let's drive up to the factory and grab some stuff." Todd said, "Oh no, I don't think we should. There's no such thing as a free lunch." Robin was devastated. Todd and he were buddies and had been partners-in-Hoovering. Now Todd had changed his mind about it and Robin felt betrayed. But both of them came into an affluent team environment compared to the hand-to-mouth existence we originally had to contend with. We veterans still felt we were lucky to even be there. The new guys felt they deserved to be there because they were good skiers. I believed then, and still do, that you never *deserve* to be anywhere. You've got to pay your dues, earn your keep, and be very, very lucky.

6. Eating My Liver

I was the rawest of rookies when I first went to Europe with the team. I had never even seen a World Cup race on TV, only the Olympics, so everything was completely new to me when we arrived at Val d'Isère in France for the first event of the 1974-75 season. We came into the town at night and the whole place was really hopping, jammed with people jabbering away in foreign languages, and I wondered if there was some kind of festival going on. In the morning, I looked out the window of my hotel room and saw thousands of people lining the route of the course and this was only for the inspection and training runs. I had no idea the sport was so popular in Europe.

It was a quantum leap for the kid from Don Mills. I was amazed to see fences around the course, until I realized they were there to hold back the huge crowds and protect them from flying skiers. The start was way up in the clouds above the tree-line and it was a struggle for me to even pronounce the names of course landmarks, like Waldeinfahrt and Zeilschuss, let alone tackle them on skis. The veterans on the team laughed at my dumb questions and told stories that didn't necessarily put me at ease. They talked about one really bad compression turn where one Canadian was so scared he literally shit his pants. This wasn't from dysentery, but sheer terror. In later years I told the same stories to rookies and would rub it in about how Collumbin's Bump at Val d'Isère got its name: Roland Collumbin, a Swiss skier, broke his back twice in consecutive years on that part of the course.

I was in both the races when Collumbin fell and "his" Bump is without exaggeration one of the most dangerous jumps anywhere.

It's up near the top of the course and you come rocketing down to this pitch, or steep drop, then onto a flat section which drops down a pitch onto another flat. If you get it right and push down, or compress, properly at the right time, you land on the pitch, before you hit the flats. Collumbin blew it, overshot the pitch and landed on his back on the flats, cracking vertebrae two years in a row.

Another part of the course, The Compression, isn't much easier, as Dave Murray once demonstrated in Crazy Canuck fashion. The rules say you have to be able to see from one gate to the next and at The Compression they had to double the height of the eight-foot gate poles to make them visible to oncoming skiers. Mur came whipping around the turn, kind of messed it up a bit, and, as he was flying through the air, he had to turn his skis so the tips wouldn't hook on the flag on top of the gate. He was 16 feet in the air going about 70 miles an hour and trying to miss the top of the gate. Mur survived, with clean underwear, but this is scary stuff for a rookie to contemplate.

My mind was filled with horror stories as I went up the lift for my first races at Val d'Isère but I made it down in one piece, finishing 46th in the GS and 31st in the Downhill. Not bad considering my start number was near the back of the pack in the 80's. In the finish area, I saw a crowd around the Downhill winner and I recognized him – Franz Klammer. I was in heaven . . . there I was actually on the same course as the great Austrian racer. He was surrounded by about 50 or 60 photographers, all clicking away like mad, and I thought, this is ridiculous, how can they all want a picture of Franz Klammer? Why doesn't one guy take his picture and give a print to everyone else? I was completely ignorant.

I had no time to reflect on my first World Cup races as we immediately hit the road for the next hill at St. Moritz in Switzerland. Then came Garmisch-Partenkirchen in West Germany, Wengen in Switzerland, and so on as the rest of the season flew by. In those days we travelled in just two vehicles for the whole team, a clapped-out Volkswagen van for us and a car for the coaches. All our skis were piled up in a pyramid on top of the van and we either froze or cooked inside. The guys in the front seats sat in front of the heater in their underwear, those in the middle seats were dressed relatively normally, and the guys in the back wore the discarded clothes of those in the front. We were a pretty egalitarian group and took turns moving around in the van to even out the discomfort.

I survived my first World Cup winter of 1974-75 in one piece and did well enough to get my name on the results sheets. The team was competing in Slalom and Giant Slalom events, as well as Downhill, and in the overall World Cup standings Jim Hunter was the best of us, finishing 33rd. The two Daves were tied in 45th place, Ken was 49th, and I was 52nd out of the more than one hundred skiers ranked. Closer to home, I won the North American and Canadian Junior Downhill Championships.

That summer, the team had another training camp where my South American misadventures continued when I was thrown in jail in Argentina. We were training in an area which was particularly security-sensitive for some reason and we were warned to always carry our passports in case of police checks. There was a curfew in effect and one night Colin Sanders (he was a ski rep then and is now manager of Sporting Life, a sports gear store in Toronto) and I had dinner and maybe a bit too much red wine. It was past the enforced magic hour of the curfew, but we were pleasantly oblivious and singing away as we walked back to our hotel.

All of a sudden these two guys walked up to us, they looked like normal Argentinians, and started blabbing away in Spanish. They held up a card and I thought maybe they wanted a game of cards. Then I recognized the word "police" and realized they wanted to see our identity cards or passports which of course we didn't have. I started giggling to myself, but soon stopped when they grabbed us and hauled us off to the jail. They slammed us up against a wall and frisked us. We had to empty our pockets, then they separated Colin and I and started grilling me in Spanish, which I didn't understand. They were real heavies just like in the movies and one of them pulled out a huge gun and set it on the window ledge. I thought, "Holy Shit! This is the real thing." Eventually they realized we were innocent Canadian ski bums and let us go. But I was scared and thankful to get out of there without a case of acute lead poisoning.

In South America every second guy seemed to have a machine gun and one night, when I came back to the hotel late, I banged on the door and the concierge greeted me by poking a gun barrel in my face. The whole place was like an armed camp, with spot checks at every turn of the road, and I was getting paranoid. I'd heard stories about some of our guys getting caught in an earlier revolution, jumping under taxis to escape bullets, seeing bodies floating down rivers, and just getting the last plane out of the airport before everything was blown to smithereens. One night, I lept out of bed at the sound of explosions and thought for sure my number was up – it was another revolution. I was petrified. Finally, I sneaked downstairs and found out they were celebrating a previous revolution with fireworks . . . .

Another time we took a bus to a beach for a day off skiing. All of a sudden we were stopped by a jeep with three guys who covered us with 50-calibre machine guns. They didn't have spit and polish uniforms like the army and just looked like a bunch of weirdos in running shoes. One of the guys on the team said, "Hey, let's get a picture of this," and pulled out his camera. I said, "Get that thing out of here, they could kill us!" I guess they only wanted to know what we were doing, but I was too busy being scared to find out. I thought some of our guys were incredibly stupid and I could have killed them myself! When we got to the harbour, Jungle Jim Hunter started snapping away at a submarine and got himself arrested. He was surrounded by a bunch of people yelling in Spanish who ripped the film out of his camera. They let him go after a lecture which none of us could understand, but I got the impression the Canucks should be a little less crazy in some foreign lands.

That camp in the summer of '75 was a major turning point in our lives because it was decided that we would specialize in Downhill from then on. It was basically Scott Henderson's idea that we should follow the European trend of specializing in certain disciplines, and our strengths seemed to be in the Downhill. Besides, we didn't really have the resources to do more than one kind of racing, and there were fewer people in Downhill. Slalom and GS had something like 120 competitors and we'd be starting around 110th. Downhill in Europe usually had about 80 racers, sometimes 50 on the more dangerous hills, so we would have a better chance starting with half-decent numbers.

We didn't yet give up Slalom and GS but we did concentrate on Downhill, and Scott's hard-nosed training techniques helped prepare us for the worst the hills could throw at us. We trained our butts off and skied in crappy weather that would force any Downhill race to be cancelled and were fitter and keener for it. It's like running with weights on your legs. When you take them off, it's such a relief you can run faster. Our all-out training made us mentally and physically tougher because we knew racing couldn't be any worse! And it helped us overcome our under-financed, under-equipped, under-privileged situation on the World Cup tour.

The Canadians were relative newcomers to the sport. That part of the ski-racing establishment which didn't resent us for trying to break into their exclusive club thought we were a joke, a bunch of hicks from out there in the wilderness who knew nothing . . . and they were at least partly right. Our team was tiny by European standards and we were pitifully poor compared to teams from the Alpine countries, who were funded to the hilt by their governments, tourist bureaus, ski industries, and so on. The European teams stayed in four-star hotels while we were booked into dumps by the local race committees. The Klammers of this world were celebrities who were good for business. The not-yet Crazy Canucks were nobodies.

In 1975, at Madonna di Campiglio in Italy, my hotel bed sagged right to the floor. I had to put my ski bag under it to make it level. The organizers of each race supplied the hotel rooms and made sure the Swiss and Austrian stars were happy, but the Canadians got the short end of the stick – the dirty end of the stick when it came to food: it was appalling, poorly prepared, and inevitably swimming in grease. A salad was like manna from heaven and we drank water because we couldn't afford extras like milk, juice, or coffee. Our team operated on something like $10,000 for each skier for the season and not much of that went for food.

At least we got free flights from the Department of National Defence to the Canadian base at Lahr in West Germany, but we didn't fly first class by any means. The military transport planes were cramped and the stewardesses, or stewards (it was sometimes hard to tell), were pretty tough cases. Maybe it was appropriate for us to travel this way because we were going to fight a kind of war.

There were a few teams down at our shoestring level, like Konrad Bartelski and a couple of other guys who made up the British team. There were always a few one-man teams, from places like Outer Mongolia or somewhere, who were usually just along for the ride against the Swiss, Austrians, Italians, French, and West Germans. The Americans and the Russians could compete with the Europeans on equal financial footing, but seldom matched them in performance. What bugged us most was that we felt we weren't being taken seriously. So our "Canadians against the rest" attitude was reinforced and some of our methods astonished the competition. The Europeans couldn't understand why we tried to help each other out on the hills, how the first Canadian down the hill would advise his teammates about the course conditions and tell them how to go faster. "Why would you help the other guy try to beat you?" they asked. It was simple: we just had to beat THEM.

It was a pleasure to be able to go to the famous resorts and see the jetset in their BMWs, Porsches and Mercedes and watch superstars like Franz Klammer in action. The top skiers had hot cars too but what I envied most was their ski reps. While Klammer and company stayed in the best hotels and twiddled their thumbs I was down in a basement away from the glitter in a grotty little room filing my skis at midnight for the race the next day. The ski rep is probably the most significant factor in a racer's life, besides talent. You can win a race without a good rep but you can't be a consistent winner.

Working on your own skis on the World Cup tour was unheard of. It's like a Formula One racing car driver acting as a mechanic on his own car. When we did get a rep from Fischer, he wasn't up to snuff, in fact a complete bozo, and it wasn't till later that we got a winning rep. But we got quite good at tending to our own skis, and Ken and Dave Irwin won races when they were working on their own equipment.

The top racers always had their reps in tow and were waited on hand and foot by a whole bunch of flunkies. We were seriously hampered in this way, wasting time and energy chasing after the clothes and training skis we had left at the top of the hill before a race. We had to retrieve them at the end of the day. Then we'd see Klammer's servants pack his stuff in two bags (that's 15 or 16 pairs of skis), and put them into a separate car, and they'd roar off into the distance. Meanwhile, we loaded all our skis on the roof of our van, standing there in the snow or rain, balancing them in a pyramid and tying them up with a rope. We tugged and heaved and jammed our bags into the back and finally putt-putted away for another second-gear session on the switchbacks. The Europeans were already an hour down the road and they were going home for the weekend. We drove for hours and hours to the next race location, booked into another fleabag hotel, and stared at the walls, read a book, or wrote a letter home. We dreamt about home-cooked meals and were always hungry. It's a wonder we didn't die of malnutrition or some dread disease from the swill we had to eat.

It was just brutal. We had a great time!

The greatness lay in the fact that we were always getting better. We had nowhere to go but up and we weren't good enough yet to have any downs. We were boot-strapping ourselves up the ladder, learning all the time and feeling positive. And for me, there was a sense of discovery. In the first couple of years, every hill was a new adventure. I'd go to the top and look down and wow! The European hills were completely outside any North American experience I'd had and it took me a couple of seasons to find out which way they went. The first time down I'd be turning left and right and come to a rise and peer over the top and wonder, "Jeez! What if there's a blind corner?" Each course is about two miles or more long and you've got to memorize it intimately to even survive, let alone race it. The race is only two minutes or so out of your life, but the fact that you run the risk of ending it lends a certain piquancy to the moment.

My first time at Kitzbühel I wondered how in hell anybody could possibly ski down it, let alone race there. On my first inspection run, I slid down slowly with my eyes popping. I stopped at this phenomenally difficult turn, barely stopped because it was so steep, and some other guys skied by. I heard them say it's not as bad as last year and I wondered how it could be worse. This turn is called the Steilhang which means steep pitch in German and that's an understatement. It's more like a cliff and naturally icy. They actually have water hydrants on the hill to make it even more so. You turn to the right through it and bounce over rollers. It's so steep that I've seen guys spin themselves around when their hands touch the hill. During my first training run, I fully expected to see the helicopters pulling bodies off the hill and the proceedings called off. They weren't and I came down in one piece . . . that time.

Anybody who loses it on the Steilhang ends up in the Bamboo Curtain. Nowadays it's a safety net, but then it was a bamboo fence set behind hay bales to catch flying skiers, one of them being Steve Podborski in a training run. I must have dropped a hand or knee on the side of the Steilhang and I spun around backward. I felt no sensation at all which meant I was flying, then there was an explosion of hay and bamboo and poof! – I landed in powder snow. I had no idea where I was and I heard footsteps crunching up. It was Scott who asked me if I was all right. I replied in the affirmative and he gathered up my skis and I went on down the hill. At the finish I took off my helmet and there was hay sticking out of my ears.

Getting down a hill safely was one thing, going up was another. We quickly mastered the no-holds-barred European technique of line crashing. They were like animals in a lineup waiting for a lift. We cut a swathe through any obstacle, hopped over railings, cut through back doors, whatever it took to get to the top. It was survival of the fittest and these battles with the crowds reflected our attitude in the World Cup: push hard, beat everybody.

Our racing attitude continued even on the road to the next event. We pushed the van as hard as it would go, 60 miles an hour maximum in a straight line, in hopes of finding a hotel fast so we could end the ordeal of driving. For years, Sullie Henderson complained about this breakneck pace and the fact that we never did any sightseeing. One day, we passed a castle and Sullie said, "Let's be tourists today." We stopped beside the road, walked up to this pile of rocks, looked at it for 30 seconds, Sullie took a picture, and we drove away. We never stopped at a castle again. At night, we very seldom went carousing and stayed in our rooms, reading or hanging out. We couldn't afford to get hammered and wouldn't have done it anyway because you'd die young if you went out on those hills with a hangover.

We were often homesick and I wrote bushels of letters to help keep my spirits up, long letters describing my mostly miserable state of affairs. Our headquarters in Europe was in an inexpensive little hotel in Zurich, smack dab in the middle of the red-light district with a porno shop on the corner and sex theatres just up the street. One day I walked out and there was a girl lying on the pavement bleeding. She'd just jumped out a window and was very dead. There's a dearth of rough areas in Switzerland but this was one of them and no place for a teenager from Don Mills to be walking around at night.

But I was impressed by Switzerland: it must be the cleanest, best-organized country in the world, but a little too slick and polished for my taste. I admire neatness and have been known to pick up plastic bags and debris from ski hills, and the garbage in places like New York City astonishes me. But the Swiss have a neatness fetish. I preferred Austria, which is neat, tidy, and works well too, but the people are more open and fun. Most of our time in West Germany was spent in army bases which gave a kind of skewed aspect to my impressions. I felt awkward in Northern Italy because the resorts seemed to be in poor areas and the contrasts between the haves and havenots was vivid. We were poor too, but rich compared to the locals there. And France . . . well France is France.

Our team uniform off the hills was jeans and we didn't care about all the latest après-ski wear. But we wanted to look like a racing team and a lot of the time we didn't have the right stuff. It was very frustrating for us to get clothing that didn't fit, was substandard in quality, or just badly designed. All the other teams were outfitted in the latest superslick duds from the European sportswear manufacturers, who weren't interested in us, and we had to make do with clothing from home where the ski clothing industry was still in the dark ages.

We were still very much the boys from the backwoods feeling our way around, sometimes going slightly off course, but we were getting noticed. On one of my early visits to St. Moritz, I was flying down the hill and came whipping off a jump about 10 degrees off the proper line. As I rocketed into the air, I looked down between my skis to see three cameras with big lenses pointing at me and three startled photographers' faces behind them. Then I saw three cameras with no faces behind them because the photographers were running for their lives. They thought I was going to kill them. I landed safely and continued, laughing.

We didn't have any preconceptions about these courses and developed our own ideas about how to ski them. We thought, what if we tried this? The Europeans would say, "Hey, you can't do that, it's never been done before." We'd try it anyway and sometimes we were right. In the beginning, we were mostly wrong, often very wrong. But that's how you learn, by making a mistake once. Providing you don't get killed making it, you learn – fast. We did a lot of learning because it was *all* new. We had to learn to speak German, how to relate to our reps, how to get equipment, money, the works. We had to learn how to sleep in different beds. The coffee was different, even the toilet paper. The toilet paper was wicked, you had to be careful not to poke your finger through it.

My entire world was turned topsy-turvy. The guys on the team who knew Europe gave me some clues and guidance but they couldn't live it for me. They couldn't teach me about the toilet paper. It was sometimes literally overwhelming for me and I felt I just could not handle it. In those early days I was in a daze half the time, I'm sure, and the others just sort of led me around. I can still picture myself in the van, rolling along with absolutely no idea where I was, completely disoriented, and unable to even find myself on the road map. On one trip after we landed at Lahr in West Germany and drove to somewhere in Austria, I had my first confrontation with a down comforter, or duvet, in my hotel room. The chambermaid had folded it down so there was a little opening, and I crawled in there thinking it was a sleeping bag.

When I was really upset or lonely I controlled it by reading endlessly or writing even more letters. I never considered packing it all in and just drifted, carried along by the course of events which began to improve with our results on the hills. For the 1975-76 season, Ken Read and Dave Irwin were in the Downhill first seed, the top 15, and I had moved into the mid-20's. There was some resentment in Europe over this because our rankings came from a summer race in Argentina which the International Ski Federation (FIS) had designated as a special points event. The Europeans felt Ken and Ir had come in the back door through cheap racing. But we showed them up in a real hurry at the beginning of that season at Val d'Isère on the 7th of December, 1975, where Ken won and we had four guys in the top ten. Ir was fourth, Jim ninth, and I was the tenth fastest skier down the hill.

When I came to a stop at the finish area and somebody told me I was tenth, I literally just about fainted from shock. I had been 27th in training and now, suddenly, I was right in there. I wasn't sure if it was a fluke, maybe I'd done it by mistake, but on that day I was one of the best Downhillers in the world. I was really impressed! The French press brought me down to earth when they spelled my name wrong. They'd never had to write Podborski before and they stuck a "y" on the end of it instead of an "i." I was labelled for life that way in France and it pissed me off, though we have the French to thank for the "Crazy Canuck" label, which they gave to us after our breakthrough early in that '75-'76 season.

Serge Lang, a French journalist who writes about skiing for *L'Equipe* and some Swiss papers, was one of the founders of World Cup ski racing when it began in 1966. He's tall and wide, over six feet tall and nearly as wide, and he ran the tour like a dictator until quite recently. When Ken won and our team showed so well at Val d'Isère, Serge Lang wrote about our boldness and aggression. The newspaper headlines said "There are new stars in the heavens, the crazy Canadian ski team." From then on we were the Crazy Canucks.

Ken was the first Canadian male to win a World Cup event and the Europeans were amazed. At Val d'Isère, he'd beaten famous favourites Herbert Plank of Italy and the Swiss Bernard Russi, who were second and third, and it was like a major earthquake on the Richter scale of the ski world. There were reverberations around the continent. We didn't realize the magnitude of it, but we decided we should probably celebrate in some way. Back at our hotel we got some champagne, toasted ourselves, then started packing: just clink, glug, and go. It was almost anticlimactic. We didn't have anybody to celebrate with us or for us.

Some thought Ken's was a tainted victory. We were on Fischer skis and so was Franz Klammer, and one of the top guys from Fischer mumbled something about Klammer winning if he hadn't fallen. That really got our backs up and we made him eat crow. We had videotaped the race on TV, we were the first team to do that, and so we studied the runs of Klammer and Ken. There was a clock ticking in one corner of the screen and we picked the same reference point for each skier and proved that Ken was faster than "The Kaiser." Besides, if you fall, you don't win. Period.

To add insult to the injured Austrian pride, Dave Irwin won two weeks later in Schladming, right on Klammer's doorstep. Ir just walked it, completely crushed everybody, over 1.5 seconds ahead of the Austrian Klaus Eberhard. That's miles in front and the Austrian fans were now convinced Fischer had given Ir a faster pair of skis than anyone on their beloved home team. They got quite nasty and were spitting on our rep's car and rocking it, even though he hadn't touched any of our skis because we wouldn't let him. But Ir had really worked over his skis the night before in a kind of competition with Ken. They were trying to outdo each other: one guy would file an edge, the other would file his more, and so on. When they'd finished trying to outwax each other, there was nothing left to do so they started filing their bindings to take off any microscopic protrusions that would affect aerodynamics. It was ridiculous and partly clowning around on their part, but it indicated how keen and competitive we were.

We were super-motivated and determined. Jim Hunter was incredibly determined. It's a shame he never won a race because it was the very focus of his being. Dave Murray was an absolute powerhouse of desire, not as obvious about it, but probably keener. Ken was fiercely determined and Dave Irwin would never let any-body else get ahead. Some of our aggression was directed at each other, but most of it went against the opposition with the help of the coach who helped us channel it there. There was never a time that we doubted we could do it. And one of the most remarkable things was that nobody told us we couldn't do it. So we just kept doing it.

After Ir's win, we whooped it up a bit more in our hotel in Schladming. It was as though we realized Ken's win was no fluke and Ir's made us legitimate. There was a bit more champagne, but it was still subdued because I think partying needs some anticipation, it's hard to do it spontaneously. You need time to savour it and we seldom had that. Jim Hunter wasn't in a party mood anyway on that day in 1975. He'd finished 15th, but was very depressed and frustrated and wanted to retire then and there. He went into close huddle with the coaches in the hotel lobby and I felt really sorry for him. He'd been the best skier on the team for years and all he really lived for was to win a World Cup race. Now two others had done it, guys who I think Jim perceived as not having paid the same dues as him.

I never thought about winning until the day I actually won a race. I only thought about improving and I still felt I wasn't good enough, strong enough, determined enough compared to the others on the team. I also wasn't yet quite prepared to be crazy enough to go that far. To be winning World Cup races requires a certain kind of madness, not just in the risk-taking sense. You have to be so single-minded, like a ski monk, and step into a different world where you file your bindings if you think it will help you get the advantage. That's what winning is, doing more than anybody else is prepared to do. That's what the other guys were ready to do, but I hadn't reached that stage yet. In a sense I was still a kid playing at ski racing.

We went back to Canada for Christmas, back to the country whose name was plastered all over Europe because we'd won races with the Maple Leaf on our uniforms. Of course, nobody in our native land knew a thing about it.

There was a communication gap for me in Canada in those days. During that 1975-76 season I was beginning to get noticed in Europe with some top-20 results. I was getting interviewed and being recognized as an up-and-comer in the press, yet when I came home at Christmas, or between races, nobody knew or cared. I'd come back with these great stories of thousands of people on the hills cheering, and media scrums of 350 reporters trying to get to the winners in the finish area. Back home nobody even knew what a finish area was or looked like, or what I was talking about. There were no common reference points and I had to translate all the jargon. My stories limped along pathetically until eventually I just gave up trying to explain and retreated into a private world. At home my mom and dad would say, "Steve, talk to us, get back to reality."

I had to be two different people. Being on the team was a completely selfish experience. All you did was try to get better as a skier. There was no consideration for time, mood, or convenience. Even if it was inconvenient, but nevertheless improved your skiing, you did it. And everybody around you did it for you. It was always me, me, me. But when I came home into other people's lives, I had to consider them. I came to understand the need for this, realizing they had no way of knowing what it was like over there. Besides, I was still learning myself.

In the New Year, the season resumed in Switzerland, a double-header at Wengen, where the Crazy Canucks were brought down to earth with a bump, a big bump. On consecutive days I placed 11th and eighth, but Ir had an almighty crash. He lost it at 75 miles an hour and bounced a long way, as ABC's *Wide World of Sports* telecast showed in slow motion. Ken had fallen in the same place moments earlier and radioed back up the hill to the coaches: "Ir's skis and equipment destroyed, blood-filled goggles." Our assistant coach Wayne Gruden brought Ir's blood-covered helmet and goggles to the finish line and we wondered, is he going to live? It was very serious stuff and very emotional for the team. We hugged and kissed each other at the finish line, for reassurance and for mutual support. A ski race is an emotion-charged event, with people screaming and yelling, bells ringing, reporters pulling and grabbing at you and sticking cameras in your face. In the middle of this crazy environment, Ir was flown away unconscious in a helicopter and it was very traumatic. As it turned out he suffered a very severe concussion; he really knocked his marbles around, fractured his ribs and had cuts and abrasions on his face caused by his shattered glasses. Our confidence was shaken by this first serious injury on the team. We'd been rocketing around, doing everything right, and winning by pushing right to the edge of our limits. Suddenly, one of us had gone right off the edge and it hurt all of us.

We were feeling skittish and the accident actually served to draw us closer together to become even more of a team. Of course the crashes also reinforced our Crazy Canuck image and the press played on it more than ever. We were the wild men from Canada, but the papers pointed out that we could ski too, saying Ken Read and Dave Irwin were great skiers, Murray and Hunter were right up there too, and then there was the kid Podborski. Everybody had a nickname. Hunter was called Jungle Jim because he was built like Tarzan and liked to perform antics like walking on his hands. We called Ken Lance Romance sometimes because of his matinée-idol looks and press image, though he wasn't really the latin lover type. Murray was Mur, Irwin was Ir, and I was Pod.

We had some comic relief at the next race at Morzine in France when I fell off a toilet seat. We were staying in a high-rise hotel complex that was falling apart at the seams. I went into the bathroom, sat down, and went flying. The toilet seat was broken and I was flopping around on the floor with my pants around my ankles and yelling WHOOA! That got a few laughs. Then Ken and I went down to dinner and asked for milk. The waiter screamed at us, saying "MILK? Milk? Milk is for children!" We got our milk, but the food was disgusting. Even we couldn't eat it, and we complained so bitterly the race committee agreed to let us eat with the workers who drove the snow-moving vehicles. At breakfast we were having our croissants and coffee and one of the snow-cat drivers came in for his morning meal. He had a cigarette hanging out of his mouth, his eyes were bloodshot, and his breakfast was a huge glass of red wine. We nearly threw up.

From Morzine we went to Kitzbühel, where my blossoming career was nearly nipped in the bud. It happened on a training run through the Hausberg section and I was concentrating on being relaxed. Maybe I was too relaxed on this left hander because my knee popped as I went through a compression at about 70 miles an hour. My right knee just let go and suddenly my feet were turned underneath me and I found myself airborne at a 90-degree angle to the sidehill. I had to come in for a landing on a wing and a prayer. My bad leg wobbled when I came down and I knew I was in big trouble as I accelerated to 80 miles an hour standing on one wobbly leg and trying to turn. I was spreadeagled, with my good limb way up in the air. There was only one solution. I just tucked my head in and fell – KABANGO!

I tumbled, rolled, and bounced along with equipment flying in all directions. My goggles were smashed to bits, my nose was broken, and I really got the shit kicked out of me, just beaten to a pulp. After what seemed like an eternity, I rolled to a stop and waited for my skis to hit me, which often happened in those days before we had brakes to stop wayward skis. They missed me and I lay curled up in a ball in the soft snow. The wind was knocked out of me and I was in agony. I didn't even notice my knee because I was in such pain all over. Tony Sailer, then coach of the Austrian team and a former skiing great who'd seen it all, came along to ask how I was. I said I was ok and he just shook his head, saying it was a really bad fall. At least I impressed him!

It took me about half an hour to get myself together and for people to find my equipment. The aches and pains faded into a tolerable overall soreness, except for my knee, and I felt well enough to refuse a tobaggan ride to the bottom of the hill. I clicked on my bindings and gingerly set off, hoping my right leg would follow instructions. It wouldn't and seemed to have mind of its own. I was skiing very slowly and it wavered around aimlessly, not following directions from above. It was completely shot. A doctor checked me over at the hotel and said two of the four ligaments were badly damaged and I would have to go home immediately to have it fixed.

Back at the hotel, everybody was sitting around me, the guys on the team, the coaches, Sullie, and some race officials. Suddenly, Rob Safrata came charging into the room and he was totally devastated. He was on the Canadian Europa Cup team over in Kitzbühel to race GS and Slalom to prepare for the '76 Olympics in Innsbruck. Rob had just found out what had happened to me. We had been looking forward so much to being in the Olympics together. He started bawling his eyes out and I couldn't hold back the tears. Until then I had been very macho about it and didn't want to show my disappointment. Missing the Olympics was part of it, but I had been really aced out by the experience of a big, bad fall and was probably suffering from shock. I'd had enough and when Rob let go, I did too. I bawled like a baby along with him and the others shuffled slowly out of the room.

Jim Hunter offered to drive me to the airport in Germany to catch a flight home for my knee operation and we set off in his yellow Porsche, the "Yellow Volkswagen." He was sometimes difficult to get along with because of his self-righteous attitude and occasionally pissed people off with his preaching. I roomed with him quite a bit and would say, "Jim, I don't want to be converted tonight. Just go to sleep." But he must have forgiven my sins and felt sorry for me because he actually let me drive his precious Porsche along the autobahn to Munich. It was a real Christian act, giving an 18-year-old kid a turn behind the wheel, and it helped take my mind off my troubles.

At the airport, I was starting to feel more shock and was so dazed I had trouble phoning my parents to tell them I was injured and on the way home. I was able to walk all right so I had difficulty pleading my case with the airlines people about needing a good seat. Luckily I got a bulkhead spot and was able to keep my throbbing knee elevated. In Toronto, I was beginning to get really spaced out and for the first time in my life the Customs people decided to search me. No doubt I looked suspicious, I was completely exhausted and kind of reeling around with my eyes crossed. I explained to the girl I was in very bad shape. She believed me and just opened and closed my bag. I was operating on automatic pilot using a kind of survival technique where you just focus on the next need and don't worry about the big picture. My next need was bed and mom and dad took me there.

I spent the following night in Toronto General Hospital where they starved me, shaved me, and got me ready to roll for the operation in the morning . . . . All my operations seem to have been at 8:00 am. They gave me a shot in each cheek and I began to relax, really relax. They threw me on a cart like a sack of potatoes and wheeled me down to the area outside the operating theatre where I lay for some time. The tourniquet on my leg, which cuts off the blood supply, had broken when they tested it and they had to send over to Sick Kids across the street for another. I was higher than a kite and when people passed by, my head would leap up from the bed and say, "Hi!" Finally, they knocked me out and did what they had to do to my knee.

Suddenly a nurse in a mask was yelling in my face, "Try to wake up!" But it was the unbelievable pain that finally roused me. I was in the hospital for about five days and got a painkiller shot every four hours. They were effective for about three and one half hours, near the end of which time I would be chewing the pillow with pain, tears streaming down my face. It was some kind of morphine derivative and I needed those babies bad. I later found out I bear pain very well, but this was staggering. I kept ringing the bell for my shot if the nurse was even a few seconds late. I'd want to ream her out but would just roll on my side and turn the other cheek. I loved that needle and would do anything to get it.

I wasn't in the Orthopedic section and the other poor guys in my ward had something done to their insides and were all really sick too. A lady across the hall screamed all night and my parents told me she had asked them to help her escape. It was a hell-hole of sorts and I wanted out too. When I was well enough to sit in the TV room, I watched *The Sword of the Lord*, a film about the team featuring Jim Hunter. In one sequence, filmed in our hotel room somewhere in Europe, Jim was doing one arm push-ups (he could do 50 or 60 at a time) and I was in bed in the background reading a book. The title referred to Jim's religious orientation, and watching that film in the hospital made me somewhat nostalgic for the team.

My parents had been planning to go to Innsbruck for the Olympics to watch their boy in action. Of course I wouldn't be there now, but all their travel plans were locked in and they couldn't cancel. They were leaving Monday. On Saturday, I told the nurse I was going home soon and asked her to get my prescriptions ready.

My parents brought me home and set me up in the basement. On Monday morning, my surgeon Dr. Palmer called: "Hello Stephen, where are you?" I was supposed to still be in hospital and had skipped out without getting his permission. But he left me where I was, alone with our dog. My brother Craig was away skiing somewhere with the Ontario team, so my only companion was Beau, a charming beast of mostly Beagle extraction and a great family pet for many years.

I had a huge cast from ankle to hip and was virtually marooned in the basement. My parents had left me food, but I was barely able to hobble upstairs to the bathroom – I hadn't yet mastered the art of crutching. I was in tremendous mental distress, wallowing in self-pity about my wrecked leg, lying there alone, upset, sad . . . the complete spectrum of miserableness. One evening, I decided to fight back with one of the exercises I'd been given to keep my leg strong. I must have done 3000 leg-lifts and suffered terribly the next day. I made a very bad cripple and, about the third day in the house, I had a kind of nervous breakdown.

A week before I had been whizzing down slopes in Europe, full of energy and living a kind of life I'd always dreamed of. Suddenly I'd been kicked in the butt and could hardly move. A huge cloud of depression descended on me and I lay in bed for a whole day, feeling as if I'd dropped into a bottomless black hole. I have no memories of that day other than lying in that stupid bed enveloped in a kind of nebulous dark hell. I was taking industrial-strength narcotic derivative painkillers and decided to quit them cold turkey to see if that would restore my mental equilibrium. Major withdrawal symptoms hit me like a ton of bricks on one of my laborious trips to the bathroom. I stood at the top of the stairs hanging onto my crutches for dear life, swaying, sweating, dizzy, and nauseous. I made a superhuman effort not to fall and gradually got a grip on the situation.

Downstairs I had a serious talk with myself and decided to stage a revolt against the slings and arrows of outrageous fortune. I reviewed my state of affairs: I like skiing, so far I've trained a little bit and done well, but I've been dabbling at it and just having fun. Maybe I got injured because I wasn't strong enough and not really serious about skiing down hills fast. Here I am at rock bottom, crippled, depressed, nearly a drug addict . . . it couldn't be much worse. But I want to ski. I'm going to come back and do this thing right.

By this time I had more than the faithful Beau for company. In high school I had met a girl named Kim Crouch and she had contacted me again when I was in the hospital. She took pity on me and came to visit me at my house and we chatted and giggled a lot. She was a gem, a buoyant, optimistic person and we developed a very strong affection that lasted for four years. Kim came to me in a time of trial and understood the depths to which I had sunk. She helped pull me up and out of the gutter with her compassion and concern. It was my first major relationship with a girl, but it ended poorly and I feel sad about that. We had a lovely time together then. Later, when I got to the top of the ski racing world, misunderstandings came between us. It's very hard to deal with the pressures up there, hard for the skiers and everybody around them.

Six weeks later, I went to the TGH Emergency section, Emerg as I came to call it, to have my cast taken off. The doctor used a device that resembled a skill saw and I was sure this sawbones was going to cut my leg off – *Buzzzzzz*, right up my leg and I expected to see the blood start spurting any second. Then, like a magician, Dr. Palmer pulled the cast off and my mouth dropped. My leg was gone! It had just withered away to a shrivelled-up length of skin and bone. There was a six-inch-long scar on the inside of my knee where they had gone in to sew the ligaments: two of the four had been damaged in my accident, one ripped in half and the other torn off at the bone. A long wire, used as stitching, poked out of the scar. Dr. Palmer grabbed the end of it and ripped it out.

There was no pain, but it was shocking for me – particularly the way my leg looked. It was totalled and my knee was stiff as a board. I got around on crutches for a while, then a cane, and I plunged full tilt into physiotherapy. I was told I couldn't ski again until training camp in South America. For the next six months I relied on the expertise of doctors, surgeons, physiotherapists, chiropractors and kinesiologists (body movement scientists), anybody who could help me get back on my feet.

At first, neither of my legs would work properly. The left one had done nothing for six weeks except hold me up. I had to get the muscles in the right leg functioning to the point where I could even straighten it out. When I first tried this on my wrecked right leg, it just twitched and bounced around a little. I rode the stationary bike with my good leg, using every ounce of energy just to will the muscles to turn on. The physiotherapy room at the Fitness Institute in the Willowdale area of north Toronto became my second home. I was determined to have some fun there and did.

I had no pity now. After all, everybody in the place was hurt. They weren't there because they felt great. So why make a big deal of it? Enjoy yourself was my theory. I walked miles and miles on the treadmill making it whine as if in protest. I plodded along going nowhere, watching the clock on the wall and vowing to get well enough to join the people running by outside in the workout area. Grunt, grunt, grunt, whine, whine, whine. I sang to myself and joked with the man and woman who looked after the physio room. In this chamber of hurt bodies and broken dreams I was the optimist. Some of the others thought I wasn't working out seriously enough because I appeared to be enjoying it too much. But I flogged myself like a slave driver.

I warmed up on the treadmill, did a complete stretching routine, then tackled a full body program with exercises for every muscle. I lifted weights until, by summer's end, I could squat nearly 400 pounds. I did this two hours a day, five days a week at the Fitness Institute. About six weeks after starting this regimen, I hopped on my bicycle and rode about 300 feet from my house and was completely exhausted. My brother belonged to the Queen City Cycle Club where George Stewart, a former Canadian champion cyclist, had helped Craig recover from injured knees a couple of years earlier. Under his guidance Craig developed as a bike racer of some note, winning a Canadian championship. George helped speed up my recovery by taking a personal interest in me. He worked closely with me, on my weight program as well, and kept charts of all the miles I biked in a riding regimen tailor-made for my bad knee. He was, and still is, an excellent motivator. Soon I was cycling a minimum of 120 miles a week. As I improved, my mileage was sometimes 240 a week, with occasional 100-mile rides on Sundays and regular 40- to 50-milers on Tuesdays, Thursdays, and Saturdays.

My goal of getting back on skis in time for training in South America was within sight. Watching the 1976 Olympics on TV had helped my resolve. Though the team was out of the medals, Ken was fifth, Ir eighth, and Jungle Jim tenth – quite respectable results.

Ken felt the course at Innsbruck was too icy. I had never heard him complain before, so I thought the conditions must have been very severe. I watched Klammer's incredible winning run and wished I was there – not necessarily because it was the Olympics, but because it was a ski race and I was a ski racer. But many times during the next few months I regretted having chosen this profession.

7. Uphill All the Way

Hell Season is how I describe the winter of 1976-77. It was the worst time of my life, much worse than my knee injuries. Ken and Ir were still in the first seed and I was second seed just behind Mur, but these proved to be the seeds of doubt and discontent. From total non-entities we had suddenly become marketable commodities and people wanted to cash in on us. Manufacturers paid money to have us use their products, something new to the team and to our administration.

Rubberized suits had been introduced by the Italians and their superior aerodynamic properties helped very average skiers become front runners. The suits prevented air from getting in to slow the skiers down. When this was understood, everybody hopped on the slippery suit bandwagon. But the suits slid on snow as well as through the air and people who fell started rocketing through fences and over cliffs. The rules were changed for safety reasons: all suits had to have mandatory abrasive fabric on the outside and rubber inside. The revamped suits were supposedly just as fast and when we signed on with an Italian manufacturer we figured we were away to the races.

But our results were pathetic. We tried harder, but they just kept getting worse. Some of us finished in the teens at the first race in Val Gardena, then we all plummeted into the thirties at Garmisch and Kitzbühel. We blamed ourselves, then the equipment, then we ganged up on the coaches Scott Henderson and Wayne Gruden. We stumbled from race to race until everything came to a head at Kitzbühel in January of '77. We'd trained and tested and experimented with waxes all week, trying everything we could think of.

We wondered if it might be our suits, so Ken got a Swiss suit and I wore three Downhill suits in layers trying to stop the wind from coming through. Our results were a disaster. At least I made it in one piece down the same hill where I'd crashed last year. But I was devastated at finishing 32nd overall.

The others had fared little better and we were sitting around in a blue funk having lunch when Wayne walked in and told us we had skied on an untested wax. It was some kind of wonder wax Scott had told him to slap on just hoping it would help. It was a desperation move that didn't work. Kitzbühel is a hill where a good, brave skier can sometimes overcome inferior equipment, but nobody can ski on the wrong wax. The atmosphere around the table deteriorated, nobody would talk to Scott, and I decided to get drunk.

I ordered one of those half-liter steins of Austrian beer and proceeded to have a liquid lunch. I got pissed and got my name in the papers because of it. Matthew Fisher was covering us for the *Globe and Mail* and also doing some radio reporting. I think it was a radio interview, but I was too hammered to remember, let alone speak coherently. I believe Matt's report said I had 12 steins which is six liters. I passed out in my room and woke up at dinner time with a colossal hangover . . . and the same problems as before. I never again tried to solve problems with booze.

Everybody had gone into withdrawal and there was very little communication. We knew our problems were much deeper than the wax screw-up and our major adversary now threatened to be a serious lack of confidence in our own abilities. Our search for scapegoats had come full circle from ourselves, to our equipment, to our coaches, and back to us. The Crazy Canucks were going downhill fast in the rankings and in danger of losing our places in the seeding. Our slide would hit us financially, especially Ken and Ir who were starting to get an income after their second year in the inner sanctum of the top 15. Contracts with manufacturers are based on seed position and we were finishing way down in the third-seed area where money was scarce. There were mutterings of discontent from the equipment suppliers which helped get us back on course as a team. The old "us against them" scenario came into play again.

We dug in and fought back. We plugged away at searching for solutions. Our foreheads were nearly flat from banging our heads against the wall. We just wouldn't quit. The determination was tremendous. We refused to give up on the slow-suit theory and finally had a confrontation with the manufacturer. We maintained the air must be flowing through the suits and slowing us down. They denied this and their rep tried to demonstrate we were wrong by blowing cigarette smoke at the suit. No smoke came through, but one of our guys took a drag from the cigarette and slowly blew it toward the suit. Wayne, who was standing on the other side of the suit, waited a moment then sucked in . . . and blew out cigarette smoke . . . .

We proved our suits were permeable: the wind whistled through them and dragged us down like an anchor. Later, tests in a wind tunnel showed the Canadian suits had 15 per cent more drag than any others. Air passed through the front of the suits and ballooned out the back as we crouched in our tucks, adding as much as three seconds to our times. That realization came too late in the season to help very much, but from then on we never compromised on equipment for the sake of a few bucks. The suit people paid maybe $10,000 to our administration, so we had worn their suits, but who knows how much it cost us. We might have gotten less money to wear better suits in the beginning, but it would have paid off in the long run. The best manufacturers invest in teams that win. Results make money. This made the administration realize that performance is what it's all about. If the racers don't perform well everybody suffers, including the administration. The mission of the whole organization is to help the racers win. Period.

We salvaged our seed placings with better results near the end of the season and were thankful most of the blame for our setbacks could be laid at the feet of inferior equipment. We learned valuable lessons from what we called "reality therapy." We had been living in a dream world where everything was going well, then reality came along and kicked us in the shins. It was a character-building year for all of us. I came out of the '76-'77 season seeded 25th in the World Cup Downhill and was Canadian Slalom Champion and North American Junior Downhill Champion. I still dabbled in other forms of racing, but was a much tougher World Cup Downhiller. I vowed never to be substandard again, neither in equipment nor in the physical or mental approach to skiing down hills fast.

In 1977-78, we had the same suits as the Austrians and quickly began making up for lost time. Ken and Mur were first and second at Chamonix and I crept up the order each race, capped by a tenth at Kitzbühel. It was no big deal on the score sheets, but a miracle to me only two years after my crash. I was seventh in the World Championships at Garmisch, but missed my big chance to be a TV star because of a beer commercial. I was the best of the North Americans by a mile and the ABC network cameras were on me during my run. So far no one had seen me on TV in Canada. At home, my parents nearly went through the roof when the network threw in a Budweiser commercial when I was doing my thing. They only saw me throwing up snow at the finish.

Right at the end of the year, I was fourth and sixth at Laax in Switzerland and was classified 15th overall in the Downhill for the season. Next year, I was going to be one of the guys that counted. Ken was clearly the best skier on the team, in fact he finished fourth overall in the Downhill standings, Ir was coming back from various injuries, Mur was right up there, and Pod was not far behind. We were a force to be reckoned with again. In Canada, there were occasional newspaper articles and pictures, particularly about Ken, and I was mentioned in dispatches.

The intensity of my training was always influenced by the results it produced on the hill, so I trained like a madman that summer. I biked 'til I was blue in the face, lifted weights 'til my eyes popped, and generally pushed myself into a state of superfitness. It helped that I was getting more support from my family and friends who were beginning to understand my somewhat antisocial behaviour.

Next season, 1978-79, we got our names in the paper right off the bat at Schladming when Ken and Mur were first and second. Ir was seventh and I was ninth. I came away from the next event, a doubleheader at Val Gardena, Italy, with tenth place in the first race and a slightly broken back in the second. About 30 seconds out of the starting gate, I was howling through an 80-mile-an-hour left hander when I hit a rock so hard it chopped right through my ski. That ski slowed from 80 miles an hour to a dead stop in an instant. I wore Marker bindings in those days and my foot stopped so abruptly the aircraft-quality tensile wire snapped in two. I still have the remains of the binding as a souvenir of one of my worst falls. I did a violent face plant that knocked the wind out of me for three minutes and tumbled halfway to Rome before crashing into a fence.

Dave Murray was next to start and watched the whole thing. He thought for sure I was dead. It was a very dramatic crash. I really ate my liver. I also suffered cracked vertebrae when my back contorted violently following the intitial face plant. I found this out when I had it x-rayed during our Christmas break back in Canada. It wasn't that serious as back fractures go but might easily have been. My doctor and I kept it a secret because there was no point in alarming people like equipment suppliers and coaches who tend to get very nervous when any of their athletes get hurt. It would have been good for a few laughs to have been able to say, "It's nothing really . . . just a broken back," but I suffered in silence for a month or so until it healed itself.

In January, we came to Morzine in France with new Downhill suits similar to the Swiss team. These featured several layers of fabric glued together and we had decided they were faster than the ones we had been using previously. Suit technology was as volatile as the race for the atom bomb and new creations had to pass rigid tests before they were approved for racing. It was felt rubberized suits were unhealthy since they were airtight and made you sweat as if you were in sauna – so you froze when you stood around in them. It was decreed that a certain amount of air must get through, and when approved for permeability a suit was marked with a small clip. Though our new suits hadn't yet been tested, our manufacturer told us they were identical to the approved Swiss numbers. We had never even trained in them. I decided I didn't want to race in an untried suit, so I wore my old one.

The Morzine-Avoriaz resort is located near the border between France and Switzerland and noted for its carnival atmosphere when the Downhill circus arrives. But there's no clowning around on the Piste des Hauts-Forts course because it's one of the most technically demanding, with several high-speed turns and varying snow conditions down its 1.8-mile length. You're only on the hill for about 100 seconds but you need to have your wits about you all the way, particularly on the upper part where the major turns are. Through the lengthy Carousel bend and the tricky S-Turn, you need perfect execution to gain and/or maintain speed for the final, straighter run to the finish.

Kenny had already gone down and done a really good time, and up in the start area I was distracted somewhat by our new masseur, Terry "Toulouse" Spence, who had just joined us. He was rubbing my legs in the usual pre-run ritual, trying to get them loose, working his way up my thigh when he felt some foreign object and gave it a tug. He thought it was a roll of plastic we often stuffed down the front of our suits to use as protection for our skis when we arrived in the finish area. This time it wasn't plastic, which Toulouse realized to his embarrassment when I yelled. He tried to calm me down but, who knows, the inadvertent tug on my privates might have inspired me because I finished that race second to Ken Read.

We celebrated with champagne, but the toasts to the winner turned out to be for me, not Ken. Someone had protested his suit. It was tested and failed to pass the permeability requirements and I inherited the victory. The suit people apologized to Ken and gave him a beautiful consolation prize, a $3,000 watch. They explained that this particular bolt of cloth had too much glue which was used to laminate four layers of material together. Mur's suit, similar to Ken's, was also found to be illegal and he was disqualified too. But losing this win may have cost Ken Read the World Cup downhill title that year.

So I backed into my first World Cup win and had no illusions about it. Sure I got 25 points for coming first and the Fischer ski company had to give me the bonus money. But Ken got nothing and he had done all the work, setting the fastest time and standing there on the podium with the cup and holding up his Fischer skis for all the world to see. Beyond that, conceivably those 25 points might have helped him win the whole ball of wax that year, and that's a tremendous tragedy for him because Ken Read, instead of Steve Podborski, could have been the first Canadian on top of the world in Downhill racing.

Ken had really gone very quickly at Morzine, beating all of us by a significant margin and, as one of the Austrian coaches said, he could have won the race wearing a business suit. Our team was bewildered by the course of events, happy about my inherited win, but wondering if there wasn't some kind of conspiracy to prevent us from succeeding. At first no one knew we existed, then we won a bit, now it seemed the Europeans were saying we'll show these upstart Canadians whose game this is. It was as if they were banding together to keep us back where they felt we belonged. As usual we bore down and tried even harder.

I had top-ten finishes in the next couple of races. Then we came to Villars in Switzerland where Peter Mueller won with some help from the weather in his native land, and some of his Swiss countrymen. The Jury, which decides whether or not it's safe to race, is usually composed of five people. One of them is always a local guy who knows the weather and the hill, and the others are coaches and officials who are supposed to be completely objective. But they've been known to make political decisions in favour of local heroes.

Earlier, this kind of "judgement" call cost me a win at Schladming in 1976. I was fastest after 30 skiers had gone down the hill, when the jury cancelled the event because of rain. The fact that I'd beaten the Austrians was generally believed to have tipped the scales of injustice. However, a lot of skiers were relieved about the cancellation, among them my brother. Craig, who was at Schladming on one of his periodic outings with the team, told me later he was happy about my fast run, but not unhappy when the cancellation came before his number came up on the rapidly deteriorating and dangerous track.

When my number came up in the starting gate at Villars, some time after Mueller was safely down with a good time, a full-scale blizzard was in progress. The wind was blowing up the hill and I launched myself into a blind tunnel of swirling snow. I was tucking my buns off and suddenly came out into daylight to find I was 65 feet off course and skiing straight toward a sheer cliff. I managed to slow down, turn back in, and cruise to the bottom to finish 38th. It was ridiculous and I was lucky to be alive. It happened to a lot of others and Ken, who had done really well in training and was a favourite to win, was so mad he skiied down a gravel-covered road and wrecked his skis. He was angry at the conditions and at his skis, which he felt were slow. That's how frustrated you can get in ski racing.

In February of '79, we came back for the Canadian National Championships at Lake Louise where I was a miserable seventh in the Downhill. After racing World Cup, I could never get myself up for the Canadians. It's probably not a patriotic thing to say, but those races just weren't important enough for me to try hard enough to win. I didn't figure this out for many years. Yet, Ken won them year after year, a remarkable achievement. They were usually held at his home ski club of Lake Louise, but that's not the whole answer. All things being equal, the guy who wants it most is usually the guy who wins.

The final World Cup event of the '78-'79 season was at Lake Placid, New York, making it a pre-Olympic race. Dave Murray was third, Ken was seventh, and I was eighth. Tragically, Leonardo David, an Italian racer, collapsed in a coma from which he never recovered. He had fallen ten days earlier in his national championships and hurt his head. At Lake Placid, he came down behind me and in the finish area I thought he looked strange, then he just fell over. He died a few years later. An American had been killed in my first Can Am race at Whistler in '73-'74, but it made no impression on me. I probably chose to ignore it in a kind of subconscious self-preservation strategy: nobody ever gets killed ski racing, at least not me. It's like driving down the highway and seeing a bad accident. Most people don't even stop. You slow down momentarily, hope nobody is seriously injured, then drive on, trying to eliminate it from your mind.

It seems callous, but we used to entertain ourselves by watching replays of ski crashes on video and TV. It was a big laugh to see somebody chew, tumbling end-over-end, whacking into fences, hitting people. It was probably a way of releasing tension. Frequently, the stars of these crash-and-burn shows were the Crazy Canucks so it wasn't as if we were hard-hearted ghouls. We knew all too well what it felt like. You have to laugh. If you don't, you'll cry.

As widely experienced crashers ourselves we knew who was likely to fall, particularly some of the members of the Third World Cup who tended to lose their equilibrium spectacularly. The Third World Cup was our name for the small, often one-man teams from non-skiing countries like Mexico and Senegal. An Austrian, Prince Hubertus von Hohenloe, skied for Mexico because his mother was Mexican. A black African representing Senegal was overheard by Toulouse, one time at Kitzbühel, talking to the Prince in the start area prior to the race. "Do you believe in God?" the Senegalese asked the

Prince. When the Prince replied that he did, the African said, "I sure hope he believes in us." Neither of them fell that day: the Prince made it to the bottom and the man from Senegal skipped the race and went straight to the disco instead.

One of the classic crashes of all time was at Val Gardena, or Gröden as the Germans call it, in the late '70s. A French skier was howling through a section called the Camel Bumps. He completely blew it, rocketing off the first hump, and thumping down on the third in a sitting position. He hit so hard he somersaulted up into the air like a rag doll. He finally splattered down to earth, on his back, slid along, then, just before he stopped, he tried to stand up. He wobbled for a few seconds, looked around a bit, then keeled over, swooning like a Three Stooges character. It was hilarious, though he'd cracked a few vertebrae.

Then two policemen came along, rolled him onto a toboggan and started hauling him down the hill. Meanwhile racers were still flying by, one of them being Jay McKim, a racer in the Canadian Training Squad who was trying to make our team. He was a late runner and the course was badly rutted. Jay hit a rut about 165 feet away from the toboggan haulers, flew out of control, and smacked into them, scattering bodies everywhere. The impact broke the back of one of the cops, fortunately not too badly, and Jay's face was hamburgered. We watched all this on the video in our hotel with the French team and laughed like maniacs. One of the broken-up viewers was Konrad Bartelski, who skied for Britain and was a particularly good friend of our team. He often trained with us. Konrad used to say a spectacular fall is as memorable as a win in the public eye.

After Lake Placid, there was great excitement in the media about the Olympics to be held there the next year. With our team's good showing there in the World Cup race, big things were expected of us for the 1980 Olympics. More important to us was our World Cup stature, in the rankings and in the European media. Ken was ranked fourth in the world again and I had finally made it into the first seed and was ranked tenth, tied with Mur, in the Downhill after '78-'79. The Crazy Canucks had become a force in skiing in Alpine Europe. Our celebrity status abroad still went largely unnoticed in Canada, though we did crank out a book called *Ski The*

Nancy Greene with "her" Ski Team at Craigleith in 1968: that's Leo Vogrin on the left, Rob Safrata sixth from the left, Nancy in the centre, and the Podborski boys, Craig on the right and me third from the right.

"The Kid" leaving home again in 1972, off to another ski race somewhere.

(BELOW) Early days in Austria, 1975: left to right, Bev Davidson, Dave Irwin, Steve Podborski, Russell Goodman, Alain Cousineau, Dave Murray, Gary Aiken, Ken Read (behind skis), Giles Walker, Jim Hunter, John Dyer, and Bob Donnelly.

(OPPOSITE) Skiing like a Crazy Canuck (at about 80 miles an hour) at Val d'Isère in 1975.

I did *not* fall! – willpower overcame gravity (at 80 miles an hour again)
– and I recovered from near disaster at Schladming in 1975.

I *did* fall! – very badly, at Kitzbühel in 1976 – out of control and out
for the season with my first wrecked knee.

(OVERLEAF) The anatomy of another fall, at Kitzbühel in 1977, when I
pushed too hard on the Steilhang and paid for it . . . part of my
contribution to "Hell Season" for the Crazy Canucks.

(ABOVE, left to right) Ken, Pod, Mur, and Ir – the Crazy Canucks at Lake Placid in 1979. (RIGHT) Craig, Mom, Dad, me and the faithful Beau in our chalet at Craigleith in 1980. (OPPOSITE, TOP) Groggy but grinning after winning at Kitzbühel in 1981, I prepare to try to explain how I did it in several languages. (OPPOSITE, BELOW) A frantic moment at Kitzbühel in 1981 . . . skis bending, hand touching the snow at 70 miles an hour, I hung onto the Steilhang this time and won.

Facing a challenge in front of the Eiger at Wengen in 1982 . . . great scenery, but no time to look at it.

(OPPOSITE) Airborne at over 80 miles an hour, I try to qualify for my pilot's licence at Val Gardena in 1982.

Tony Duffy, All-Sport

(ABOVE) Kitzbühel, 1982: a good day for Mr. Fischer (on the left) when Ken was third, I won, and Franz Klammer (on the right) was second.

(BELOW) Kitzbühel, 1982: some of the stuff that helped me win, with coaches Heinz Kappeller and John Ritchie, and the famous Terry "Toulouse" Spence.

(ABOVE) I hadn't *officially* won the World Cup yet, but we celebrated anyway with a few friends at Whistler in 1982.

(BELOW) Ann Rohmer helps me put on a brave face at the hospital in 1983, despite my third serious knee injury.

Wayne Cuddington, The Ottawa *Citizen*

(OPPOSITE) About to become an Officer of the Order of Canada in 1983, along with Bruce Cockburn, Morley Callaghan, Cardinal G. Emmett Carter, and others.

(LEFT) Go For It! – out of the starting gate at Val Gardena in 1984, my last season.

(BELOW) After 11 years on the hills, heading for the finish line at Wengen in 1984.

Steve Podborski, 1987.

Canadian Way, written by Ken, Ir, Mur, Pod, coach John Ritchie, and his brother David.

When we went our separate ways that summer, I threw myself into training harder than ever. I felt next year was going to be a good one and I got very, very fit. I probably trained harder than the others, except for Ken, who was always in good shape. I cycled like a Tour de France competitor and emphasized the weight-training program that George Stewart and I had perfected. When we went back for the new season I had muscles in my eyeballs.

In keeping with the roller-coaster ride our fortune seemed to take in those days, the winter of 1979-80 started off on a downer. In the first race, at Val d'Isère, Mur was ninth, but Ken and I both fell. At least I was able to cheer on my brother Craig, who was over for a few races, and he finished 60th. Then, at Val Gardena, there was a worse disaster. Our new-found stature as contenders meant we were no longer waxing our own skis. Fischer did it for us and, while their chief engineer Hans Stroi was a brilliant ski designer, his ability as a waxman at Val Gardena proved to be considerably below the genius scale. We had skis with four or five different kinds of bases for varying conditions: new snow, old snow, wet snow, spring snow, old snow with new snow on top, and so on. And snow can change several times down a two-mile hill, with different altitudes, sun exposures, wind-driven snow, and many other factors affecting the conditions. The ideal is to choose the right base, then wax it so it suits the snow conditions perfectly. Done properly, it puts you on at least equal footing with your rivals. Done badly, you can find yourself almost skidding to a halt because of the wrong wax. I skidded into 45th place in Val Gardena.

Fischer had come up with a new wonder wax: the dreaded wonder wax again, and we wondered why in hell they did it. I was extremely pissed off, absolutely livid. I was embarrassed. I hadn't come 45th for years! It was absolutely ridiculous. I could have walked down faster. I used every expletive in my repertoire at the bottom of that hill, even cursing my dad for depriving me of the right to learn more swear words as a kid. I got my revenge by refusing to hold up my skis with the label on them at the finish line. Come to think of it, I may have done them a favour. Nobody would have dashed out to buy a pair of Fischer skis after seeing my performance that day. I felt a great deal of loyalty to Fischer before and after, but not then. I was one of the first of our guys to come down and I radioed news of the disaster up to the others. They scraped frantically at their skis, and Ken actually managed to finish seventh and Tim Gilhooly from our "C" team was eighth, amazing results considering the wax fiasco.

We never let them wonder wax our skis again, though we had a battle royal when they tried to do it again at Kitzbühel. John Ritchie backed us up in what became a full-scale screaming match, but we won. In fact, Ken won at Kitzbühel and was first and second at the next races in Wengen, where I was eighth and third. Wengen was a doubleheader to make up for a previous race at Morzine which had been cancelled because of bad weather. I had fallen at Morzine, before the race was called off, and again at Kitzbühel. I remember those falls as well as the races at Wengen.

Morzine is really a bugger of a course and that year it was fast, icy, and dangerous. In training, I was whipping along down near the bottom, having a good run, when I caught both edges at the usual 80 miles an hour . . . . I never seemed to fall at slow speeds. I pitched forward on my hands and knees and my extremities slid along the ice like four high-speed curling rocks. I was quite pleased about not hitting anything. Gradually I started to notice a heat build-up in my hands and knees. They got hot, then they burned! I managed to flip over onto my back and continued on my merry way at scarely abated speed. I skimmed along, now on grainy snow, and my back began to burn like the blazes. My body was getting cooked! Finally, I came to a halt, jumped up and the crowd cheered me like crazy. They figured I was just another Crazy Canuck living up to his name.

Fortunately the Morzine race was cancelled so my fall cost me only a slightly burned skin and ego. But the experience helped broaden my understanding of the chemistry of skiing. Skis work by building up friction, so there's a layer of water between them and the snow and they slide on that. This principle is less effective when you try it with your body. The next time I ate my liver, at Kitzbühel, I learned more about the physics of skiing, or rather, falling.

On the Hahenkamm hill, I was fastest on one of the timed training runs and felt confident. In the race, I later learned I was fastest in the top section. I had been going like gangbusters until I came into The Road, an easy connecting section of the course. Nobody ever has trouble here, but I somehow managed to catch my edges and veered head-first off the course like a human dart. I immediately impaled a snow fence, with my head poking through the slats. Then I flipped over so I was hanging by my helmet suspended above a forest far below.

The Austrians had never seen anything like this in the long history of Kitzbühel and they were running around in circles gibbering away in German trying to figure out what to do with this dangling skier. My skis and goggles had been knocked off and my eyes were full of snow. One of the fence slats was jammed right up into my helmet beside my nose. But I wasn't hurt and I just hung there swaying in the breeze for a while. The rescue operation seemed to be going nowhere, so I finally reached up and broke away some slats, undid my chin strap, and plonked into the soft snow below.

From my point of view, the main casualty at Kitzbühel was a precious ski from a prized pair of Fischers that I had used through-out my career. When I first got them, they had tested well at the factory and, later on, they proved to be the fastest pair they ever had. The base was perfect and their stiffness was ideally matched to my weight. Over the years, with countless waxings and filing of edges, they seemed to get even better. Nobody knows why this happens, but skis can mature into greatness.

My confrontation with the Kitzbühel fence had snapped a tip clean off. I was devastated. But my trusty rep Hans assured me they could be mended. He took them back to the factory where they were straightened, glued, and re-pressed. And they worked. I used them regularly for years and still have them, though the edges have been filed away to near invisibility.

I managed to stay upright in the next races, back-to-back events at Wengen – the tremendously challenging course which runs over two and a half miles down the side of an alp. It starts in a snow field way up in the peaks and the run seems to go on forever. Half the time it's like falling down an elevator shaft and in one place you go blasting through a railway tunnel under the tracks. This was featured in Robert Redford's movie *Downhill Racer* and I laughed inside my helmet one day when I went under there with a train going by overhead.

Wengen just goes on and on, through forests and fields, past little Swiss chalets and farm buildings, until you fall over a final cliff to the finish. You've been skiing for two minutes and about 30 seconds, but it seems like two and a half hours. Ken won in just over 2:31 here in the first race. The next day he was second to Peter Mueller by .02 seconds, while I was .07 behind Ken. That works out to a few inches separating the top three.

I was glad to get back up on the podium at Wengen after falling so much in the earlier races. In fact, that third place began a very long streak of top-seed finishes for me. Prior to this I had been Mr. Chew himself, pushing too hard and falling because I was skiing over my head. I thought I had to push myself over the edge, ski beyond my ability, to win. I was convinced I could get a win if only I went far enough out on a limb to get it. But I was going too far. My theory worked in part: I was winning a lot of the timed runs in practice, but then I pushed harder in the race – and fell off the mountains.

8. *On the Loud Pedal*

We came back to North America to finish the '79-'80 season, but first there was the matter of the Olympics to be attended to. Though I became the first Canadian male skier to win an Olympic medal, my adventures at Lake Placid in February of 1980 were not an entirely positive experience. In Europe we were masters of our own destiny, our coach was the boss, the lines of communication were wide open to him, and we were a streamlined, efficient, and tightly knit unit. The Olympics brought two extra layers of bureaucracy into play: the Canadian Olympic Association, who were running the whole show and felt it was their gig and we were bit players; and then all the officials from the Canadian Ski Association head office in Ottawa. The CSA people signed the cheques but we seldom ever saw them during the year. Now they saw this as their moment of glory to show how well they ran *their* ski team which was going to win medals, no question about it.

We felt that outsiders were sticking their noses into our business but we played along. After all, it was only another ski race. We found out otherwise as soon as we came to the American border on our bus from Montreal. I'd been to the States a gazillion times and as soon as you say you're from Canada, you're off to the races with no questions asked. This time you might have thought we were a busload of Russian spies. They searched everything with metal detectors, asked stupid questions, and were rude about it all. So much for welcoming the world to the U.S. Olympic experience.

What should have been a three-hour bus trip took five hours. When we finally trundled into Lake Placid, they said we couldn't take our bus into the ski area and would have to carry tons of equipment nearly a mile to our wax room. Eventually we persuaded them we weren't terrorists and they allowed the bus through. By this time I was getting rather grumpy, I hadn't eaten for a long time, and the whole thing was becoming a royal pain in the butt. Then the athlete's village was like a prison camp, with guards patrolling everywhere, police dogs, and more handguns than I'd ever seen in my life, even in South America. Then our huge Greyhound got stuck in the snow and we messed around for hours sorting that out.

Meanwhile, we had to fend off a berserk media contingent. In Europe, everybody knew the rules and understood the whole business of skiing and went about getting their stories in an orderly fashion. Here, every single press person, and they seemed to outnumber the athletes, figured they were unique and they demanded instant cooperation. As we were putting our bags into our rooms, a photographer barged in and wanted us to pose there and then. I explained to him that we had to eat first and we got into an argument. He was insistent, and I told him we were here to race and do well and that food was important for our performance. He got hostile and talked about having a wife and kid who had to eat too – so pose!

The other guys on the team were on my side, but an official from Ottawa butted in and said do what the photographer wants. I felt betrayed. This bureaucrat wanted publicity and had forgotten the whole point of our mission, to win medals, not to be media darlings. I told him how I felt in no uncertain terms and stormed off in a high dudgeon. Besides, the photographer was a first-class prick, obnoxious to the nth degree, and I wouldn't have given him his picture anyway because he was such a shrub. The Canadian media ran amok with fantastic predictions about our medal chances. Downhill racing was the glamour event and the stories soon began that the Crazy Canucks might be able to win. A few days later, we read that we were likely to win at least one medal, then two and finally, according to the press, we were guaranteed a clean sweep of gold, silver, and bronze. We tried to explain it wasn't a foregone conclusion. There was a slight matter of about 100 of the best skiers from around the world standing between us and these predictions. But it was to no avail.

A couple of days before the race, my least favourite bureaucrat from Ottawa said there was an important press conference at 5 o'clock and we had to be there. This was at 4 o'clock and I pointed out that every second of our time was programmed, beginning at 5:00 am in the mornings. We had to juggle our schedule like mad to accommodate this precious press conference where all the important Canadian sports editors were lined up to cover "The Story of the Games" as we were now being billed. This would be a switch because previously, during all our successes in Europe, only junior reporters and starving freelancers had been assigned to cover us. All the fat cats and big name scribes were busy with hockey.

So the Crazy Canucks came face to face with the cigar-smoking gentlemen of the Canadian press. The first question put to us came from the sports editor of one of the biggest papers in Canada. He wanted to know how ski racing worked: "Do you get disqualified for hitting gates?" "How old are you?" "How do you spell your name?" "Aren't you a little small?" There we were, Ken Read, Dave Irwin, Dave Murray, Steve Podborski, four of the best skiers in the world being subjected to a barrage of embarrassingly inane questions. We were professionals surrounded by complete amateurs who hadn't even done their basic homework from the tons of files and press releases available to them. Later on, when I had more clout, I made a rule that the first question put to me which had already been answered in the press kit would be the last question from the floor. That was in effect at the next Olympics, but at Lake Placid we answered all the dumb questions. We told them what we had for breakfast and what colour our underwear was. And it really wrecked my day

The Olympic Association kept herding us into cocktail parties to show us off to dignitaries. We began to feel like prize cattle being paraded around the ring at a fall fair. We were getting pretty stressed out by all the Olympic hoopla. We walked out of one banquet without eating when we found out it had nothing at all to do with us, that it was simply another self-congratulatory event for the officials. Getting up early to go training was more important than grinning and stuffing your face with rubber chicken. It's unlikely anyone noticed our departure amidst all the back-slapping, horn-tooting, and flag-waving. The ballyhoo reached its zenith at the opening ceremonies the day before our race. It was the big moment for everybody and his kid sister, the press, all the officials, the bureaucrats, the coaches and last, and probably least, the athletes.

After another 5:00 am start, we trained on the hill in the morning then headed for the grand opening. Our bus managed to get within three miles of the staging area and we had to walk through the mud and cold and millions of people. We stood around freezing our buns off, then marched into the stadium with bands playing, then – Poof! the Olympic flame was lit. It *was* great to see my mom and dad, friends from the Craigleith club, old coaches, and so on at the ceremony, but I was still doing a slow burn over the perception that I was here as some kind of pawn being pushed around in a bizarre carnival that had very little to do with ski racing.

It was insulting to be treated like children by petty bureaucrats who thought they knew what was best for us. Ten times a year we had races that were better in quality than the Olympics (in which only four skiers from each country are allowed to compete). The competition in the World Cup has much greater depth, with countries like Austria and Switzerland sometimes fielding teams of ten skiers who all have the ability to win. We were dealing with that day in and day out, but wading through the peripheral trappings of the Olympics was harder than handling glare ice at Kitzbühel.

The Olympic course on Whiteface Mountain in the Adirondacks was quite unlike Kitzbühel, shorter by about 1500 feet and much less hairy because of its relative lack of bumps and jumps. It was fast enough, averaging about 65 miles an hour, but not particularly difficult – despite dramatic names like Dynamite Corner and Grand Canyon for some of the landmarks. On race day it was a relief to get on the chairlift, especially after having run the gauntlet through the mayhem down below; the gunslingers were out in force and you had to show your pass to everybody and his dog, spectators were running around in circles, officials were trying to organize yet another cocktail party, press people wanted to know my grandmother's middle name . . . .

I was enjoying a very peaceful interval, gliding silently up among the pines where all was cool and serene, when I glanced over to another chairlift across from mine and spotted my first coach Leo Vogrin and Bob McMillan, whom I'd know for years. They were sitting there right beside me, hoping I might notice them, but afraid to interrupt my reverie. They were so nervous for me they thought speaking to me might throw off my concentration. They wanted to support me and give me the big Rah, Rah, but I had to break the ice.

I hooted and yelled at them like I'd always done. I found their concern touching, though funny, and we laughed about it. I was in my natural element now and relaxed. I'd been doing this for years, it was my life. They hadn't seen me race for a long time and didn't know how to deal with me any more. It was amazing for me to see these grown men so unsure of how to behave, and I understood how important this event must be for them. About a half hour before a race, I would go into a kind of trance but prior to that I always had time for friends.

Up on the top of Whiteface Mountain in the start area, aptly named Hurricane Alley, it was miserably cold and snowing for the Olympic Downhill. Ken started before me and fell. I heard about it and said to myself, "There you jerks, that'll teach you." I was sure all the distractions had contributed to his downfall and my theory was further reinforced when Mur and Ir finished tenth and 11th. The press, who'd worked themselves up into a lather of medal frenzy, hadn't planned for this and would now have to eat their words. Unquestionably, the relentless pressure had gotten to me too and I defused it by cursing outside interferences. But poor old Ken, I really felt sorry for him.

We started at 90-second intervals. I stood in the gate with ten seconds to go, planted my poles into the snow, the beeper started its countdown, and my mind became as clear as a bell. I pushed away and thought: "It's over." It just popped into my head that all the Olympic phooferaw was finished, and now I was racing. When the flag drops the bullshit stops, as they say in motor racing.

I came third, but at the finish all the fuss seemed to be about Kenny falling. It was probably the most anti-climactic Olympic bronze medal in the history of ski racing as far as I was concerned, because everybody was sure Ken would have gotten the gold. I was disappointed, not so much for myself, but disappointed at the attitude of the press. They couldn't understand how the team hadn't lived up to their press clippings. Anyway, I was the third-best skier that day, but I regard my Olympic medal as symbolic of a tremendous screw-up.

On the other hand, my respect and admiration for the Olympic movement, and the goals and opportunities the Games offer people around the world, continue to grow. In fact, I'm now on the other side of the fence, on the organizational side and as a member of the press. The negative experiences of my first Olympics should be useful in helping me improve things for the new Olympians.

From Lake Placid, we went to back to the reality of Lake Louise for the Canadian National Championships and the final World Cup race of the season. I was second in the CNC event and fourth in the World Cup Downhill. Ken was Canadian Champion again, but the pressure on him continued here as he was in the running for the World Cup Downhill title, providing he won the race. As well as the usual entourage of World Cup reporters, a herd of Canadian mediamen had followed us to see if we couldn't salvage some of the reputation they had lost at the Olympics. Ken was skiing on his home course again, so they made him a cinch for the title. He didn't do well enough, finishing eighth, and the press were at a loss for words.

There's no question in my mind that the ridiculous expectations of the press bothered Ken. I know it bothered me and I was the most voluble in telling them about it. When we were in Europe, reporters would sometimes phone us up at 10:30 or 11:00 on the night before a race and tell us they were on deadline. It might be 5:00 or 6:00 in the afternoon in North America, but in Europe all good ski racers are in bed asleep. The people at the hotel desks didn't know that it wasn't an emergency and the calls got through. I would lecture the inconsiderate journalist in terms I thought he could understand: "Do you know what time it is here? It's late at night just before a race that is bigger than a Stanley Cup final. We only get ten kicks at the can in a series that is not just for the championship of North America, which the Stanley Cup is. This is for the championship of the whole world! Please call us earlier. Good Night!" Click.

My ranting and raving in their ears did some good, but the midnight callers continued to pester us as new reporters came on duty. Later on, this long-distance media attention eventually became so bad I had to put a code word into effect. No call would be put through to my room unless the caller knew the secret word, Victoria, which was a nickname of my girlfriend Ann Rohmer.

I'm pretty sure that for some time the hockey-oriented press was convinced I was a first-class weirdo. It hardly mattered that I was ranked ninth best Downhiller in the world after the '79-'80 season, had an Olympic bronze medal, was voted Ontario Amateur Athlete of the Year, and so on. They focused on the diamond stud I sported in my left ear. In 1975, my friend Andy Bryce and I had our ears pierced in a fit of blood-brother exuberance. Andy is a minister in Prince Edward Island now and quite a sensible fellow, but as an 18-year-old he was as crazy as me, and we had our ears done long before it was in fashion for males to do so. When Kim Crouch and I became a twosome, I bought diamonds and she and I wore them for several years as a symbol of our love. Apparently my sexual persuasion was questioned on occasion because of my diamond stud. Then the press did an about face and accused me in print of *being* a stud with all the ski groupies in Europe . . . .

In a way my diamond symbolized a feeling of rebelliousness I harboured because of the way others perceived my life. Nobody in Canada seemed to know what the heck I was doing, so why not give them more to chew on. For them, the diamond was just another symptom of radical madness: I was bucking the system, not even going to school, screwing around in some obscure amateur sport . . . and, scandal of scandals, getting paid for it! Oh Olympic sacrilege! Shock! Horror! Money for the skiers in World Cup racing was a long-established fact and allowed for by the International Olympic Committee. They only required that it be managed in a trust account. The rest of the sports world knew this, but it was big news to the press and the public in Canada. Those were the kinds of reactions I had to face on the home front, and they seemed primitive to someone who was mainstream in Europe. I was on a different wave length and the diamond in my ear helped reinforce that.

Later, in March of 1980, we went back to Europe and did a few GS races, one of them in Lichtenstein where I pulled off third place, a miraculous result for a Downhiller. Andreas and Hanni Wenzel, a German brother and sister who skied for Lichtenstein because their family lived there, were overall World Cup men's and women's champions, and the principality threw a huge state dinner to celebrate. Ken and I were invited and we got to hang out with royalty, the King and Queen and Princess of Lichtenstein who invited us up to their castle. It was great; a real castle with a drawbridge, places in the wall to pour boiling oil on the invaders, all the trimmings just like in the Middle Ages. Ken and I felt like kids in a sandbox, though we behaved ourselves and did not let our country down. At the dinner, we were introduced and received a tremendous ovation, just as lengthy as the Wenzels. It gave me a greater appreciation of the impact we were having in Europe and how much we were now respected there.

From hobnobbing with the royals, Ken and I turned our attention to skis. Our contracts with Fischer were due for review and/or renewal which gave us an opportunity to look for a better deal from another company. In May, we went to a factory in Austria and were given the grand tour. We saw how their skis were made, met the chief designers, then went to nearby Hintertux to test some skis. The snow was in a typical state of late-season crappiness and it was tough going on long Downhill skis. At the end of one testing day Ken and I moved off piste to ski down a relatively harmless side slope. As I pulled my skis around a turn I felt something go POP in my infamous right knee.

The pain wasn't excruciating, but I knew from experience there was probably something seriously wrong with the ligaments. I didn't even fall, which might have lent more gravity to the situation. I told Ken I had hurt my knee, though I didn't mention it to the Fischer people, whom we decided to stick with after all. I took what I thought was a realistic view that it was just another knee injury and I would be ready to race again next season. I didn't even limp when we arrived at the Fischer factory to do our deals.

Ken and I did our own negotiating and we did it separately behind closed doors. I think we came away with similar deals, which for the first time were in the same ballpark as the Europeans. I ground away at the Fischer money man until he finally said he couldn't pay me more than the Austrians. That's all I wanted. One part of my deal called for payment for a second-place finish in the World Cup standings. Ken had finished right behind Peter Mueller in the Downhill standings, yet he had got nothing from Fischer for being second in the world in the 1979-80 season.

However, my contract wasn't signed that day which proved to be awkward. A week later, Fischer read about my knee problem in the papers and were upset I hadn't told them. They refused to sign me for the 1980-81 season until I re-established myself as a top racer. I was really scuppered because it was too late to go to another company, all the budgets were in place, and I was under the gun to prove I could perform in order to be gainfully employed. But first I had to go under the knife . . . again.

By this time Dr. Palmer had gone out of the knee business and back in Toronto I signed on with Dr. Kostuik, an enthusiastic and rather eccentric fellow – characteristics shared by many top surgeons – who briefed me on his game plan. He was going to hack out a piece of tissue from the outside of my thigh, build some ligaments out of it, and sew it into my knee. He was very positive and confident about it and assured me I'd be back to normal in no time, except for an 18-inch scar and a gap in my thigh. Only later did I find out that no athlete had ever returned to world-class competition from this type of operation.

Back at my old stomping grounds, the TGH, the good doctor and his team cut me open and found the inside of my knee had totally exploded. The damaged ligaments looked like spaghetti in tomato sauce. The operation is a marvel of modern medicine but very gruesome for laymen to witness. Lauron Productions were doing a film on the Crazy Canucks for Shell at the time and they included some operating-room footage. At one particularly messy stage, with Dr. Kostuik holding up a piece of dripping tissue for a close-up, the cameraman put down his camera and left the room. He was later found passed out in the bathroom.

Even though they did a lot more hacking and slashing, there was less pain than before. And I recovered much faster this second time around, partly because I was taking megadoses of vitamins and felt stronger physically, and also because I knew what to expect. The cast, a gigantic chunk of plaster which had to be held up with a rubber strap around my shoulder, came off after five weeks and the leg muscles were less atrophied than before. I got much better on crutches thanks to my brother who was a virtuoso on two sticks. He had had two or three knee operations after ski injuries, and he instructed me on the fine art of crutching: you get a forward lean going and take a little hop between steps so that you can really honk along, faster than many people can jog.

My commitment to skiing was absolute and I trained my buns off that summer. I reclaimed my corner in the physiotherapy room at the Fitness Institute and sweated it out every day of the week, working out on the weekends on my own. The sacrifices were easier to make now because everybody knew I was a ski racer and supported my mania for Downhill racing. Even the Canadian press had started to come over to our side. It was perfectly clear that we were among the best in the world. They could feed on "the thrill of victory and the agony of defeat": we were winning races and they couldn't ignore winners, and we were sometimes falling and getting hurt so they could comprehend the incredible odds against us. Ken's Lou Marsh trophy as the Canadian Athlete of the Year and, to a lesser extent, my Ontario Athlete of the Year award were landmarks of recognition for us in Canada, and a definite turning point for the ski team.

The team was still pitifully underfinanced and we trained that fall without video equipment, it was broken and we couldn't afford to get it fixed. When we finally got videos at the first event of the '80-'81 season, in Val d'Isère, I saw that I was skiing like a grandmother. My knee was full of scar tissue and sore, swelling up every time I pushed it, so third place (Ken was second) was an excellent result. It also proved to Fischer I had regained my form and they signed my contract. The whole team did well at Val d'Isère, with Chris Kent (up for this race from the Downhill "C" Team) finishing fourth, Ir fifth, and Mur seventh. A week later, in a doubleheader at Val Gardena, I was third and tenth, very good performances on a course with long flats where a small guy like me loses out in gliding to the big hunks whose weight carries them along faster.

The next race was at beautiful St. Moritz, the original glamour resort in Switzerland. The world's first ski school was started here in 1927 and the place is steeped in skiing tradition. The course is old style: narrow and twisting with lots of bumps and jumps near the bottom where it comes right into the outskirts of the town. In training, the course was really badly iced up, it hadn't been used in years, and half the first seed ate it big on the first run. People were wiping out all over the place: the Austrian Uli Speiss effectively ended his career when he flew off a huge bump, hit his head on his knees on landing, knocked himself silly, rolled out of control for miles, and finished up with a badly damaged knee. One of our young guys, Tim Gilhooly, went on an off-course excursion through fences, over roads, into people . . . it was chaos. Ken and some of the other top skiers thought the race should be cancelled. They were really thrown by the conditions. But I didn't feel that way at all. I was actually enjoying it, having fun. On one of my inspection runs, I had a revelation: if I ski well here nobody can beat me. Not only do I have the ability to win, I *can* win.

It was an instantaneous flash of inspiration as I was sideslipping along the course: everybody else was having trouble, but I was enjoying the course. I felt in complete control and if I didn't make any mistakes I would win. It seemed such an arrogant thought. These were the best guys in the world, with everything going for them, and I was just an upstart Canadian without any great track record. But I had this insight – it wasn't intuition or a wildly optimistic spate of positive thinking – it was a matter of putting all the pieces together and having self-confidence. If I hadn't won, it would probably have thrown me off kilter for a while. But I was *bound* to win. I even blew one of the turns quite badly and still won by a tenth of a second over Peter Wirnsberger of Austria.

It wasn't bravery so much as just being a better skier in the extreme conditions that day. My technical ability gave me an edge and I wasn't scared. You don't have to be brave if you're not afraid. I would certainly be afraid if every time I flew off a bump I was unsure of landing on my feet. But I knew I was going to land right and take the turns right. I was in a really positive mood and refused to be distracted from it.

The Daves finished back in the teens and Ken was ninth and very unhappy, really quite distraught about the jumpy course. It doesn't take long for negative feelings to spread on the team when the best skier feels that way. But I was beginning to spread my wings, making up my own mind and not keying off him so much any more. As soon as he started having trouble at St. Moritz, I just subconsciously shut him off. I always compared notes with Ken and got his opinion on how to run a course. It would have been stupid to ignore a resource like him because he was a brilliant skier, one of the best, if not *the* best in the world at that time. But when it came to negative stuff, I didn't want to hear about it.

That year a lot of first-seed people got hurt and Ken was one of those calling for more controls over the races in order to make the courses safer. I didn't buy that point of view then and I still don't.

It makes for major philosophical discussions every time Ken and I meet. My feeling was, and still is, if you can't handle it, you just go slower. That's my bottom line.

I was satisfied standing on the victory podium at St. Moritz for my first genuine World Cup win but there was no jubilant war-whooping. I felt happy and enjoyed it. I'd achieved a goal, done what I had set out to do. It seemed almost routine. I always imagined a win would involve pushing myself to the limit and just barely making it. This was somehow mechanical and maybe I was the only guy ready for it. The lack of emotional build-up prevented the great outpouring of euphoria I was to experience in subsequent victories. I was like a kid with a new toy who doesn't quite know how to make it work.

We broke for Christmas and came back to Canada for another session of reality therapy, not all of which I found beneficial. Usually, I took this opportunity to help the coaches at the Christmas ski camp for kids at Craigleith. The club had supported me, even giving my family money to help finance my early career, and I was only too happy to repay their generosity any way I could. Our budding celebrity status on the home front made new demands, starting with having to handle a media scrum in the John Molson room at the brewery in Toronto. That one event, which became a tradition, was okay, but there came to be many more. It was easier to deal with the 350 knowledgeable journalists who regularly followed the World Cup tour in Europe than the much smaller group of Canadian reporters for whom Downhill racing was something of a mystery.

I was looking forward to the relative quiet of working with the Craigleith kids when my parents announced that I had to go to a private gathering at the home of some of their friends. These people had called in all their neighbours for a drink and I was to be the pièce de résistance. I wasn't Jackie and Mike's son, but rather Steve Podborski the famous Downhiller, a ski object. I got angry with my mom and dad, pointing out that I was only home for a week and they were selfish and misguided to let others use me in this way. Even they seemed to have forgotten I was still just Steve their son. They were suitably contrite when I showed them that people's view of me, even those closest to me, was changing, in this case for the worse.

On another occasion, my parents actually got into an argument over who was getting the most TV exposure. I said, "Look you guys, this is going too far. Let's not have family strife over whose turn it is to be interviewed as the mom or dad of the 'famous' skier." Earlier, when they had felt I was getting too selfish and egocentric, they brought me down to earth saying, "Steve, here's where you were. Where are you now? Come back to reality." Now, reality was harder to find than ever in my Downhill life and home was in danger of following suit. My mom and dad were getting swept up by the whole media hype, public eye, fantasy world.

Even at the tender age of 23 I knew skiing could be a dirty ego-busting business. We were very conscious of this on the team, the artificiality of hype, the tenuousness of celebrity, the fragility of limbs. Our guys had seen, sometimes felt, it all before. Heroes are made and destroyed overnight and we were very cynical about rampant egos and artificially inflated images. One poor bugger from Switzerland had skied down a few hills rather well and suddenly the Swiss press were screaming about this new Bernard Russi, a former champion from Switzerland. Sure enough, a few races later, this new guy wiped out and ripped his knee to shreds. He was gone. The pressure had thrown him off track, just blown him away. The hills are littered with has-beens who are ignored by everybody. You've got to watch the whole star-trip syndrome: you read in the papers that you're great, people start telling you you're great, and you start thinking you're great. If you start believing it, you're dead meat.

Believing in yourself as a skier is one thing, believing you're good because you have your name in the paper is another. I regarded myself as a damn good skier and that's about it. You need a well-developed ego to do what I did, and I could have easily been swayed by the trappings that surrounded me. I was awed by the huge investment made by the equipment companies just so I could ski faster than anybody else. But I knew they did it not because I had a winning smile (though my mom thinks I have), but because I could win on skis. You've got to separate the media personality from the reality. Just because my name was well known, I never expected I should get free lunches. I got them, and still do, but I never expected them. It's all right for others to be star-struck and it's often flattering. But I kept my feet on the ground by remembering I was just some dork from Don Mills who could ski fast.

After Christmas, we started in Garmisch-Partenkirchen in West

Germany where I'd fallen during my tailspin period the year before. That time I had an agricultural excursion into the trees and wound up pounding my fists on the ground in frustration. Now I was determined to stay upright, and I had good training runs: in one of the upper turns called the Ice Hang, an icy cliff, I was fastest. I was the only one using a step turn there, transferring my weight from one ski to another instead of just holding on and switching edges. This maneuver, which requires great leg strength and balance, enabled me to accelerate faster out of the turn.

There are a lot of flats at Garmisch, where I shouldn't have done so well because of all the gliding required, but my fast turns gave me more speed to carry into the flats. Near the bottom, there's a superfast, icy, rough, and very long turn called the Gates of Hell where you have to tuck. Tucking and turning are usually mutually exclusive in a fast turn, and hell to survive. So I went for it on this wicked hill, put it all together in the race, and set a new course record. There were a lot of people there and the Germans liked me, so my third World Cup win, and my second in a row, was a fairly big deal.

But the celebrations for my win at Garmisch were very subdued because Ken had had a bad fall and really destroyed his knee. At the finish line, Serge Lang congratulated me on winning then told me about Ken's fall. He said the press weren't being allowed near Ken and I must find out how he was and report back to him immediately. He picked me because I was small and could worm my way through the crowd more easily. Serge has a very strong personality, he growls and waves his arms around a lot, and is the godfather of the World Cup, so I did his bidding. It wasn't easy getting near Ken because of the enormous crowd around the finish area, most of them intent on getting a piece of the winner of the race.

I finally barged my way through to Ken's ambulance and hopped in beside him. He was covered in blood and looked a complete mess. He'd broken his nose, cut his head open, and had leaked blood all over his beautiful yellow suit. It was a very painful contrast between a winner and a loser and I knew exactly how he felt. He said his knee was sore and he was devastated, so I tried to reassure him that everything was going to be ok, which of course it wasn't.

He'd torn the ligaments in his knee, his first bad injury in seven years with the team, so I was all too familiar with the difficulties facing him. As it turned out, his knee injury was even worse than my first one, but Ken had what it takes to come back and he did, though he never won again.

One of the ways I was able to help him was to do his final packing. It was one of the rituals of the team, a very depressing one, that you packed for the guy who was injured. I had been packed for twice before and it is not a happy time because conceivably you might not be back. You have to strike a delicate balance between optimism and the hard facts. You try to make light of it and pretend you're just doing the guy a casual favour, avoid references to the future, and just tell him to hang in there. The packer was always someone the injured party could relate to, so I went to Ken's room and did his packing. He lay there on his bed with his head swathed in bandages telling me which bag to put his underwear in and so on. It was awkward for both of us, neither one wanting to admit the seriousness of the situation, and I hated it.

While Ken's dreams had been shattered, mine seemed to be coming true. After the first five races, it was obvious I was on some kind of a roll while Ir and Mur hadn't placed in the top ten since the season opener at Val d'Isère. Various theories were put forth as to why this was happening. Coach John Ritchie thought my injuries might have given me a psychological leg-up, maybe even a physical boost. The team had skied and skied for years and years, so there was a distinct possibility of burnout. But I had been forced to rest twice due to injuries, reflect on my situation, recharge my batteries, reconfirm my commitment to skiing, and train like a madman to get fit again. Coming back from my injuries gave me a new lease on life and a very strong body. Whatever the reason, I was building up a tremendous momentum and felt confident enough at Kitzbühel to play mind games with the opposition.

I did well on the first timed training run and won the second, despite slowing up near the finish. I stood up for the last 900 feet and made big sweeping turns out of the bottom section. All the coaches were watching and were sure I was just jerking around. I knew I had a great run under my belt and I wanted them to think I could win with my hands tied behind my back. I deliberately cruised the final section so the coaches would tell their racers it was no contest because Podborski had stood up for ten seconds and still beat you.

Then Kitzbühel turned around and kicked Joe Cool in the teeth on my last training run. I wasn't hurt, but it knocked the cockiness out of me. The course was rougher than my first run and I ran wide and poked a tip in a fence, not a clever move at 60 miles an hour. One leg wanted to stop abruptly, the other didn't, and their argument sent me armpits over bindings down the hill at a considerable velocity. Eventually I stopped tumbling, dusted off my wounded pride, and began to pick up my scattered stuff. A Russian came flying by, very close to the fence, and he was so scared I heard him whimpering as he shot past me.

Strange as it may seem, I had never really watched skiers tackle Kitzbühel close-up, or any Downhill for that matter, and I joined John Ritchie down at the Oberhausberg where he was timing people. Suddenly, I heard a banging, crashing, and clattering like a battered old pick-up truck on a gravel road. It was the next racer, none other than Franz Klammer, and he flew by in a blur. "Jeeezus! John, do I go that fast through here?" I asked. "Oh no," said the learned coach, "you go faster." I just about had a baby! I was just blown away. I had no idea of how spectacularly fast we went down this amazingly difficult course. I was super impressed. I think John handled it the right way by presenting the news to me matter-of-factly. Klammer, one of the greatest racers in the history of the sport, looked really scary and I could have been thrown off. But I soon decided I was faster because I was smoother, thus more in control. At least I hoped I was more in control.

I still think it's a miracle to win at Kitzbühel. Even skiing down it in one piece is a major triumph. The place has such an aura, a mystique, and just saying the words Mausfalle and Steilhang gives a real ski enthusiast the shivers. I remember every detail of the race in January of 1981 and still shudder at how close I came to screwing up by giving up. My journey down the two-mile Strief hill into the charming little Austrian village of Kitzbühel took only 2 minutes, 3.76 seconds, but shortly after the race started I was ready to end it prematurely.

In training, I had been technically perfect in the upper sections of the course and this was where my advantage supposedly lay. Out of the starting gate, I whipped through Mausfalle right on form, then headed down into the trees for Steilhang. I felt supremely confident as I shot across the hill toward the right hander where you either turn or plow into the fence and/or safety net. Technique is essential here, you have to be locked into your turning timetable, because if you think you're not going to make it, panic, and try to change horses in midstream, you either lose speed or crash, usually the latter. I rattled around the Steilhang with the wind whistling in my helmet. My mind projected my path ahead and it decided I was not going to be able to make it. No way!

I was convinced I was on a collision course with the net surrounding the outer limits of the turn, the one which protects the trees from victims of the Steilhang. I was moving much faster than the speed limit on Canadian highways, but my destiny came toward me in slow motion. Turn – turn – turn! I commanded my skis. TURN – TURN – TURN! I refused to give in to the seemingly inevitable coming together of myself and the net. I held my line and went right round the turn with my skis about one inch from the net . . . as captured by the televison cameras. I came out of the exit of the turn at about 50 miles an hour and dropped down into my tuck to pick up more speed. You can take a little mental break through this flat section and I had a serious chat with myself. "Steve, you just blew it. After dominating training up here you've just gone through Steilhang in probably the slowest time in the history of Kitzbühel. Stop right now so you won't die of embarrassment at the bottom."

Maybe it was taking the turn in slow motion mentally that made me so sure I had lost speed. But I wasn't brought up to be a quitter and the idea of stopping was wiped away before it had a chance to manifest itself. Besides, I was going too fast to stop with dignity now. I bore down again and skied the lower part of the course really well. The TV cameras show me whipping across the finish line and throwing my hands up in a gesture of futility, my body sagging in despair, as I kicked up a shower of snow to stop. Then I saw I was half a second faster than anybody else, leaving superstars like Peter Mueller, Peter Wirnsberger, Herbert Plank, and Harti Weirather in my wake. I'd also clocked the fastest time ever recorded on a speed trap at Kitzbühel – 90 miles per hour.

There was some fairly serious partying that night. It was such an unexpected win for me, on the same hill where I'd wrecked my knee, and on the most difficult course in the world. I had been skiing well and winning, but this win, my third in a row, meant I'd really arrived on top of the skiing world because I had beaten the best on the Downhiller's Downhill. Oh boy, was I happy! The whole of Kitzbühel is set up for mainline après ski craziness and we weren't about to put a damper on things. Headquarters is The Londoner, a pub run by a mad Englishman who issues special passes in a futile effort at crowd control. Whenever an English-speaking skier won, the champagne was on the house, literally, because most of it got sprayed. It hurt when you got it in the eyes – but it's really a gas.

The Londoner is a madhouse with 100 per cent too many people, a lot of them rich and famous. The free champagne gets the owner free publicity and that night it was reported in the international media that 200 bottles of champagne were demolished and the winner of the race got hammered. It was a riot with people yelling, singing, and dancing on the tables. I spent most of the night standing on a table, there was no room to even fall on the floor. When I was pushed off the table, I just fell into the crowd and they would set me upright again. When it eventually fizzled out and the last champagne glass had been smashed to bits, I went back to the hotel and stood in the shower in my clothes to wash off the booze, blood, sweat, and tears (the blood came from those who were cut by broken glass). It was wonderfully silly and therapeutic to go completely nuts before getting back to business.

The gossip columns and the sensationalist press like to emphasize that part of ski racing, and many people are under the impression we partied harder than we skied. It's completely untrue, but John Ritchie used to say: "Tell them what they want to hear since they won't believe the truth anyway." So I do. These days, when I'm called upon to make a speech and people ask me what life was like as a Crazy Canuck, I make a joke about a typical day in my World Cup life: I roll out of my bed with its silk sheets, my dresser helps me slip into an ensemble of designer race suit and warm-ups, and I descend to the breakfast room of the luxury hotel where fawning waitresses serve me champagne and orange juice. Pursued by hordes of beautiful jetset groupies, I stride to the ski lift, signing autographs, posing for the paparazzi, and blowing kisses all the way.

I ascend the hill, my retinue of attendants and my ski man bow respectfully before me. The enormous crowd watching my every move hushes as I throw my designer warm-ups in the snow, don my goggles, and attack the hill, my descent accompanied by an earth-shaking tumult of noise raised by my adoring fans. As usual, I collect my strongbox full of gold at the bottom, and reverential crowds part before me as I make my way to the post-race celebrations held in my honour. My dazzling blonde companion and I leave the party at dawn, jump into my turbo Porsche, and roar off to the next race.

At this point in my speech, I tell the audience if they believe what I have just told them they might be interested in buying some swamp in Florida. It's always good for a few laughs, but the truth was seldom funny. That party after Kitzbühel was an exception and in reality my life was getting harder instead of easier. With Ken out of the picture, and Mur and Ir fading from the front lines, it was getting rather lonely at the top.

9. *Skiing My Buns Off*

The next race of the 1980-81 season was at Wengen, where I would be hard-pressed to continue my winning streak. The course required a lot of gliding and my 158 pounds weren't nearly as glidable as the bigger guys. Ken Read recently came up with another theory about Wengen: they used snow machines on the course that ground up the granules, chewed them, and spat them out in a flattened and perfectly smooth finish. Ken thinks this billiard-table surface made it easier to stay in your tuck, placing less emphasis on skiing technique, and more on just gliding. In effect, this emasculates the hills, making them easier to ski, while a place like Kitzbühel, where snow machines feared to tread, still required balls and brains to handle the natural terrain and snow conditions.

I came away from Wengen with a respectable third, then got another at St. Anton (which we always called Stanton). Pictures of me taken at that time show suitcases under my eyes and the effects of World Cup pressure written on my face. I'd been on the road since who knows when and was getting to the end of the proverbial rope. I was the focus of attention now, even in Canada with CBC TV following my adventures and a couple of newspaper reporters on the tour full time. I was public property and I waged a constant tug-of-war battle to stay private in order to maintain my advantage in the run for the World Cup title.

The last European race, at Schladming, was cancelled because of bad weather and we headed back to North America for the season finale at Aspen. I made a detour to Whistler to visit my ski-boot guru Dave McPhail. Dave, a building inspector at Whistler, was and still is (he and I are working on a revolutionary ski-boot design) a genius on making the foot and boot work together optimally. Dave did his thing to my boots and then I headed south down through the mountains to Vancouver.

I was alone in my car, it was about 8:00 in the morning, and a light rain was falling so I had my headlights on. I came around a turn and saw another car heading straight for me in my lane. The escape route on my right was barred by a rock cliff, but I was sure the other car would veer off. It did not. At the last moment, I turned sharply left, but it was too late. The impact spun my car around and I stopped just short of going over a 40-foot drop to a railway track below. The other car was completely pulverized. It was eerie as I ran over to it: the only sounds were my feet slapping on the wet pavement and the stereo in the other car booming away.

Gas and oil were dripping all over the place and in the front part of the wreckage I saw a girl slumped down with her long brown hair draped over the upholstery. She was breathing; then I realized there was another girl inside. The impact had driven her from the passenger seat into the back behind the driver's seat. I saw she was alive, then I realized we were all in danger because their car was in the middle of the road on a blind curve. I ran down the road and intercepted a whole line of traffic. I flagged them down, got somebody to chase after ambulances and police, and kept asking 'til I found someone who knew first aid.

Later, I found out both girls were reasonably ok, though both needed plastic surgery for facial injuries. They remembered nothing of the accident and no one knows why they were in my lane. At the time, people shielded me from any of the details and my immediate problems included dealing with severe whiplash and bruising in the neck, shoulders, and upper back. I was very sore and so weak I couldn't carry my briefcase in my left hand. Shock set in and I spent most of that night vomiting in John Ritchie's house in Vancouver.

I flew to Toronto the next day for a guest appearance on *Front Page Challenge*. The people who met me at the airport were shocked at my appearance and threw me into a hotel room until it was time for the show. Fred Davis and the *Front Page Challenge* panellists were quite impressed that I'd shown up when they heard about the accident. After the show, my parents took me home to bed again, where I stayed for some time. I got a lot of heat from the organizers when I missed a GS and a Slalom in the Canadian National Championships – which really pissed me off. I might easily have been killed, but as long as I was still breathing these idiots wanted me at their race.

A couple of weeks after the accident (what a gallant trooper I was), I did show up at Lake Louise for the Canadian National Downhill Championship where I was seventh – which is a giant step backward from being first in World Cup Downhills. I watched videos of that performance and my timing was way off, just about the worst thing that can happen. I was missing turns, hitting all the bumps, and getting thrown around like crazy. The next day, I was second in the International Ski Federation (FIS) Downhill at Lake Louise, which proves I could pull up my socks when I was worried about my form. But the fact was the car accident had thrown me for a loop.

I was a mess when I arrived in Aspen. John Ritchie was handling me with kid gloves, coddling me on the one hand while downplaying the whole thing with the other so that I could handle the pressure more easily. I was fully aware of what he was doing, that the whole World Cup year had boiled down to these last two races, and that Harti Weirather could still beat me for the title. Sure enough, Harti won the first race and I was tenth, a crappy result, but not bad considering what I'd just been through.

The next day, I was first out of the gate and whipped off a beauty of a run that held up as fastest in the race until Harti came down skiing his buns off to beat me by .28 of a second. I went over to the new holder of the World Cup title and hugged him. Harti was a great skier, a good friend, and a genuinely nice guy. I was also supportive of him because he used Fischer skis. I wouldn't have hugged some of the other guys if they'd just beaten me, but Harti was a good man, a gracious man. He'd overcome tremendous odds and pressure to beat me and I thought he deserved the title.

I wasn't at all devastated. Canadians weren't supposed to be within a million miles of where I was. I'd gone further than I'd ever dreamed of and I'd done it without the built-in support systems and advantages the Europeans have from playing their own game and performing in their own bailiwick. At the beginning of that season if anybody had predicted I would finish second overall in the World Cup Downhill, I would have laughed in their face. It was completely preposterous that a shrub with a bionic knee from the relatively flat landscape of Ontario could beat the men from the Alps who are born with ski wax in their ears. My whole season had been like getting bonus points on a pinball machine: bing, bing, bing – Crack! – another free game . . . it was great fun!

In May, I was cycling with my brother in North Toronto when I had another confrontation with a car. The lady behind the wheel turned right in front of me at an intersection and I plowed into the side of her car, hitting the roof support with my shoulder. I bounced off that baby and whoomph! – I landed on my back on the pavement and my shoulder hurt like hell. I sat up for a moment, then just lay down. I couldn't believe it. Another crash, and my shoulder felt like it was broken into teeny little bits. People were dancing around, the lady was wringing her hands and saying, "Oh My God!" Somebody called an ambulance and my brother called my mom. As soon as she put down the phone, a radio station called her to get her reaction to her son's latest accident.

There's nothing worse than lying there feeling miserable with a bunch of concerned faces staring down at you. They threw me in the ambulance and I think I insulted the attendants when I told them I hoped I would never see their likes again. They were nice guys, but riding in an ambulance is a very negative experience. At the North York General Hospital, a grumpy nurse insisted I lift a weight so that the x-rays would show how much displacement there was. I protested because it hurt like crazy. I said, "Give me a break!" She said, "You've already got a break, hold the weight!" The doctor recommended immediate surgery on the separated collar bone, but my parents and my brother took me to the TGH to get a second opinion from my personal knife man. Dr. Kostuik suggested that a program of aggressive therapy, without an operation, would be just as effective, and it was.

From the point of view of results that '80-'81 season proved to be my best, even better than my title year. My three wins in a row was the first time it had been done since Franz Klammer had pulled it off in 1976. My high finishing rate, never out of the top ten, resulted in me being given the number-one ranking in the Downhill from the FIS. Things went very well on the home front too. I was Ontario Athlete of the Year, winner of the John Semmelink Award from the Canadian Ski Association, and recipient of the Norton

Crowe Award for Canadian Male Athlete of the Year. The most useful pieces of booty came from being voted Athlete of the Month by the Sports Federation of Canada in December, 1980 and January, 1981. For this I received passes from CP Air which I made good use of by flying to Hawaii to unwind and recuperate from a tremendously trying season.

It was very satisfying to be receiving real recognition in Canada after flying the Maple Leaf on the road since I was 16. I heard about most of these side benefits after the fact in letters from home. But really, the recognition factor at home took second place to standing in the finish area at a race in Europe and being mobbed by thousands of people, and to the vastly improved lot of our team. It seemed that literally everybody in the Alps now knew who we were, including the proprietors of ritzy hotels who fought among themselves to have the Crazy Canucks on their register.

Our entourage had grown with more support staff and we had a succession of vehicles to play with, too many to handle on one occasion. We were given a gaggle of little white cars by the Honda Motor Company, identical except for the licence plates – though after a few miles we were able to keep track of them by the different dents in the bodywork. We had piled into our Hondas to make a hasty exit from St. Moritz and, a few days down the road, somebody noted the cars were packed with more people than usual. We did a head count, then a car count, and realized one of the Hondas had been lost in the shuffle. It was later found sitting in the parking lot at St. Moritz.

We were on the road constantly and there were a lot of near misses and occasional hits. We weren't necessarily being overly "Crazy Canuckish" behind the wheel, but we did conduct ourselves at speed on the road as well as on the hills. After years of trundling around in slow-moving vans, we really motored with our new machinery, though there was usually a practical reason for our joy riding. When there were long breaks between races, it was easier to stay in Europe and train than to return to Canada and lose several days to jet lag. One of our favourite destinations was the island of Elba off the coast of Italy, a warm and sunny place for dryland training.

One time on Elba, we were outfitted with Saab 900s (Slabs we called them), rather ungainly looking devices but real movers. We had had a lengthy dinner one night with plenty of fermented grape juice after which one of the reps asked John Ritchie if he could have a go in a Slab. John, in a benevolent mood, said sure and away we went in convoy with some other team Slabs. I was in the rep-driven car with John and several others, and the backseat drivers got excited by the chase and yelled at the driver: "Bump him! Pass him! Step on it!" Of course he listened to us, which was dumb since we were cruising along a sheer cliff with the Mediterranean crashing on rocks 500 feet below, and it would be SPLAT! in our Slab if there was trouble.

We slewed around a blind right-hand turn and everybody yelled WHOA! in unison because a gigantic Elba boulder was approaching us at a terrific rate of knots. We bounced off the boulder and ricocheted into the side of the cliff – Whomp! Whomp! the lights went out and we sat there in the darkness, upright and unhurt, but somewhat shaken from what was a very sobering experience. We crawled out of the now slab-sided Saab, it was totalled, and John was hopping mad. He couldn't really chew out the rep or Dave Murray and me, who were among the instigators, because we weren't his employees. But Toulouse, our masseur, was, and poor Terry Spence bore the brunt of the coach's wrath. John really gave him the gears for egging on the rep, whose name I won't mention to preserve his otherwise untarnished reputation.

We pushed the remains of the vehicle off to the side of the road and in all the confusion Toulouse disappeared. We thought he might have hitched a ride with some of the others, but when he didn't show up at the hotel I began to get worried. Suddenly I got the idea he had jumped off the cliff. I thought he had been pretty distraught at John's harangue and I grabbed Joey Lavigne, who had been on the team and was now a coach, to go and look for Toulouse or his body. We arrived at the crash site and I hung on a vine over the edge of the cliff and yelled down into the crashing waves: "Toulouse, you jerk, did you jump?" I was really worried, but also pissed off because we'd searched the whole area for hours. Then we heard noises coming from the trunk of the Saab. I opened it up and there was Toulouse curled up and snoring peacefully. I could have throttled him. To complete the saga some of the locals stripped the Saab later that night and the whole episode probably did little for relations between Canada and Sweden where Saabs are a prized export.

There was an unofficial priority list of drivers on the team, based on seniority and the idiot factor. Everybody was paranoid about letting rookies fresh from Canada get behind the wheel because they tended to be madmen, not having sorted out the differences between the brake and gas pedals and when to apply them. It took me a while to learn this and when I did I became a very poor passenger. I often drove the equipment vehicle for Toulouse who was content to sit there while I exercised my right foot. It was usually a Volkswagen panel truck, faster than our early vans, but still the last vehicle to arrive at the hotel.

My seniority and racing success meant I no longer had to engage in the battle for the best hotel rooms, a battle that raged among team members for several years. It was vital to arrive early to get the best choice of rooms and we raced up and down corridors comparing accommodation and arguing over beds. Eventually the coaches assigned rooms, the best going to the better racers – not the fastest in the hotel corridors, but the fastest skiers. This was a terrific motivator in inspiring better performance and ranked right up there with World Cup points as a tangible indicator of your arrival as a top skier.

Roommates were rotated regularly, though I still bunked with Ken most often and we began to get along quite well. He and I had both matured and I tore up the list of pet hates I'd made when we first met. He reformed his aggravating habits after hints were dropped (never by me, I didn't have the nerve). We all bugged each other in little ways and hints, sometimes broad hints, were usually enough to get the point across. For someone to tell you point blank that you were out of line was to be avoided if at all possible. Ken's insistence on always navigating us on the road ended when the rest of us got to know where we were going and somebody just took the maps away from him. While we remained individuals, we soon learned it wasn't a one-way street and you had to work together as a team 24 hours a day. Everybody had to make sacrifices for the common good. You couldn't be self-centred and insular and say to hell with you, I'm here to race, not to win friends and influence people.

I never went to charm school, but I was forced into learning how to be nice to the media and to smile for the cameras, not always an easy task after my 1980-81 season. It had been fun to that point and later on I was able to enjoy it again, but at the height of my career I found the media madness a very tough go. It got totally out of hand when I had to talk to at least 50 reporters every day, and I had to develop a kind of shorthand technique in the interest of preserving my voice. They flocked around me in bunches, one guy would throw me a question, I would field it, and everybody scribbled or recorded my answer. Another question, another response, and so on, with everybody interpreting it in different ways. The poetic licence some reporters take can be amazing. I gave individual interviews if someone was doing a feature, then ran for the safety of the hotel. The European press knew this was sacred ground, but our privacy was still often invaded by newcomers from North America.

Good relations with the media are very important on the World Cup tour. These guys can make or break a reputation fast and as soon as you become a winner they start examining you with a microscope, particularly the unscrupulous types who try to dig up any dirt that will help sell newspapers. One Austrian journalist somehow took a dislike to me, probably thinking I was just too nice to be true. One time in the start area at Kitzbühel, Toulouse told me that Franz Klammer was winning the race. I said that was great, and that now I would have to ski really hard if I was going to beat Franz. The big-eared journalist in question overheard this and in his report twisted my words around so that I was quoted as saying I had the race in the bag and didn't think Klammer was good enough to win. Klammer is one of Austria's greatest heroes and there were big headlines in this very influential Austrian paper trumpeting the fact that the Crazy Canuck had dumped on The Kaiser. I had also won the race.

It was potentially a very damaging situation because the whole of Austria was getting the wrong impression. When we came back to Austria for a race at St. Anton, I spoke to Heinz Pruller, a very respected ski and motor racing journalist, who's a good friend of mine. I explained to Heinz about how his colleague was giving me the gears and being unfair. Heinz had been at Kitzbühel and agreed the other guy was wrong. I suggested Heinz have a heart-to-heart talk with the other journalist, explain to him that I was upset, and if he continued to screw me around I could make his life miserable too. We both had a job to do and it would be much easier to get them done without friction. Heinz asked him to lay off and it worked out fine after I had established my point of view. In many ways playing a role for the press is a kind of game. Yet I played it with a clear conscience. I always tried to accentuate the positives, but never tried to hide the negatives. I felt it was the responsibility of the media to present a balanced picture.

For years, I got tons of fan mail, five or six letters every day at home in Canada and a lot more in Europe where they would be waiting for me at every race. The European magazines often printed my home address and there were boxes and boxes of accumulated airmail at my parents' house, most of it from ski-struck teenage girls. I'm sure the mailman in Don Mills grew to hate the name Podborski. I tried to answer them all, a nice mindless activity, though deciphering the curlicue of flowing German script was frequently like plowing through a difficult crossword puzzle. I developed a high-speed technique of ripping open the letters, copying the return addresses onto a stack of autographed Podborski postcards, which Fischer had made up for me, and dumping the lot into the nearest mailbox. I spent a small fortune on postage since few well-wishers thought to include a stamped, self-addressed envelope.

Some of the keenest fans of the team in Europe were young ladies, a few of whom were fanatics. One Swiss girl painted her car the same colours as our suits, yellow with red stripes, and with a huge Maple Leaf on the hood. She asked us to sign her car which we did, in large letters with permanent ink. Most people were content with ordinary autographs on paper, but they went to great lengths to get them, often standing patiently in line for some time. The Crazy Canucks were much more approachable than the European teams and our accessibility made us a major focus of fandom.

They built up an heroic image of us in their minds, big brave men in the crazy sport of Downhill racing. When they finally met us, their minds went into overdrive and they would go for it, not wishing to miss what they saw as the opportunity of a lifetime. It was flattering, yet unsettling, and sometimes very bothersome. At one point I developed distinctly anti-fan sentiments when I couldn't walk more than a few feet in any direction without being engulfed by a swarm of them wanting autographs or conversation. Everything I did in public took twice as long and I felt harassed and sometimes showed it.

Then I sat back and analyzed their behaviour and mine. I realized I was responsible for striking some kind of chord with these people and if I moved them enough to overcome their inhibitions and approach me, then I owed them at least a few moments of my time. I could empathize with fans because I've been one myself. Meeting Bruce Cockburn reduced me to a complete blithering idiot, even though I was a supposed "celebrity" too. I forgot that famous people are just ordinary people who have become well known.

However, during my really successful years, there was nothing in my life besides skiing, and plain old Steve from Don Mills disappeared from view, buried under an avalanche of public exposure. My face was plastered around the western world now that North America had hopped on the Downhill bandwagon. ABC's *Wide World of Sports* televised my two wins at Kitzbühel and the total international audience each time was larger than the Super Bowl. I was a grinning guest in the living-rooms of the whole world of jockdom and the notoriety meant I had perks coming out my ears. Sure I got upgraded to First Class on many of my flights, but I paid a price.

On planes, instead of keeping my head buried in a good science fiction book, I had be to nice to the attendants and talk to the passengers. The airline got their money's worth in publicity. In restaurants, the proprietor might insist on giving me a meal on the house but I was expected to sing for my supper by acting as the floor show, with patrons watching every bite I took. Since I eat quite normally, they must have been disappointed. Often it seemed I signed as many autographs as I took mouthfuls of food.

I learned how to play the role of the token celebrity and chose to play it straight: in the public eye I tried never to be anti-social. I could never be out of character and signal my displeasure to the jerk who had just cut me off in traffic, nor bawl out a waitress if she spilled soup down my pants. I left a tip no matter if they watered the wine because if I didn't, I would be forever labelled a tightfisted twit. When you're put on a pedestal, there are always vultures waiting to chew you up if their expectations are not met. They expect you to be perfect and it's a tremendous drain on your vitality trying to live up to their image.

Satisfying the demands of our fans could have been a full-time job, but we were still in the business of ski racing and to survive in this goldfish-bowl atmosphere we were forced to spend a lot of time avoiding public scrutiny. We developed highly refined techniques of scooting through crowds faster than they could react. The procedures varied according to the density of people. A favourite technique was to have an intense look of preoccupation on your face as if the fate of the world was in your hands and you had to attend to it immediately. You always moved very fast, looking down with your eyes fixed at a point ten feet in front of you. In airports, I would sail along with my baggage cart in front of me to repel boarders. I scowled and never acknowledged any of the yells of "Hey Pod!" "Mr Podborski!" "Steve!" The trick is to never even flinch, even if it's a beautiful blonde . . . well maybe a slight flinch in her case.

Handling sidewalk traffic was a little easier, the open field situation offered more room to maneuver. Here too it's fatal to stop; if particularly aggressive celebrity hunters see you coming, they'll do anything to arrest your progress, stand in front of your face, even trip you. Occasionally, we called our back-alley or underground technique into play. This was developed at Whistler in B.C. where it's possible to walk through the whole village in underground garages. Wherever we went we checked all the exits and prepared the escape routes beforehand. The Whistler garages could get you all the way from the hotel to the ski lifts without surfacing.

The finish-line shuffle was our main method of movement at the end of a race: you put your skis over your shoulders and, without actually using them as a battering ram, you charge the crowd in a forceful manner. It's easier to be physical in Europe where pushing and shoving crowds are de rigueur and there is a certain amount of bouncing off people, gentle nudging, and occasional stepping on toes. But if your timing is right, you're gone before they can strike back. You develop a kind of subconscious radar system and spot potential holes in the crowd before they even develop. You adjust your stride length frequently to adapt to conditions and kind of go with the flow. One time, my parents and my girlfriend Ann Rohmer came to Schladming and I led them out of the multitude by having them hold onto my jacket. It takes quite a lot of practice and rookies can be swallowed up by the mob.

Handling the attentions of our "groupies" was not a heavy chore. I hesitate to call them groupies because that implies they threw themselves at our feet. Most of it was very innocent, they saw our lifestyle as being glamorous and exciting and wanted to be a small part of it. We spoke to them and they gave us gifts of dolls and teddy bears and took pleasure in just hanging around the periphery of the team. Really, they were little more than persistent fans and we gave them more attention only because they were there more often. We didn't encourage intimacies and there were strict rules that no outsiders could have dinner with the team or stay with us.

Most of the time, our monk-like existence provided little opportunity for meeting members of the opposite sex, let alone dallying with them. We didn't even have much contact with the Canadian women's team, which was totally separate from us. They had some very good skiers. Gerry Sorensen won a Downhill in Austria in 1980, the first Canadian woman to do so since Nancy Greene. Laurie Graham won her first Downhill in 1983 and Betsy Clifford, Kathy Kreiner, and others did well on the women's World Cup tour. Their races were usually held on different courses, though we occasionally trained together, which made for interesting comparisons. We were very impressed, then aggravated, to find that the girls seemed to get more desserts at mealtimes! It seemed their coaches liked desserts more than ours and found ways to fit them into their team budget. There was some compensation in travelling with them because it gave us a chance to fraternize and speak English with new, and much prettier, faces. There was very little more than just companionship, although Ken eventually married Lynda Robbins, who was a member of the ladies' team. That was after they'd retired from racing, and for the most part we were strictly committed to skiing. Heavy romance might have interfered with that.

At one point, some of us wanted to have our girlfriends with us. In fact, Ir and I tried it but it just didn't work. We were such a closely knit group, incestuous in a way, with everyone having learned how to deal with the others, that newcomers caused trouble. We catered to each other's whims: Dave likes this, Ken doesn't like that, the other Dave likes this, and so on, and you were never, never late. Inevitably a girlfriend over from Canada would regard it as a

131

holiday and, if she took a leisurely approach to applying her make-up in the morning, there would be some very upset ski racers waiting to get the show on the road. Women in the team caused tensions and even when people were married, they hesitated to bring their wives.

Our lives were dominated by skiing 24 hours a day: even when you took a coffee break, it would be with someone like your rep. All team conversation was ski-related, except at dinner where the rule was no ski talk. This proved to be a great strain and sometimes a lot of us read books at dinner. There were times when you felt you would go absolutely nuts if you didn't find some escape to avoid burnout. The discipline was largely self-imposed, the coaches didn't have to whip us into line, but the red-blooded young Canadian males who were the darlings of Alpine Europe frequently had profound inner struggles to keep the forces of nature at bay.

I grew up on the ski team. My last cultural milieu had been high school in Don Mills where the constraints of society at the time meant that parking with a girl in a car was a big deal, and if you got beyond petting it was a miracle. My first miracle occurred when I was 16, but I was still a relative saint when it came to the opposite sex. When I began to travel with the team, the constraints were removed and, when I became a celebrity, the opportunities for miracles with girls were multiplied and I occasionally took advantage of them. But I never went berserk – none of us did – despite the popular conception of raving rock and roll groupies who would break your door down, rip off all your clothes and do horrible things to your body.

I had great respect for the mating ritual and felt there should be mutual admiration as well as physical attraction. Another consideration was your roommate on the team: the logistical problem of double beds in close proximity to each other meant you couldn't just grab some chick off the street and whip her up to your hotel room. The time factor also worked against romance on the road. We raced on weekends, travelled on Monday and/or Tuesday, and practised and trained the other days of the week. If you went out and howled at night, it ruined you for the next day. We were in Europe to be ski racers and, unlike some rock stars who might choose music as a means to an end of wretched excesses, we wanted only to win races.

The press loved to play up the groupie factor in our lives and their fiction was inevitably more entertaining than our reality. Only once was I the recipient of advances made in the way it might happen in a soap opera. We were having dinner in our hotel in Austria when a knockout blonde sidled up to our table, handed me a note, and took off. Everyone looked at me and, with some embarrassment, I read the message. She had invited me to meet her at a bar later on. I didn't show up at the proposed rendezvous and was in bed, alone, as usual by 10:30.

For the most part, the others on the team shared my views, but Ken had the matinée-idol image and it used to bug him, it still does, when we called him Lance Romance. He's extremely good-looking, so the girls tell me, and witty and articulate in three languages. But he preferred to be recognized for his skiing talents. One time, when a photographer suggested he should consider a modelling career, Lance was very insulted.

Our pursuers weren't always nubile young wenches, nor were they necessarily unattached. One tremendously wealthy Swiss woman hung around the team for some time and I'm sure she regarded us as another trophy to flaunt at her jetset friends. She wore a wedding ring and also the biggest diamond I've ever seen in my life. It was so huge she had to cut a hole in her ski glove to get it on, and to show it off. We were often collected by celebrity headhunters and tolerated it if the rewards warranted it. In her case, this meant being invited to her gigantic estate to sip Dom Perignon at a sumptuous feast. That was another rendezvous I didn't keep, I heard about it from some of the others. I regarded this as just another little blip in my life to be kept under control so it wouldn't affect my performance. It was usually the guys lower down in the rankings who took advantage of these perks.

I did attend the annual cocktail party hosted by Mr. Fischer before the race at Kitzbühel. Everybody who was anybody in the top echelons of European society would be there, princes and princesses, the rich, the famous, and the fashionable, posing and strutting their stuff and decked out in enough fur and glitter to pay off the Canadian national debt. It really was an incredible spectacle with all these beautiful people going ga-ga over Joe Ski Racer who to-night might be dressed in scruffy jeans, a shirt that hadn't been washed in two months and a jacket that had been crushed in a suitcase, but tomorrow would risk life and limb on the Hahnen-kamm. Cocktail parties have been called a civilized form of bottom-sniffing, akin to behaviour in the canine world, and this la-de-da gathering of prize poodles was a heady mixture for a boy from Don Mills to comprehend. I sniffed all the perfume and the money in the air, but I also got a whiff of the absurd: all this fawning over people just because they can ski fast.

It was fascinating for me to watch and learn about people while on the road. When I left home I assumed everyone was like me and had been brought up with the same sense of values. My beliefs didn't account for the differences being rich can make. On one occasion, the Swiss lady with the rock on her finger complained about Austrian schillings cluttering up her purse. To me the coins were money, to her they were garbage, and my "a-penny-saved-is-a-penny-earned" upbringing was challenged. It wasn't exactly the school of hard knocks, but I was learning.

One of those who befriended us was Walter Wolf, the Austrian native who came to Canada and made a fortune in construction and oil. He was an enthusiast of high-speed activity with a stable of exotic cars and, for a while, his own Formula One racing team. He had homes around the world, including a villa in the south of France and a ski chalet in Austria, where his entourage included Franz Klammer. Walter has a theory that winners attract winners and, when Ken and I began to win, we did indeed meet a lot of successful people – one of them was another friend of Walter's: Gilles Villeneuve.

We were training up in the mountains in the South of France, about a hundred miles inland from the Côte d'Azur at Pra Loup, when two guys on snowmobiles started ripping up the hill. Ken got caught in one of their ruts and was about to give them a tongue-lashing when he learned one of the hooligans was Gilles Villeneuve who lived nearby. The fellow-Canadians were introduced and Gilles came to our hotel to meet the rest of us. Ken and I watched him perform at several Formula One races and he was great fun to be with. After one Long Beach Grand Prix in California, we went to dinner with Gilles and his wife Joanne. His Ferrari teammate, the South African Jody Scheckter, came along and we soon had 12 people at our table. When we were finished, Jody suddenly stood up and said, "Well thanks for dinner, Gilles," and left. Everybody roared but Gilles paid for us all.

Another time, I went to watch him at a Grand Prix in Belgium, at Zolder, the same circuit where he died in 1982. I was standing around in the Ferrari pits during practice when Gilles came storming in for some new tires and sat there with his helmet and hands poking up out of the cockpit, the only human element in this sinister red racing machine. The mechanics swarmed over his Ferrari and it was all deadly serious. Then I caught his eye and he winked at me.

There was a certain amount of affinity in our professions and we could relate to the kind of public pressure Gilles was under. Formula One racing is more international and has more glamour, money, and danger, but the car racers seemed to think we were in similar circumstances and we were accepted into their inner circle. World Driving Champions James Hunt and Nelson Piquet sometimes appeared at The Londoner celebrations in Kitzbühel and at their races we hung around the paddocks in the luxurious motor homes of the teams and sponsors and enjoyed the atmosphere. I never became a really close friend of Gilles because we usually met under racing conditions and I knew from experience that you operate on a different wavelength there than you do in private life.

In an interview following his death in May of 1982, I was asked to give my opinion about performing in a sport where you might lose your life. I quoted Gilles who said that if he wasn't racing he wouldn't be really alive anyway. The standard layperson's response to that is, "You're nuts." But I could really relate to Gilles' philosophy. Ski racing made me. I devoted my life to it, put every last bit of my energy and desire into it, and was rewarded with a heightened sense of my own being. Undoubtedly the risk factor amplifies this state of affairs by concentrating all your senses in an effort to control your own destiny. Only when I came skiing down a hill as fast as I could possibly go was I really completely alive.

I was glad to be able to commiserate with Joanne Villeneuve after Gilles was killed. They had two children, Melanie and Jacques, and the boy was quite a good skier. One time she brought him to Val d'Isère to see me race and afterward I took Jacques to play Space Invaders at a pinball parlour which helped distract him from dwelling on the loss of his father. My experience in dealing with death was very limited, but Joanne seemed to think I could understand better than some and we talked a lot about life in general.

Our celebrity status opened the doors for us to meet other famous Canadians. I first met Pierre Trudeau with Ken and Gerry Sorenson from the girls' team. We were introduced in the Parliamentary Gallery and thus got our names in Hansard, which is an honour of sorts. Then we were taken to the Prime Minister's office. He seemed very self-assured, which I admired in someone in his position. I'm not very good at taking any heat but he seemed entirely capable of handling himself in hot water. I was very impressed by his intelligence and alertness and by his grasp of facts, even obscure ones like my name. Whenever we met after that he always got my name right. I have a habit of saying, "Hi, I'm Steve Podborski," to avoid having people get embarrassed should they forget my name. That was never necessary with Pierre Elliott Trudeau.

I finally met Jean Claude Killy when we worked on a promotional project together. Many people think he was probably the greatest skier of all time and, at the very least, he was the outstanding figure in the sport during his era, the sixties. He won everything in sight, including six World Cup Downhill races and gold medals in the Slalom, Giant Slalom and Downhill in the 1968 Olympics. Then he retired at the age of 24. He was just as successful in business as he had been in skiing, with his own line of clothing and a host of enterprises that made him very wealthy. I was impressed that success hadn't spoiled him and that he still had all his old friends. He also told me he'd written three books, two how-to-ski publications and an autobiography. He told me I should forget about my life story and write instructional books because they made money.

"King" Killy once told the press that he was thrilled to win Olympic medals, but his real wish was to win the World Cup title. His wish came true in 1966-67 and again the next year. Based on the results of my 1980-81 season, it didn't require a great stretch of the imagination for my wishes to be fulfilled. Harti Weirather and I had each won three of the ten races. Only twice was I out of the top three and the mere five points separating me from Harti in the final standings amounted to tiny fractions of seconds on the hills. I could win the Downhill title . . . if I skied my buns off again.

10. On Top of the World

Going into the 1981-82 season, I felt that if I was ever to become the World Cup Downhill Champion, this was it. Last year was a dress rehearsal, now for the command performance. The team now included Robin McLeish, who was promoted to join the four regulars, and various members of the "B" and "C" teams were to race with us at selected events. We were being treated like winners now and we took advantage of that at the first race, at Val d'Isère, where we asked the organizers for an out-of-the-way hotel, and we got it. We chose it because it was near a lift that went up the back of the race hill and we could avoid the crowds. In the race, I managed to avoid most of the crowd, but three of them finished in front of me. I was fourth again a week later in Val Gardena, Italy: not bad on a course I never liked because of its long flat section where I always lost time.

I was slightly worried because those first two results put me behind my pace of the previous season. But, because I was always a slow starter, I convinced myself this was par for the course. So I was raring to go at Crans Montana, Switzerland, a rolling sort of soft and turny hill with no real screaming stuff on it, but fun nonetheless. At the time, I believed, along with most others, that I needed a really hard, fast course to do well on, so I had to aim higher than usual to hit my target at Crans Montana.

Everything started on a high note when we checked into the best hotel in town and were treated like kings. Then I fell from grace on a training run. I was fooling around in the wide open spaces of the upper hill in about a foot of newly arrived snow. I was cruising along about 60 miles an hour when I came upon a partially buried fence. The procedure here, in fact the only option, is to hop over it. This I did, but the hop wasn't high enough and I hooked a tip and took off, flying through the air about three feet above the ground in a prone position. I sailed merrily along like Superman for a considerable distance, then landed – poof – in the soft powder. It was hilarious, though I was somewhat chastened to find I'd dragged the fence about 50 yards down the hill.

Obviously the experience left me none the worse for wear because I won the race over Peter Mueller, and Ken's third place here (following a fifth in Val d'Isère) was great on his comeback from injury. I felt good about this race, I hadn't skied brilliantly, yet was good enough to win. If I was brilliant at Kitzbühel, where there were back-to-back races scheduled, I would be in good shape.

Kitzbühel is the pinnacle of the Downhill experience. You've got to attack the Hahnenkamm. You go to war with the hill. If you win the battle, you can win the race; if you lose, you can get hurt. I had both of those experiences, but I never pussyfooted around because that puts you at the bottom of the results. The course is icy and rough and can be as intimidating as hell if you let it.

Standing in the starting gate, you look down between your ski tips and see a void in space. You shoot out of the gate and hang a right, then a quick left, which is also a compression – a sudden change of terrain where it becomes very flat – leading to the Maus-falle (which means mousetrap in German). It means big jump in any language and you have to pre-jump it – actually jump into the air before you hit the bump – and you land 100 feet or so later. If you screw up and take off too late, you jump higher into the air and might conceivably finish up on your head in downtown Kitz-bühel. When you get it right, you land on a long steep section which immediately flattens into another compression. The G-forces here are enough to ram your tongue down your throat and the sudden deceleration makes your quadriceps ache, but you've got to take a sharp left at the bottom of this pitch, or steep section.

Another abrupt right, then left, and you're face to face with the Steilhang (steep wall), the toughest part of the course. It's so steep that snow won't stay here, so they carry it in and glue it to the rock face with water which freezes the stuff in place. The right turn through here, which falls away over very rough terrain, is probably the most difficult in ski racing. Get it wrong and you're out of control at over 75 miles an hour heading for the Bamboo Curtain. A safety net covers it now, but when I first rammed into it, it was built of branches, snow fence, and hay bales, and it hurt. Assuming you've got it right, your inside ski is up around your waist and you're hanging on for dear life with your left. Your exit speed of about 50 miles an hour picks up during a 45-second ride through the Alte Schneise, a long, narrow trail between the trees. The trail ends in a bumpy side-hill section where you judder up and down like a jackhammer at something like 80 miles an hour. If you're still mobile, you're about halfway down the Hahnenkamm.

Tucking away like mad, you shoot through the Larchenschuss, a long, flat section that's an alpine meadow in quieter times. It ends in a big, sweeping right-hand turn down through a little valley where a stream flows in the summer. After a hard left, then a sharp right, you're in the Oberhausberg, named after the quaint wooden house there which always has photographers parked on the roof. They're focusing on the Hausbergkante and with good reason. You're really howling at this point and you have to set yourself up exactly right as you tear through the right turn because, after you fall through space at the Hausbergkante jump, there's a sharp left with a compression. You have to press it and land turning to the left. If you misjudge it, the photographers get some terrific crash shots – as they did of me in 1976 when I lost it here and wrecked my knee for the first time.

Now comes the fastest and hairiest part of the course as you shoot along a steep side hill, make a right, and launch yourself into orbit off the lip of the Zielschuss. You jump from light into dark because the sun never penetrates into the hole after your take-off point, and you're travelling at about 80 miles per hour, at least I always was. The launching ramp is very rough and you have to push down hard as you leave the ground, otherwise you'll fly forever. It's a very difficult maneuver and this is where Todd Brooker's career ended in 1987. You fly for maybe 130 feet, but it seems forever and you have to fight your body's tendency to want to just lie down and die. You push forward and float like a ski jumper, and when you finally hit terra firma the impact throws you right down onto your skis. You land in a compression at 80 miles an hour and, like hitting a pothole in your car at that speed, it's very hard on the shock absorbers, in this case your legs. Five seconds after you come down from this high, you cross the finish line.

What a wild course! The coaches told me that I talked to myself coming down Kitzbühel, yelling and cursing all the way . . . mainly whenever I made a mistake. But some of my verbalising might have been from sheer exhilaration. Kitzbühel was probably my favourite race because of its challenges, its atmosphere and drama, and because it was so exciting. When I won here in 1981, I was clocked at 90 miles an hour on one of the speed traps, the fastest ever recorded . . . it sure felt like it!

Now, a year later, I was nearly as fast in the first race, but not quite as fast as Harti Weirather, who beat me by .69 seconds. Second place at Kitzbühel was a noteworthy achievement, as was Ken's third-place finish, but we both knew from experience that one of the worst possible things in a doubleheader here is to have a good result yet not win in the first race. Some of the psychological edge is lost when you have a good result here, you tend to feel satisfied with your performance. Then the demands on the top finishers in places like the Londoner Pub make it tough to peak the next day. However, we managed to avoid any distractions that night and the results the following afternoon showed Ken third for the second day in a row and me a winner at Kitzbühel for the second year in a row.

I felt I was really back on top form with back-to-back wins on two completely different kinds of course: the rhythmically jumpy hill at Crans Montana and the cliff-hanging nailbiter at Kitzbühel. I was skiing very well in varying conditions, my skis were performing nicely, and all bode well for a good season. Then we went to Wengen.

Wengen is the most beautiful course and the most physically trying because it's the longest Downhill run at 2.64 miles. Trying to maintain your tuck here meant you were squatting for nearly three minutes (though times improved over the years and it's closer to two and a half minutes now). Racing began here over 60 years ago when Sir Arnold Lunn and some of his British friends staged a competition. The place is steeped in tradition. The village, perched on a plateau high above a valley, is accessible only by rail and the ski racers take the train to get to the start of the famous Lauberhorn run. It drops over 3000 feet and you're much too busy to appreciate the splendid scenery in the shadow of the mighty Eiger peak. You're tucking and turning, jumping and tucking, bobbing and tucking, weaving and tucking, and you're hanging on for dear life . . . it's a gas!

The start is in a snow field high above the treeline. You skate out of the gate and push and push to build up momentum over a series of rocking and rolling undulations and turns. You tuck and tuck into a huge 180-degree right-hand turn that's doubly difficult because you've got to jump up out of your tuck and force yourself into the change of direction, otherwise you go rocketing off splat into the rocks on your left. You skid around, throwing up a giant roostertail of snow, losing speed as the turn gets tighter and tighter. You enter at about 80 miles an hour and exit at around 30. Then you turn left and swoop through what we called the "Cat's Nuts," two enormous rocks that loom on either side. There's little room for error here as you've only got about nine feet to play with between the feline's gonads.

Because Wengen has been around so long, the FIS bends the rule stipulating a minimum course width of 30 meters (98.4 feet) and shooting the gap between the Cat's Nuts is one of the biggest thrills on the World Cup tour. You immediately drop off an incredible jump, which I always said was like disappearing down an elevator shaft. Many people fall here when the elevator doesn't stop at their floor. Then you enter a section named after a skier named Joseph Minsch, who had trouble on this drop, and it ends in a compression. The Minschkante is a jump and a tight 160-degree fallaway to the right and it takes your breathe away. Ken and Ir both fell here in 1976 and Ir was badly hurt when he bounced off the course at over 75 mph. When Ir woke up in the hospital at nearby Interlaken and couldn't remember anything just before or for several hours after his accident, he figured that was probably just as well.

The course narrows again after the Minschkante, following a tiny goat track that's barely wide enough for the brown Swiss cows that graze here in the summer. I always had difficulty navigating this section, something to do with my speed of 50 miles an hour no doubt. Next comes a barn-burner of an S-turn, right and left, and over a bridge across a tumbling alpine brook. Mercifully, at this point all the gyrating through the scenery has slowed you down to about 20 miles an hour as you scrape the edges of the fence with your skis. But when you consider that the average speed of the course is 60 miles an hour, you realize the fun has only begun. So you grit your teeth and drop into your tuck again to tackle the Langentreien where you veer off into the tunnel under the railway track. In Robert Redford's movie *Downhill Racer*, two skiers converge on this tunnel side by side and one of them gets elbowed off line and goes *Kerthump!* against the stone wall. Hollywood took some liberties with reality in that film, though the time I went under the tunnel with a train passing overhead would have made an entertaining film sequence.

We've now descended into the trees and the course cuts a swathe through them, swinging back and forth in a series of big S-bends. It's important to carry your speed through here and once after a training run I asked a Swiss coach, who knew it like the back of his hand, how I looked going through this section. He told me I looked rough and not very good at all. Nevertheless, I had an excellent time on his Swiss watch and that's what counted. Things get quite exciting again as you zip over a bridge which recreational skiers go under on their way down from the slopes to Wengen. They would be well advised to keep their distance now as we rocket over the bridge at a considerable velocity into the Hanneggschuss, turning right all the time and flirting with potential disaster in the trees which crowd up to the course. The route straightens out slightly and you go faster and faster past Seilerboden, Wegscheide, and other complicated-sounding landmarks until the dreaded Osterreicher Loch makes its presence felt.

The "Austrian Hole" is a series of three big rolls with a severe compression, where most of the Austrian team wiped out one year. But this section plays no favourites and claims victims of all nationalities. By now you've been on the road for too many minutes and your legs are crying stop! Instead you tuck, tuck, tuck, and fly over the rolls, then sweep around the last S-turn which the perverse Swiss water down so that it's glare ice. It's a real test of stamina to remain upright, let alone negotiate the bends which are banked in reverse camber – in opposition to the direction you're supposed to turn. It takes five or six agonizing seconds through here before you know if your maneuver has been successful. If it is, you gather the remains of your strength and courage for the final dash over the

Zielschuss, a fairly serious cliff immediately before the finish line. You need to summon up a last gasp of energy to come to a halt from your quite considerable speed here. Occasionally, people have nothing left and they end their race at Wengen by bonking into the fence at the finish.

This year, at Wengen, it snowed heavily and the course conditions deteriorated throughout the race. When I got a late start number, I knew I was in trouble. I skied my heart out, but still finished nowhere, way back in 11th, my worst result in two years. Ken had an uncharacteristic result too, finishing in 23rd place, and we stood at the bottom of the hill moaning in unison. Sure we were victims of the weather, and everyone is at the mercy of the elements, but we were unable to console ourselves by being philosophical. Harti Weirather won and conditions at the top of the Downhill standings became rather crowded, with Peter Mueller hovering in the background waiting to pounce on Harti and me.

After Wengen, we took time out from the World Cup tour to visit Schladming where the Austrians have been skiing since the turn of the century. This season of 1981-82, it was the site of the World Championships – like the Olympics, just another ski race (which doesn't count in the Cup scoring), but given a fancy label so the bureaucrats of skiing and the equipment manufacturers can trade on it. The officials from the team office in Ottawa came over and ran around madly in all directions organizing press conferences, cocktail parties, and dinners. There was bare ground showing in the finish area and there were delays while the organizers made snow.

Schladming was not a particular favourite of mine, though it was one of the fastest courses on the tour, with speeds averaging over 70 miles an hour from a standing start. That's really honking, but it's wide open like an autobahn – at least 100 feet wide in most places – and consequently rather sterile and without the character of Kitzbühel or Wengen. It's like driving down a six-lane highway as opposed to a twisting mountain road, though the vertical drop of 3270 feet over 2.23 miles at Schladming makes it one of the steepest courses. The surface is manicured by snowcats so it's very smooth and not particularly demanding technically.

However, like all the famous Downhill courses, Schladming is indelibly imprinted on my mind and I can conjure up a run with my eyes closed. From the start, you drop down a steep pitch right – turn left – off a little jump onto a really steep pitch, roll off it – turn left along a traverse, or flat – right – left – right – left to the bottom of a hill – right again – jump over a road and land in a tree-lined avenue – left – right – left – hard right – left – right – over another road and straight along another pitch – pop over another road – hard left – shoot up to another right-hand turn onto a fallaway with trees on either side – left – hard right – hard left, a big sweeping left-hander – onto the last pitch at about 90 miles an hour – finish . . . .

As I stood at the top waiting for my turn in the starting gate for the World Championship race at Schladming, there was a mighty roar from the crowd at the finish line over two miles away. Toulouse, always in touch with the latest news by radio, asked me if I wanted to know what all the fuss was about. We had the option of hearing about rival times, disastrous falls, and the like, or not, in case it would distract us from our run. I always wanted to know, even if a teammate had had a bad fall. It may sound cold-hearted, but I figured knowing about it might prevent me from doing the same thing. Besides, it seemed to me that the best way for me to aid a fallen comrade was to get to the bottom of the hill as fast as possible.

Toulouse told me the noise at the finish was in celebration of local hero Harti's fast time. I filed that away, took off, and soon knew it wasn't going to be my day. My timing was way off and I skied like a dog. The finish area at Schladming is so fast the only thing you hear is the wind screaming in your helmet. When you slew to a stop, the noise of the crowd takes over, but this time there was complete silence at the completion of my run. Then the patriotic Austrians erupted in an incredible din and I didn't even have to look at my time on the board. I knew they were cheering because I'd lost. Harti was "World Champion" and I was ninth, but at least the race didn't count in the World Cup.

I got serious again at the next event, in Garmisch, though Fischer threw an obstacle in my path in the form of a new trick ski. The geniuses in the design department had created the Band Ski which had a metal strip along the top to hold the tip up. At speed, a ski vibrates up and down and the theory was that the strip would stop the downward motion, thus absorbing wasted energy. I immediately evaluated the Band Ski as a piece of crap. I maintained that skis permanently bent up at the tip wouldn't turn properly and felt that the lack of downward motion meant the dissipated energy had to escape somewhere else. To find out where it went I clamped a ski to a table, set a coin where the boot went on the ski, bent up the tip, and let it snap back. The coin flew up in the air, which meant the skier's foot would absorb the energy on a Band Ski, making it difficult to control in a turn.

There were heated discussions and Fischer insisted we use them. I have great respect for Fischer, I think they're the best ski company because they do more testing and work harder than anybody else at improving their products in a scientific manner. But sometimes they get carried away and I objected to being used as a guinea pig in an important race. If they wanted to experiment, it should be on members of the Europa Cup team, the junior series. Finally, I gave in and we tried them in the first training run, but only after they agreed to put extra insurance on us. That proved to be quite unnecessary as the Band Skis were so slow it would be impossible to get hurt wearing them. We went back to our regular skis and got down to business.

Garmisch and Partenkirchen are twin resorts of about 10,000 people in the Bavarian Alps, an hour's drive from Munich. They've had ski races there since the 1936 Winter Olympics and huge crowds are part of the tradition. The course is not outrageously difficult, but some lengthy, steep, and icy sections make it quick and interesting. The upper part is sometimes better suited to the World Speed Skating Championships, or maybe combined speed and figure skating, as it twists and turns on glare ice. You need razor-sharp edges to cut figures and make turns on your skis here, especially on one hard left-hander, the Icehang, where you have to grind away like mad to stay on the rink, yet come out of it with as much speed as possible. When I finally mastered this turn, it was one of the main reasons I was able to win three times at Garmisch.

From here, you risk the danger of going to Heaven. The Himmelreich (Heaven Jump) is complicated by the need to hang a right as you leave it and you zip down a long bowling alley of a straightaway between the trees. You sashay through some big sweeping turns and into a section of more abrupt changes of direction punctuated by icy pitches, all this skied in the neighbourhood of 70 miles an hour. You bounce and bounce and bounce, swing a hard right, then a left with an entertaining jump in the middle of it, and you're ready to test your tuckability in a vast right-hander. You whoop through this baby at better than 70, and you fight G-forces and common sense to stay hunkered down in a tuck. Another left with a jump, then an 80-mile-an-hour right-hander, left, and left again, and you exit Garmisch-Partenkirchen as you began, on a pitch.

That was a perfect run at Garmisch, but I had several less-than-perfect runs there during my career. On one occasion, while perfecting my technique, I got somewhat out of shape in the Icehang and cut some figures worthy of my world champion figure-skating friends Underhill and Martini. My uphill ski went astray, throwing me off balance, and I sailed along with one ski askew like an outrigger on a canoe. The outrigger sideswiped a hay bale, scattered some timing equipment, and parted company with my foot. Now I was on one ski and one boot, not the most desirable situation at something like 80 miles an hour. There was no other course of action than to fall, which I duly did, and shortly thereafter my progress was slowed, but not completely stopped, by a safety net strategically located for just such a purpose. The strain of my arrival proved to be more than it could bear and I shot through it and landed on the other side, quite a remarkable achievement since the gaps in the the thick nylon rope are about the size of my fist. I had a lot more trouble trying to get back on the course than I did getting off it. I was completely unhurt and chalked the experience up to just another aspect of learning the ropes.

Now I was thinking positively as I waited in the start area at Garmisch. Toulouse informed me that Harti had just done an absolute flyer of a run, a second and a half faster than anyone else had *ever* gone on this course. With him out there in the twilight zone of performance, I would have to pull out all the stops and probe the outer limits of my resources.There are several levels of excitation and risk that you program into your head in ski racing, and this called for a full-fledged Crazy Canuck attack on the course. It's really being crazy like a fox in that you rely on your cunning and technical ability as much as your instincts and reflexes. It's akin to running across an ice flow or a log boom where you're confident your forward momentum will prevent you from falling victim to your constant defiance of the forces of gravity. You make continual minute adjustments to maintain progress and speed, but if you falter or fall in the Downhill, you can get hurt or, worse still, lose time.

So I turned on the after-burners and did a screamer down Garmisch. Caution to the wind, balls to the wall, I picked up two or three tenths of a second on the upper part of the course, and more at the bottom when I tucked like mad through the last turn at what felt like a million miles an hour. It was tremendously exhilarating and satisfying. I felt there was no part of the course I could have skied better and the scoreboard agreed with my assessment. I won and set a new course record. Harti was third and Mueller sixth, so I'd consolidated my grip on the title. Then we returned to Canada, where I had one of the best runs of my career, though I didn't win.

We arrived at Whistler to find a full-scale media blitz in progress with most of the bombardment aimed at me. The press, radio, and TV people had decided I was going to win the World Cup title and they were set to document this great moment in Canadian ski history from all angles. There were stacks and stacks of messages waiting for me each time I got back to the hotel and the message light on the phone in my room flashed all night long. I was under the gun at every move, with media types camped in the lobby and seemingly intent on following me everywhere, even to the bathroom. I felt like a fugitive on the run and made extensive use of the underground escape route from the hotel to the hill.

Though another hill at Whistler later became one of the best, the course we raced on then fell somewhat short of world class. It was easy, too easy, just one long glide from top to bottom. As a non-glider, I didn't like it and the Austrians liked it less. They complained at the lack of challenge and Harti's quote to the press summed it up: "I think I must be in the wrong place. This is not a Downhill." Downhillers thrive on tackling varied terrain and turns that tax their complete repertoire of skills. This hill tested your gliding ability and not much else, a kind of passive maneuver where you drop into your tuck and stay there. The outcome of a race on this type of course is usually decided by the law of physics which says that the bigger the lump on the skis, the faster the time. As a smaller lump, I was at a distinct disadvantage against people like Peter Mueller, Mr. Glide himself.

I tucked into my run on a course which was made even slower by a heavy snowfall. In one of the upper turns I dropped a hand into the snow, a stupid mistake made perhaps from lack of con-centration, which slowed me even more from the 50 miles an hour or so I was going. I kept on tucking, my turtle-like pace affording me the opportunity to view the crowds along the route. At least they were on my side here and I hoped to give them something to cheer about. I tucked and tucked seemingly forever and squatted across the finish line to a roar of approval. Miraculously, I was second to Peter Mueller. I was completely tuckered out, but this result virtually assured me of the World Cup. With the best five results over the season counting in the final tally, my three wins and two seconds gave Mueller and Weirather only very remote chances of winning.

People assumed that this should have been the greatest moment of my life and that I should go stark, raving bonkers with unbridled euphoria. It didn't happen that way. My results the year before had been so far outside my imagination that they may have used up my supply of euphoria. Then, I'd skied well enough to win and only fate had stood between me and the title. Now, it was tremendously satisfying to realize that I'd done it, for myself and for the people around me, but it wasn't a surprise. I started this year very deter-mined to win the title and if I hadn't won it, I wouldn't have considered the season a success. My attitude was, this is what I do; my life is skiing; if you ski as well as I skied, you win races; if you win enough races, you win the World Cup Downhill Champion-ship: a natural result of the circumstances. But that pragmatic point of view doesn't mean I'm a partypooper.

The whole team did well at Whistler: Dave Irwin was right behind me in third, Todd Brooker was fifth, Ken seventh, and a bunch of our younger guys got their first taste of World Cup competition. So a major celebration was in order. Dave McPhail, the ski-boot genius, proved to be also a connoisseur of champagne with a great sense of occasion. He produced a giant Jeroboam of bubbly with a cork the size of your fist. About 30 of us swigged it down in my room in a great outpouring of effervescence. The festivities then continued at the awards ceremony in the Whistler village square, where I picked up trophies for second place and top Canadian, and learned a bit about what it must be like to be a rock star.

The square was jammed with people surrounding the awards podium. When somebody handed me a microphone, I felt like Mick

Jagger. Since I can't sing or strut around a stage very well, I led the crowd in cheering: "Let's hear it for Whistler! . . . Let's hear it for Canada!" They responded with deafening roars and the power I seemed to have over this mass of human energy was scary. I quickly relinquished the spotlight and sprinted for the relative safety of my hotel where pandemonium reigned, a great deal of it in the corridor outside my room which was packed with revellers who had been whooping it up and chug-a-lugging it down all day. When we finished packing, we had to get to the team bus parked in front of the hotel. Briefly, I considered jumping down into a pile of snow outside my window, but decided against it in deference to the three-storey height. We decided to form a human battering ram with five guys in front of me and three behind. We made a run for it and I arrived panting at the bus with just one of my bodyguards in front and one behind. The others were tripped, tackled, or otherwise waylaid en route.

The extracurricular madness was even worse at Aspen for the last two races of the season. John Ritchie ran interference for us, deflecting as much media attention as he could by giving interviews to people, most of whom wanted to know how much money we made. This seemed to be the barometer of success for the North American media. They could only evaluate the validity of our sport in terms of dollars and the only way we could prove how good we were was to open our wallets and let them see inside.

One persistent lady journalist hounded John about my income, but he wouldn't budge, telling her it was an impolite question. She pestered him until finally he asked her how much *she* made. To his surprise, she told him her most intimate financial details, but John held firm and told her my earnings were none of her business. I learned to handle the tricks of the trade employed by the money-grubbers. A favourite technique was to rapid-fire questions at me, then trip me up with a loaded dollar question: "How old are you? – What's your mother's name? – What do you have for breakfast? – *How much do you make?*" My standard reply was like John's "None of your business."

I could handle the pressures of ski racing until the cows came home and dealing with the attentions of the media were part of the game. But all season long I also had to respond to the gung-ho enthusiasm of well-meaning well-wishers. It's like being in the com-

149

pany of a tremendously enthusiastic person at a party. They're hell-bent on having a good time, and demand that you do too. Though you may wish you were at home in bed with a good book, you feel duty-bound to perform as expected. Certainly my reaction was self-inflicted, but that's the way I was. The alternatives were to be branded a spoilsport or become known as a big-headed jerk.

When Canadians won internationally, it was usually a team effort with several people sharing the burden of public scrutiny. For several years, all of us on the Crazy Canucks did just that, even revelling in it to a degree. But in my World Cup winning season everybody wanted a piece of me. The other guys were a tremendous help, but I was the focus of attention – which began early in the year and multiplied with my success: "Steve, you've won at Crans, Kitzbühel, and Garmisch!" "You can win the World Cup!" "Steve, I'm so proud of you!!" "Steve, you're going to win!!" "STEVE, YOU'VE WON!!!" "FANTASTIC, YOU'RE THE BEST DOWNHILL RACER IN THE WORLD!!!!"

Most of this hype happened in brief meetings with people who had worked themselves up into a lather of good will. They might never get a chance to encourage me or congratulate me again, and they put everything they had into it. This happened literally thousands of times and I tried to match every superlative: "Yeah, thanks a lot!" "Yeah, great, sure!" "Thanks, I really appreciate it!!" "Ok, right on!!" "WOW, YEAH, GREAT!!!" "SUPER, AMAZING, UNBELIEV-ABLE, WHOOPEE!!!!"

Aspen is famous for its après-ski activity and its attractive position in Colorado's Roaring Fork Valley, where goldrush fever helped start the town in the late 19th century. The Aspen course is similar to many others, flat and easier on the top, and more difficult near the bottom. The place is typically North American in that it seems new and bright and shiny compared to the more weathered and worn European sites. The crowd reactions are different too: the Americans go YAHOOO! – more an expression of excitement than the Austrians' HUP! HUP! HUP! which is intended to encourage skiers to go faster.

But Aspen in March of 1982 is just a blur in my memory. Here and now I can hardly remember it. Then and there I thought I was really up for the races, training with the other guys, watching videos, and so on. I thought I'd done everything right and I wanted to win. What happened at Aspen confirmed to me that ski racing is so much of a mental sport: even with all my advantages, the best equipment, a winning season under my belt, and *thinking* I was ready, my mind wasn't up to it.

Mentally, I had stopped skiing at Whistler. My results at Aspen, 14th overall in each of the two races, are a reflection of that and an indication of my stressed-out state of mind. I just went through the motions, operating on reflexes to get from one situation to the other.

I was too zonked to even appreciate Todd Brooker's excellent second place in the second race. I hardly noticed that Ken was disqualified for a start-line infraction in that race, and the fact escaped me that these events in Aspen were the last races in the careers of two of the Crazy Canucks, Ir and Mur. Peter Mueller won both races, while Weirather was second and fourth. Harti had needed to win both races to take the title and, though Mueller actually tied me in total points, the title was mine because of my higher finishes earlier in the season.

I'm afraid the newly crowned king of the Downhill didn't make very colourful copy for the press. When my rivals failed to knock me from my perch, the press moved in for breathless quotes. All they got were mumbled clichés: "It's a very strange feeling." "I'm sort of in a dream world." "It's a moment that's been floating around in my imagination for a couple of years now." "I need a little time to put it into perspective."

The press was hovering in the background when Prime Minister Trudeau called me with his congratulations. When I put down the phone, I couldn't remember a word he said and told the press I was sorry. Later, I read what he had said after some enterprising reporter got the message from his office: "All Canadians are proud of you. You've done a lot for young Canadians. They will try to emulate you and that's a big responsibility." Of course, he was right and that responsiblity did not rest lightly on my shoulders. In fact, I think I had an over-developed sense of responsibility and the effort of trying to live up to the expectations of the public was largely responsible for my post-title shell-shocked state.

After Aspen, I was just dead, completely buzzed, yet obligated to make an appearance in the end-of-season Nor Am races. I missed one of them, suffered some criticism for that, and staggered down the hill at Panorama, B.C., to finish fourth. The only bright spot then was some fairly comprehensive partying before the team broke up for the summer. Since Dave Murray and Dave Irwin were retiring, their passing could not go unnoticed. We had a big dinner in Ir's Okanagan Valley stomping grounds. We were staying in a hotel in Vernon and that night Ken used our equipment van to take his girlfriend (now his wife) Lynda Robbins back to her hotel where she and the rest of the women's team were staying. We were all rather zonked in the morning when Ken phoned to say the transmission in the van had conked out and he was marooned, along with all our equipment.

Immediate chaos. Though I was absolutely pooped, for some reason I was responsible for getting the show on the road and Ken's call had come less than an hour before we Easterners had to catch a flight from the local airport to Calgary to link up with CP Air for Toronto. I rushed around like a chicken with its head chopped off, gathering up people – my girlfriend Ann, Robin McLeish, Todd Brooker, various other people and their bags – threw the lot into our station wagon, and roared off to the airport about as fast as my record speed down Kitzbühel – 90 miles an hour. I dumped everything and everybody in a pile at the airport, zoomed back to find Ken sauntering casually around Lynda's hotel looking for a newspaper. I reminded him that he had the keys to the van and imparted my sense of urgency to him. We proceeded to unload the ton of equipment into the station wagon and journeyed posthaste to the airport, arriving with seconds to spare.

Somebody told CP Air I had just won the title and they put Ann and me in the privileged section. They gave us free champagne which we took back to the others and we partied high in the sky across the prairies. We were met in Toronto by my parents, Todd and Robin's girlfriends Lisa and Anne, and my friends Paul and Vikki Fredricks. Everybody was invited back to my parents' house for more champagne. Rob Safrata joined in the fun and off we went to dinner at a restaurant run by some Swiss people. They pulled out all the stops and showered us in free schnapps, aperitifs, and cocktails. Wine flowed freely at dinner and there were numerous liqueurs and everybody was in very high spirits.

When we finally called it a night, it was fairly late the next morning and Rob found himself locked out of his house and was nearly arrested for climbing in an upstairs window. Another friend tried to go to work the next day, but fell asleep in her car while waiting at a red light. Then I got a call from the head waiter at the restaurant who told me I'd tipped them far too much above and beyond the call of duty when I had paid for the meal. He asked me if I wanted to adjust it downward slightly and I did.

That was my impromptu World Cup celebration. It was totally overdone. Just nuts. But great fun, a commodity I was to see little of again for some time.

11. Fringe Benefits

For the next several months, the first non-European World Cup Downhill Champion did at least one ceremonial and/or promotional event per day, sometimes three or four. Some of these appearances were to receive awards like Canadian Male Athlete of the Year (again), *Ski Racing*'s Canadian Alpine Skier of the Year, the World Champion Award from the Government of Canada, and the Excellence Award from the Government of Ontario.

I was in big demand as a public-speaker-cum-guest-of-honour at breakfasts, luncheons, and dinners, cocktail parties, receptions, golf and tennis tournaments, and gatherings of all kinds – and the media interest intensified. I handled most of the arrangements and bookings myself, since the team frowned on people having anything like a full-time manager or agent in those days. The only reason I ever turned down a request was if I was already booked for another event. I felt it was my duty to do whatever was asked of me, which was easy for a good cause like the Canadian Paraplegic Association. I became the figurehead for the Ontario division of the CPA and was able to help them raise a lot of money. The dangers of ski racing made this a subject close to my heart. Later, when my public obligations as a fundraiser got completely out of hand, I restricted my charity work to the CPA and our association continues today.

I believed I owed a debt to society and took the Prime Minister's words about being a role model seriously. My achievement had received unparalleled recognition and I felt I had to pay something back. I recognized the need for people to see me and talk to me. It seemed I was most effective in group situations and was conscious of the ability I had to motivate people. When you have this ability, it is vitally important not to abuse it. So I tried to do good works and put everything I had into interviews and appearances. It was very intense and emotional for me and incredibly draining because I drove myself as hard as I did in skiing. Unlike skiing, or most jobs where you can work off the tension, the pressure of maintaining a public persona can't be easily diffused. I was really resentful at the time that nobody could understand the magnitude of the demands being made on me.

One of the major distractions for me that summer was a dispute we had with the Canadian Ski Association (CSA) in 1982 when they tried to make us pay for the privilege of being on the team. Somehow they had a shortfall of $200,000 at headquarters in Ottawa and didn't have enough left in the kitty to get the racers through to the end of the season. That was galling. There we were, the best ski racers in the world, winning races and thereby bringing money into the team. Beyond that, we attended endless banquets and fund-raising dinners, made TV appearances begging for money for the skiing program, and generally raised by far the largest chunk of money Canadian skiing got. On the other side of the coin were the fat bureaucrats in Ottawa with nothing to do but spend the money we earned and keep track of that expenditure. When they screwed up, they asked us to pay for their mistake.

I was in a towering rage for some time over this absurdity, at the stupidity and injustice of this proposed levy. I was particularly incensed that I was being asked to pay because I was the World Cup winner who had heaped glory on Canadian skiing. Granted, I got more out of it than anybody else, but I didn't want to be penalized for that because I also put more into it than anybody else. The name Podborski counted a lot in fund-raising and I hustled my buns off as an unpaid volunteer. I sat down and worked out the time I'd spent on behalf of the CSA that year, hypothetically charging a few bucks an hour for my time, and came up with a sum that would enable me to retire comfortably for life.

The CSA was already taking 25 per cent off the top of any deals that went through the team, by far the lion's share, and the poor racer was low man on the totem pole when everybody had taken their cut. For instance, if a jeans company decided to put Steve Podborski inside their product and have him pedal their ads around for a fee of $10, $2.50 went to the CSA immediately, leaving $7.50

up for grabs. When an agent or manager was involved, he took 20 per cent of the gross, leaving $5.50. The government took 50 per cent of the full amount in taxes, and poor Podborski is left with 50 cents rattling around in the pockets of his jeans. Podborski may be a Crazy Canuck, but he's not stupid, nor are the other guys on the team.

We knew the only reason people in Canada started watching ski racing on television was because we won races. That meant money in the pocket for Canadian skiing, exposure for the advertisers/ sponsors, and so on. The only reason the team went from a shoe-string-budgeted bunch of starving yokels to a well-funded group of Downhill racers with cars and all the trimmings was because we put Canada on the map in the sport. Now they wanted us to pay a levy of $2,065.00 for the honour of wearing the uniforms on the team we had brought to the top of the world.

The financial fuss between the racers and the team office really began in 1979 with the publication of our book, *Ski The Canadian Way*. All the Crazy Canucks contributed and we had chapters on the World Cup tour, skiing technique, training methods, and so on. It was fun to do, particularly when I got to write most of the photo captions and was able to criticize everybody else's technique. In typical go-for-it Crazy Canuck fashion we just went ahead and did it, signed a contract with a publisher, and became authors. Suddenly, there was a mighty uproar from the team office when they saw that we might be making money from the book. A long and bitter battle ended when we agreed to give them a percentage of the royalties. Though nobody made a pile of money, it started the controversy over how much of the racers was owned by the team office.

The book was a fairly cut-and-dried situation compared to the complicated scenarios that typified our other commercial activities. To illustrate the kind of thing that went on I like to use the services of my favourite character, Fred Leadbeater. Fred is a great guy and the best skier in Canada. When he skis, Fred wears Smooch lipgloss because that company is an official supplier to his team. But Fred is quite a man about town back in Canada and in the summer he's approached by another lipgloss company, Smack, to wear their product. Smack offers him $5 to keep his lips glistening and sexy in the off-season. Is Fred legally bound to wear Smooch year round?

Because Smooch supplies the team, do they own Fred's lips? If he does sign with Smack, how much, if any, of the $5 should go to the team administration? Poor old Fred's lips purse and quiver as he twists on the horn of the Smooch and Smack dilemma. Because he's winning races Fred Leadbeater's handsome face is the one everybody sees on television, but the Smooch and Smack turmoil in his tortured brain makes it hard to force his lips into a winning smile. There's also the distinct possibility that the lipgloss gefuffle will gum up Fred's performance unless it's smoothed over fast.

Like Fred Leadbeater, our team had skied for years before we found a balm for our chapped lips. We were able to breathe easier, financially speaking, when we started to win in Europe, but even when we were on top of the world we operated at something less than full throttle compared to the Americans and Europeans. In 1982, the Canadian Alpine Teams had $1.7 million at their disposal, that's for men and women's teams in several different categories. About half of that came from the government through Sport Canada and most of the rest came from fees paid into the supply pool by manufacturers. It's safe to say that the bulk of the operating budget was generated by the results of the Crazy Canucks. When the Canadian media discovered we were newsworthy, it attracted Canadian companies into the fold. It was a pleasure for us to get this response on the home front and refreshing to work with people we could communicate with in the same language and on the same wave length. One of the biggest new sponsors was Molson Breweries and, rather than being some huge machine that just churns out beer, these were real people, wanting to work with us to help beat the world in skiing.

When it became public knowledge that we were actually earning money from ski racing, it gave more credibility to the sport in the eyes of some. Formerly, people would ask me when I was going to stop fooling around and get a job. As soon as the press started talking about our incomes, you could see the gears grinding away in people's heads as they made the great leap away from their image of a bunch of kids playing games in the Alps. Now they saw athletes getting paid to perform and the race was on to find out exactly how much we made. But ski racing is a different game than most, steeped in European tradition and values which include a certain amount of discretion when it comes to financial matters. While the

157

Crazy Canucks broke a lot of new ground in skiing, we dug in when it came to spilling the beans about money.

I've spent a lifetime ducking, bobbing, and weaving around the money issue. It's a real fight sometimes, but there are a lot of people in my corner. All the ski-industry companies I've dealt with have stressed that confidentiality is of prime importance in our relationship. I was never "a millionaire in blue jeans" as the press was fond of saying, but I might have been had I pocketed what it cost to fund my 11 years on the team. By the time I retired, it was estimated that $50,000 a year was needed for each skier on the team. None of that came to me personally and my peak earning power only lasted a couple of seasons on either side of my World Cup year. I paid other dues in the form of three knee operations, car crashes, a very weird lifestyle, and working a lot harder in a job that most people would not willingly do for any amount of money. There are no guarantees in the sport: no performance, no pay. Probably only half a dozen guys make a decent living out of it. Downhill racing is a real crap shoot and I was lucky.

In 1981, Ken and I were among the top earners in the sport, which was a big breakthrough for non-Europeans. A couple of years earlier when Ken and Ir got into the first seed, they went to negotiate a contract and were given a pittance of something like $5,000 by the ski company. We learned later that that was unbelievably low money for first-seed skiers, but at the time they were happy to get anything. Part of the problem came from Ken and Ir suddenly shooting into prominence after the manufacturers' budgets had been allotted for the next two years. Contracts are renegotiated every two years, but even at the next renewal of the cycle there was a real struggle to convince the Europeans we were worth as much as their local heroes. Our reasoning was that we were among the most recognized skiers, we were multilingual, and we were universally popular – unlike the Austrians who were hated in Switzerland and the Swiss who were hated in Austria and so on. We legitimately claimed that we had the most international marketing capability because we had exposure in North America where the Europeans were unknown. So we asked them to recognize the facts and deal with us accordingly.

We sat down with Fischer, Lange, Tyrolia, Carrera, and the other top companies and we'd grind away at it until finally we got them to say they couldn't pay us more than the Austrians. That was ok with us, in fact that's all we really wanted. The equal-pay-for-equal-work deal meant we also earned victory premiums for winning races on top of the base fee. Each team member handled his negotiations individually, another part of the established tradition. The ski companies also frowned on anybody representing the athlete, probably thinking they could outsmart a dumb skier more easily than a sharp agent. We were able to wheel and deal quite effectively, though the personal contact might have cost me something. Negotiations sometimes got fairly heated and I had trouble pounding my chest and saying, "Look, I was the best Downhill racer in the world last year, pay up! I can speak more languages than your Austrians. I'm from North America and I'm going to blow your markets away around the world . . . ." In fact, I never said anything like that at all. It embarrassed me to toot my own horn. I just talked in generalities and I think I banged out a fair deal. The important thing was to be in financial territory similar to the European racers after being so downtrodden as Canadians for so long.

Winning a race was worth from $10,000 to $25,000, depending on the prestigiousness of the event, with Kitzbühel in the top category. It was difficult to win more than three races a year, so the base salary was the important factor in bringing home the bacon. Depending on what kind of results you had the previous season and providing you had no distressing personal habits like picking your nose in public, you could establish a reasonable base so that your trust fund might have $75,000 to $100,000 in it at the end of the year. These were not big numbers in North American terms, when guys like Marcel Dionne were getting six or seven times that just to lace up their skates.

However, that was a respectable sum in Europe where commercialism is not nearly as rampant. There's little advertising on television, most of the networks are state-run, which makes it all the more important for skiers to be seen on the hill in a race – best of all on the winner's podium. These circumstances also dictate that the ski sponsors take a shotgun approach to funding and spread their money among the largest possible number of potential winners. A year after I retired, the FIS opened up the commercial potential of ski racing to allow sponsors' logos on helmets and these days the big stars can earn up to half a million dollars a year.

In my day, ski racers certainly weren't breaking the bank, but some Canadians seemed to think we were breaking the rules by earning anything at all as amateur athletes. There was no trouble with this in Europe, where most of the Olympic establishment is from, because they know how the world works. They set up the trust funds and we operated entirely within the rules. Certain naive people thought it shocking that we made money, then, perversely, when they found out the amount, they thought less of us. These are the people who measure the worth of an athlete by his income. They also judge a sport this way and there was no way ski racing could compare with traditional North American sports on financial terms. So ski racers were a contradictory bunch to the-rank-and-file sports fan: these ski bums make money even though they're amateurs, but they don't make much, so skiing down hills in a funny suit can't compare with baseball or hockey or basketball. Money was like a minefield and we tiptoed around it. We still do.

We weren't necessarily skiing mercenaries, but we were like explorers with machetes hacking through a green jungle of uncharted financial territory. As members of a more commercially oriented society, we had the potential to go further down the road than the Europeans because we could more easily endorse products outside the ski industry, and we were pioneers in that area. We learned all the time and it was very exciting to discover the business side of skiing. We broke new ground there as we had in racing. Money was another motivator, so it became more important than ever to ski well.

It might be argued that I was a money player. By the 1980-81 season, I was pretty well maxed out as far as my base contract with Fischer was concerned. I was earning as much as the trade could bear and the only way I could supplement my income from them was through victory premiums. I won three races, was second twice, third four times, and never finished out of the top ten. I had a real dog fight with Harti Weirather to see who was going to break the bank at Fischer first. They had to spend a fortune on victory premiums, far more than they had budgeted for. It became a running joke at the finish area that when the Fischer guys saw Harti and me standing on the podium, they'd fumble around feeling their pockets, protesting that they were empty. But our results sold a lot of skis and, increasingly, that became an important part of Downhill racing.

Becoming a wage earner was a new experience for me and I had to learn how to handle it. At first, I just spent it, not frivolously, but on things I could never afford before. I bought bicycles and paid $5,000 for a Datsun 280Z which I kept for seven years. I went out to dinner more often and was able to rent my own place in Toronto. I got along well enough without money for years and having it turned out to be no big deal, just another fringe benefit to make life a little easier for a ski bum. But I wasn't about to give it all away.

In May of 1982, I was recuperating from my World Cup win on the beach in Hawaii when I got a frantic phone call from Ken. He told me I had to come back to Canada immediately because the CSA wanted to take everything. A new guy who had come into the administration was saying they owned us and, if we were lucky, we might get 25 per cent of the action on any commercial deals we made. Because we had to pay income tax on our share, this meant we would wind up with next to nothing. What a disaster! My holiday was ruined. I tried to blow away the gloom by windsurfing, but it was no use. I sat in my hotel room just shaking my head in disbelief. I had never made any money in my life and now, when I had the opportunity to make a few bucks, these guys wanted to whack 75 per cent off the top. I was completely devastated and Ann said, do something about it, you're driving yourself crazy. So I took a day off, bought some paper and a pen, and wrote out all my arguments in detail. We flew back to Canada and I went to Ottawa for the confrontation.

Ken couldn't make it, so it was Podborski versus the Canadian Ski Association. I sat down across the table from two of the bureaucrats and listened as the new guy who thought he owned me did all the talking. It was a very gentlemanly discussion, but I was just burning. This guy was running around in circles like a big wheel when he was really only a small cog in the wheel. But he was convinced the CSA was responsible for winning races and they wanted money as well as glory for their labours. When he finished his litany of bureaucrap, I laid it all out for him from the racer's point of view and felt I blew him out of the water on every one of his points.

I stressed the fact that when he screwed the racers around, he was screwing himself around because the racers made everything happen, including paying his salary. If he insisted on taking 75 per cent of my personal deals, then I wanted 25 per cent of any deals he made. I wanted 25 per cent of the TV deal, 25 per cent of every clothing deal in the team pool, 25 per cent across the board on every penny that came into the CSA coffers. He said that was preposterous. I suggested my numbers were no more preposterous than his. He wouldn't back down and we were at a stalemate. Then he said something about them going ahead and doing it anyway. I replied that it would be very difficult to bill somebody who wasn't there.

There was a profound silence in the room for some time. Finally, my adversary replied that he understood my position and they would take it into consideration. The meeting was over. I was absolutely serious about being ready to quit. It would have been ridiculous for me to even consider skiing. I would have hated every second of it, just as I hated being backed into a corner by this guy. I had been prepared to come to an amicable solution and retreat gracefully from certain points, but he wanted to gun me down. So I called his bluff. It would have changed my entire life and this one guy would have had to take the flak from the hue and cry raised over Canada's World Cup Downhill Champion leaving the sport. From then on the CSA got 25 per cent of the racers' deals and that was that.

A great deal of my off-season activity involved helping to promote skiing in Canada and I worried about how this merry-go-round might affect my own skiing. But I had no yardstick to measure it with, nobody had gone through this before, and I made up the rules as I went along. That summer, I trained as much as in the past, but without the same structure and intensity, fitting my cycling, weight, and exercise programs into my schedule wherever I could. I was focused less on my skiing performance than on my celebrity role. However, I felt I could keep it in perspective and was determined to avoid losing the mental edge that had shoved me back to 14th place in the races at Aspen. I thought I had everything under control. I knew it was hard to stay on top and I had seen many people win it all and lose it just as fast. I was sure it wouldn't happen to me.

12. Peaks and Valleys

With Mur and Ir now retired, the Downhill "A" team for 1982-83 had Todd Brooker, Robin McLeish, Ken, and me to carry on the Crazy Canuck tradition. The results of our first race, at Pontresina in Switzerland, had familiar names at the top: Harti Weirather, Franz Klammer, Peter Mueller, and Ken Read, who was sixth – but Steve Podborski was 12th. I knew I was in trouble. I just wasn't skiing and, when I finished 24th, then 17th, at a double-header in Val Gardena, I was reeling on the ropes.

Those disasters were in December of '82 and I made New Year's resolutions to pull myself up by the bootstraps. But early 1983 was worse when we reconvened for back-to-back races at Val d'Isère. In the first race, I caught an edge and was tossed onto my chin, the guard on my helmet pushing my head back a lot further than it was built to go, and I slid over 300 feet on my stomach. I was badly battered and less than fit for the next race, and 34th was my lowest finish in many years. Fortunately, Ken was pulling his weight with good top-ten finishes, including a second and a fourth at Val d'Isère.

Mine was an absolutely pathetic performance and everybody was wondering what the heck was going on. In the past when I dropped out of sight in the results, I could lay the blame on bad wax or skis; now it was just me standing there on good equipment with no excuses and going downhill fast in the worst possible sense of that phrase for a ski racer. Holy mackerel! I was being beaten by guys I'd never even *heard* of. It was embarrassing for everybody. People on the team even stopped asking me how my run had gone. There was nothing to say. Even the press avoided talking to me about my performance, and interviews with the reigning World Cup Champion were of a very general nature. Everybody was on my side, there was no jumping on me when I was down, and they realized it was all up to me to get back on track.

I knew I had to transcend what had gone on before and gave myself a severe pep talk before the next races at Kitzbühel: "Steve, you bastard (sorry dad and mom), there's no way in the world that 33 guys are better skiers than you are. Get a grip! Are you a winner or a wimp? You won at Kitzbühel for two years running. It's the hardest course of all and if you ski the way you have in the past, hike yourself up to that level, you'll be all right. You know it's easier for you to do well on a difficult hill because on an easier hill, where the nervous factor is removed, everyone can ski closer to their maximum ability. At Kitzbühel more people hold back because they're not sure they're going to make it. Kitzbühel immediately eliminates the guys with intermediate confidence levels. Come on! You've got a senior confidence level. In fact, you're the World Cup champion! Get off your butt and go for it!!"

I was second in the first race at Kitzbühel and would probably have won except that the sun came out after my run and warmed up the flat section. This smoothed out the flats and helped create a layer of moisture between the base of the skis and the snow so that Bruno Kernen of Switzerland was able to glide out a .11 second advantage over me to score his first, and last, win. Then the dreaded double Downhill syndrome at Kitzbühel took over and I was ninth the next day. Right at the top of the hill in the start shack I did the next-to-impossible and stepped on the tail of one ski with the other and almost came to a dead stop. It was a stupid mental error, probably brought about because I was trying too hard to win. I went berserk down the rest of the hill, but the damage had been done and I finished ninth. It was fabulous when Todd Brooker won the race, his first World Cup victory, and Ken was third to prove the Canucks were still "Crazy" at Kitzbühel.

Off we went to Sarajevo in Yugoslavia for a race which had a lot of hype built around it because it was to be the site of the Olympics in 1984. It was a knee-trembler of a course because of the many humungous jumps that tested confidence levels. A lot of people flunked the test and put on the mental brakes. In training, they felt their way down the hill, standing up when they came to a jump to slow themselves down. Meanwhile I was bounding down the hill like a kangaroo, just rocketing, flying off the bumps, doing a quick tuck between them, then soaring airborne again for very long flights. I could have qualified for my pilot's licence there.

In the race, my aerial act had me fastest after the first seed had gone down and everybody was congratulating me on finally winning a race. I said forget it guys, the last time I was winning somebody came down faster at the end of the day. Sure enough somebody from the back seed, an Austrian named Pfaffenbichler, pulled off the run of his life and beat me by .21 of a second. That happens in ski racing when some guy suddenly transcends himself, whether from supreme effort or luck, and bursts onto the scene with a win. In fact, the majority of racers only win once or twice in their careers and I just happened to be second best on Herr Pfaffenbichler's big day, his first and last win.

With so many complaints about the course I was the media darling in Yugoslavia when the press asked the skiers' opinions about the suitability of the hill for the Olympics. Most said it stunk and wanted the bumps ironed out. I said it was great, leave it the way it is. Sure it's scary and dangerous. But that's what Downhill is all about. The naysayers said people could get hurt. I maintained it was like Kitzbühel, where those who couldn't take the heat got out of the kitchen by going down the hill more slowly. It's quite simple really. If you feel you're going to get killed, slow down. Unfortunately, I was in the minority and they took away the jumps to make it a very boring Olympic course.

A fourth-place finish in St. Anton left me with only two events, in North America, to salvage a win out of the season. I was very intense in Aspen, almost desperate, and maybe that contributed to my downfall. The organizers had to clear a heavy fall of new snow off the hill and it was piled beside the course. I came barrelling down through the Aztec and around the Airplane turn to where the course flattens out. The light was bad and I failed to see soft snow piled up: my right ski hit it and tracked off on its own. I immediately transferred weight to my other ski, which pivoted sharply to the left at about 60 miles an hour. My left knee popped and, though I was tumbling and somersaulting at a terrific rate, I was fully aware that I'd just wrecked another knee, the only good one I had left.

After a few minutes, I gathered up my remains and skied slowly to the bottom to accept congratulations for still being alive. For the first time in my career I didn't hang around the finish area, but went straight back to the hotel. In the past I always stayed to answer questions, no matter how bad my run, and I deplored the disappearing acts of others. But this time I didn't want to face the music: the prospect of dealing with another knee operation was so frustrating and upsetting that I didn't really want to ski anymore. This was my tenth year on the team – a decade. I'd had a bad season, now my knee was shot, and I faced six months of therapy and training . . . . My resolve was at a very low ebb, especially since I'd been trying my hardest to come back and only got this kick in the groin for my troubles. I asked, "Why put yourself through this? You're stupid. Just quit."

This frame of mind prevented me from fully appreciating Todd's fine win at Aspen. Back in my hotel room, a doctor confirmed what I already knew by telling me to get home fast. Denver was snowed in and I hung around airports for awhile. In Chicago, a reporter from the *Toronto Star* spotted me and called in the news that the wounded hero was returning. I didn't want to talk to anybody, just my doctor who was waiting at the hospital.

Ann met me at the door of the plane in Toronto with two RCMP constables who grabbed me and hustled me through Customs. A platoon of the local press lay in wait for me. The Mounties asked me if I wanted to talk to them. I said, "No! – I just want to get to the TGH." They whipped us out the back way to Ann's car, but just as we were getting in some of the press spotted us. We took off, leaving them tripping over their cameras and The Great Media Chase began. It was hilarious and helped distract me from my troubles. As we went up University Avenue, Norm Betts, a photographer from the *Toronto Sun*, pulled alongside, taking potshots with his camera. We abandoned Ann's car in the hospital parking lot and, with me hopping along on crutches, we barely made it into the elevator without falling into the clutches of the press. As the doors closed, the cameras were clicking away like mad.

Dr. Kostuik looked me over and said he would admit me the next day – meanwhile he would help me escape. The nurses guarded the door of his office, while Ann and I made our exit via the fire escape. We made it to her car unmolested and were driving along when a CBC man pulled alongside with his two-way radio in hand. Very kindly, he asked if I wanted to be left alone. I said, "Please," and the chase was called off until I gave a press conference later on. In the interval, I had time to compose myself. I was really very depressed over what lay ahead, regardless of my skiing future. I hated being hurt, being crippled, and not even able to walk my dog. I hated the prospect of working and working just to get my leg straight, let alone struggling to get it back into skiing shape . . . .

"Holy shit, they did the wrong one!" I woke up in the hospital, still dopey from being knocked out, and felt no cast on my left leg! My God! – I was in absolute terror for a few seconds, until I found there was no cast on the right one either. The way my luck had been going it would have been par for the course. But I should have had more faith in Dr. Kostuik who had done his usual good works, this time without any bionic bodywork being necessary. He had poked an orthoscope into the wreckage in several places and found a ligament shredded. But it still had tissue around it, holding all the fibres together, so he decided to leave it alone and let nature take its course. He knew I was a good healer and that I was an obedient patient. It would heal on its own and no cast would be necessary, but I couldn't put any weight on it for six weeks.

Dr. Kostuik is the most optimistic man on the face of the earth. He said, "Steve, you'll be back with no problem. You'll be as good as new before you know it." His positive reinforcement helped my naturally optimistic nature reassert itself: "Hey, maybe I might as well keep going, get fit again, and try to salvage something after this disastrous season." I wasn't as keen as before but, after all, the Olympics were coming up and I'd been second on the course at Sarajevo. I was still ranked 11th in the Downhill making me officially one of the best skiers around. I was still one of the guys, the lifestyle had its moments and, besides, I didn't have any other plans.

Another boost came from receiving the highest honour a civilian Canadian can get. At the house one day, I opened a letter and read that I had been awarded the Order of Canada. It was like a bolt from the blue and I was amazed and flattered. It represented recognition from my country I hadn't expected. It was self-evident that I was a good skier, but this award paid tribute to flying the flag and bringing some honour to Canada. Ski racing is an extremely selfish sport, but we were always conscious of being Canucks – the

Crazy part was another matter. It was very important to us to have the Maple Leaf on our suits and to have people know where we were from. Being made an Officer of the Order of Canada was the icing on the cake.

The Investiture was at Rideau Hall in Ottawa where I'd been a few times before for functions involving athletes. On a previous occasion, I'd fumbled my way through a meeting with Prince Charles. I was 18 at the time and totally out of my social depth. I must have looked it because the Governor General's Aide de Camp rescued me at the door and sat me down at his table. We were waiting to form a receiving line to meet the Prince when somebody summoned me to the front to start the ball rolling. I looked around frantically for an escape route, there was none, and I was first to meet the guest of honour. I wasn't even sure how to address him and hoped "Your Royal Highness" wasn't a faux pas by a dumb colonial.

The Order of Canada ceremonies were presided over by Governor General Schreyer. Morley Callaghan, Bruce Cockburn, and some other luminaries and influential people were also being given the award and I again felt out of place, though not as much as before. We wore black tuxedos and the women had long gowns and everybody swirled around in their finery in a large hall draped in fabric like a tent. It was pretty intimidating for a guy accustomed to hanging around in jeans or a ski suit. The ritual was very impressive with each recipient announced to the gathering, their achievements read out, and the reasons listed for their being asked to join the Order.

I was very moved at the Investiture. A lot of whoop-de-doo ceremonies are so much fluff and gloss with silly artificial trappings. This was the real thing, people were very serious about it, and the solemnity, pomp and circumstance exactly suited the gravity of the situation. It was a truly significant occasion for me and I hope I got the ritual right. I walked up the aisle to the Governor General, shook his hand, turned to one side and bowed to somebody, bowed again in front of Mr. Schreyer, who slammed the medal over my neck, then I backed up a couple of steps, bowed, and made my escape.

The Order of Canada helped fan the embers of desire that were smouldering away and I concentrated on getting fit for another season. It helped that I was less in demand publicly after my poor

168

results in '82-'83 and I was able to devote more time to sweating myself into shape. I began to take more of an interest in how my body actually worked and became more nutritionally concerned. My buddy Dave McPhail was tremendously knowledgeable about the effect of diet on performance and how food allergies can have a negative impact. I ate less red meat and more carbohydrates for more energy. The knee sorted itself out fairly quickly and I was fitter on the bike than ever before and puffed away on weights all summer.

Ken decided not to come back for the 1983-84 season and, with Robin McLeish back in the Downhill "B" team, Todd Brooker and I were alone in the "A" squad. For another assault on the hills, I probed the outer limits of health and fitness. In fact, Todd thought I was nuts. I carried a portable air purifier with me and when we drove through the tunnels under the Alps I would turn off all the vents in the vehicle and breathe the air from my magic machine. Todd considered me to be eccentric and I understood how he felt. I remembered I used to feel that Ken and Jim Hunter went overboard with their training and I didn't think I could ever put that much into it. But I was impressed with how willing they were to do anything to help them ski faster and eventually it rubbed off on me. Jungle Jim would work his brains out and Ken would sometimes throw his supreme effort in our faces, making sure we knew how hard he worked out. One time at Val d'Isère, he was running up and down the road in front of our hotel when he was divebombed by a big black crow. He'd been flapping his arms so much the bird thought he was a threat and attacked him. It was hilarious. But soon we all followed Ken's lead and went on our famous "psycho" runs where we pushed ourselves to the limit. Once at Zermat, I made the mistake of jogging down a mountain at the start of a psycho run and, after my uphill return, my pulse rate was 205. I was pushing myself that hard now in hopes of recapturing some of my former glory.

I started the '83-'84 season with a third at Schladming, a seventh at Val d'Isère, and another third at Val Gardena, where Todd finished just in front of me. I thought I was trying as hard as ever. But after a 17th at Laax and consecutive 20th-place finishes in Wengen and Kitzbühel, I knew I had lost the desire. I was fitter than ever, but the *need* to win had gone.

I decided to have one last attempt at resurrecting that need in the next race, at Garmisch. I had talked myself back into winning form before and tried it again. I gave in to the total mania of skiing, thinking about nothing else. I concentrated solely on the race, giving myself no respite except for reading a book in my room. I went out on the hill and just gunned it. I went through the 32 gates down the 2.06-mile Kandahar course and won at Garmisch-Partenkirchen for the third time in my career. That's when I knew I could never do it again. It had taken every last iota of my mental and physical energy and it was more than I wanted to do any more.

I wasn't saddened by this realization. I'd had a great time. I'd won an Olympic Downhill medal. No North American male had ever done that before. I'd won the World Cup in the Downhill. No non-European had done that. I'd won eight World Cup races, enough to rank me up there with some of the most famous names in the history of ski racing. I thought back to my first World Cup race at Val d'Isère in 1974: I was ready to accept just being there as a Downhill racer as the highlight of my life. What had happened since then was beyond my wildest dreams and it had changed my life. Ski racing had made me a completely different person. Now I was very much a realist and knew it was time to think about getting out of the game. I was still a good skier, but no longer had the commitment to be a great skier.

Skiing instinct got me a sixth place in Cortina, but it wasn't enough to get me a good finish in the Olympics. Sarajevo was quite civilized from the point of view of outside interference for the skiers. We had attended media-planning sessions in Calgary in the summer, and had officially aired our grievances about the Lake Placid fiasco. These were duly noted and not repeated, so we had no organizational complaints in Yugoslavia. What we did have was a really stupid course. Any thoughts I had of psyching myself up into Olympic-medal territory vanished when I saw they'd laundered the course beyond recognition, ironing out the jumps and making it a wimp's paradise. The only guy who fell during the whole week was Franz Klammer, who must have tripped over his boot buckles. A Scottish photographer, Stuart "Fitzy" Fitzsimmons, caught his fall on film and got rich by pedalling it around the world. It was the only exciting shot of the Olympic Downhill. The American Bill Johnson won, while Podborski and Brooker were out of the medals in eighth and ninth.

We had spent a lot of time with the Canadian figure skaters at the Lake Placid Olympics and we tried to see as many of their events as we could in Sarajevo. I was good friends with Barb Underhill and Paul Martini, who were in line for a gold medal. I happened to be there when they blew it. Unfortunately, Barb kept tripping and I was just dying a thousand deaths for her. It was really, really sad. I went to them later and poor Barb just looked at me. I gathered her in my arms and she cried her eyes out. She was totally distraught and I understood how she felt. I knew what it was like to fall. I knew what it was like to blow it when you're not supposed to and the whole world is watching your misfortune. But Barb and Paul became World Champions that year even though they lost out at the Olympics. They're with the Ice Capades now and we still keep in touch.

The Yugoslavian security people searched our bags when we left the Olympic village and confiscated blankets we'd borrowed from our beds as souvenirs. Todd had actually bought his from the commissary so he was rather upset about losing them. The Olympics left us all quite depressed and we attempted to cheer ourselves up with a slight party. We barely made it to the station to catch an overnight train for Zagreb. We woke up in the morning feeling horrible and our tongues seemed in need of a shave. We knocked back some railway coffee, made from sludge they must have drained from some oil crankcase and added caffeine. Todd and I still weren't terribly alert and, when the train came to a stop, we jumped off. Too late we realized we had gotten off too soon and we were marooned somewhere out in Subterania. We hiked for awhile through a grey and brown landscape and finally found the Zagreb station. We grabbed a taxi for the airport where my car was parked.

I had a brilliant red BMW 323 that cruised at 135 miles per hour. I wasn't even breaking the speed limit when we were stopped by a policeman on the autobahn in Austria. He asked to see my driver's licence, so I handed him the document from the Ontario Government that said I was legally entitled to drive a car. It's called a driver's licence in Ontario, but the cop said "What is this?" in German. He asked for an international driving permit, which I didn't have. Then he said, "You didn't do very well yesterday did you?" I said, "No, but neither did the Austrians." Then he let us go. It's the only time I've ever been stopped by the police in Europe and I know it was because he recognized me.

As Todd and I drove along, we thought we sensed something strange in the way people were driving and behaving. We stopped for food and gas and Todd bought a paper. A huge headline said: BLACK DAY IN AUSTRIA and the article talked about how the whole country was devastated because the ski team hadn't won the Downhill gold medal. Austria was in mourning. We drove on to Munich to catch a plane for home and the Canadian National Championships, thankful that the national fervour in our country would be less severe than in Austria.

I won the Downhill in the Canadian National Championships at Rossland, B.C., which wasn't terribly surprising. Ken had won it perennially and now, though Todd was coming on strong, I was still the class of the team and, in fact, was ranked fifth overall in the Downhill in the world that year, while Todd was ninth. Winning that race marked the end of a controversy that caused as much fuss as anything in my career.

Eight months prior to the race, when I'd heard that a tobacco company was to sponsor the CNC, I wrote a letter to the Canadian Ski Association outlining my position. One of the firmest convictions I have is a belief that smoking is bad for people. I don't care if others do it (though there's no smoking allowed in my house), but don't ask me to support it by having my picture associated with it. I don't want to be photographed coming across the line or standing in the finish area with huge cigarette banners dominating the scenery. I ended the letter by saying that I didn't want my positon of influence in skiing abused in this way and asked the CSA to please consider my opinion and let's work it out together.

Somehow the press got wind of my stand and the fecal matter hit the fan. I was descended upon by the media hordes who seized the opportunity to create The Great Smoke Scandal. I was accused of biting the hand that fed the team and much ink was devoted to the fact that I wouldn't be where I was if it wasn't for sponsors. They ignored the fact that it was a two-way street and that the team had a responsibility to me too, which they weren't living up to. I explained my position to them, that I simply didn't want my name associated with tobacco and that I had hoped to work it out on the quiet. The CSA responded to the press reports by telling me they hadn't received the letter – or it didn't go to the right person – or I should have written to somebody else – or, or, or. My letter had been lost in the bureaucratic shuffle and their dithering continued. The tobacco people talked to me and I told them I appreciated what they were doing for the team, but I refused to budge.

Finally, a couple of weeks before the race, I asked John Ritchie what I should do. I always valued his opinion and his advice was to go with the flow. He pointed out that I wasn't just skiing for myself. The event would be an opportunity for young skiers to race against me. I agreed to race with the stipulation that I would not accept the tobacco trophy if I won. I didn't want to be a jerk and jeopardize the future of the sport and the skiers' welfare. In the end everybody won. The team got the tobacco money, but I didn't stand on the victory podium or receive the cup, and I avoided being seen with the sponsor's message.

I have nothing to show for winning that race other than intact scruples. I got more fan mail from across Canada over the issue than absolutely anything else in my career – all of the letters approving of my stand. I was amazed at the emotional uproar it caused then, and the matter is still dragged into the press occasionally. Nowadays, I nip volatile issues like this in the bud. Recently, I turned down a lucrative offer to endorse some junk food. I don't eat it, therefore I don't promote it. It's as simple as that.

My speed on the course at Rossland helped clear the smoke out of my head. I was clocked at 84 miles per hour through the Indian Flats section and was probably hitting over 90 out of range of the speed trap. When you tuck through this wide flat area, you can really howl, hunkered down in what amounts to a little aerodynamic egg shape with your head poking out front. At those speeds you can turn by just moving your head slightly right or left which blows you across the hill so you don't even have to edge. The force of the wind is amazing and you're getting bounced around like mad, so when you drop an arm for balance it gets whipped round behind your back. You have to inch it back carefully or the wind will grab it again and spin you off course. Things like that are what make ski racing such a gas. You get intoxicated by the exuberance of your own velocity and can shut out the rest of the world.

World Cup racing continued at Aspen where I was eighth, a good journeyman result if you're on the way up . . . or on the way down. I wanted to do better in the final race of the season, at Whistler, but I caught some kind of unidentified plague and was sick as a dog. I flaked out in my hotel room, aching all over, hallucinating, and my throat was so raw I coughed up blood. I was barely human again by race time and the chances of a story-book finish to my career were dim. The race had been delayed by fog and I was hoping against hope the course would be a solid sheet of ice like an NHL rink. This wasn't to be and I tried to get down without disgracing myself. Bill Johnson won, Todd was fourth, and I was fifth in my last race.

There was no tear-jerking stuff at the finish line. I had already broken the news to Matthew Fisher of the *Globe and Mail* a few days before that this race would be the end of the line for me and everybody had the story at Whistler. I had made the final decision on our return from Sarajevo a few weeks previously. We gave our usual press conference at Molson's in Toronto and I talked to the reporters and the ski people and generally reconnoitered the situation. I went home and tossed around the alternatives: I'm not enjoying myself any more, so what am I going to do? Maybe I should quit, maybe I shouldn't. What will I do when I stop? I've been doing this for 11 years, maybe I can go for two more. What about hanging in there 'til the next Olympics? The options flipped around in my head until finally I said, "No, I've had enough. That's it – I quit."

I thought the decision was taken quite calmly and rationally, but my body felt otherwise. That night, I developed incredible stomach pains. I was rolling around groaning out loud and saying to Ann, "I think I'm dying, phone the doctor!" She soothed my fevered brow and assured me I would be all right. I didn't believe her. I had cramps like crazy and thought surely my appendix was blowing up. But she was right and I was perfectly okay after a few hours.

Obviously, the decision to retire had been a major emotional upheaval, for my stomach at least. I was 26 years old and my entire adult life had been spent on the team. Nearly every waking moment of every one of all those days I'd been thinking about ski racing. Now I had a tremendous void to fill. The whole focus of my life had changed overnight. It would have been much easier for me to continue down the familiar path. I had come to a crossroads and chosen a new route that had no guideposts.

On reflection, I think what tipped the scales was knowing I didn't want to be just another guy hanging around the first seed marking time and raking in some cash. I raced because I wanted to ski better every day. Now I wasn't getting better and knew I didn't want to get better. I'd been the best. What more could I do? Granted, former winners like Klammer, Mueller, and Wirnsberger had hung on through some lean years and won again. The point was I didn't *care* enough to win any more now, nor did I have the desire to hang in there to see if I might be motivated enough to care again.

I had to quit and it didn't matter if people thought it was a good or bad idea, timely or untimely. It was *my* time. I was very positive about it and, as it turned out, so was everyone else. The press and public reaction was very gratifying. Rob Safrata organized a retirement dinner for me and we were able to commemorate my hanging up my skis in a very positive way by using money raised at the dinner to establish the Steve Podborski Bursaries for up-and-coming skiers. We set up corporate tables and invited all the powers-that-were. Of course, all the guys were there, Ken, Mur and Ir, Todd, John Ritchie . . . and it was just great for me, very, very gratifying.

When I was a kid at Craigleith, I occasionally won things like the Jozo Weider Bursary, which undoubtedly made a difference to my career. A few hundred dollars here and there really helped my parents out because having a budding ski racer in the family is a very expensive business. In a way, the Steve Podborski Bursaries are a tribute to my parents as well as being worth $500 each to the best male and female juvenile skiers in Canada each year. We top up the fund originated at my retirement dinner by staging special events regularly and I often donate speech fees to the fund. I'm happy to put whatever I can back into the sport that gave me all I've got.

13. *Après Ski*

Some aspects of my new après-ski life were already in place when I retired. I had started working with the Sun Ice sportswear company and my Pod Line of ski clothing was being launched that season of 1983-84. I made deals to continue promotional work with several of the ski-equipment companies I'd worked with over the years: Tyrolia bindings, Carrera goggles, and others – and Dave McPhail and I had been working on a ski-boot idea for several years. John Ritchie became my manager after he stopped coaching and he helped me handle the negotiations. It was an ideal situation since he knew the ski industry and all the people in it. Most of all, I trusted him.

Ann and I were living in a rented house in downtown Toronto, but I decided I wanted peace and serenity so I bought a house in Newmarket, north of the city. Another reason for responding to the call of the wild was my dog Dante. Though he had a loving disposition, he was a Doberman and tended to frighten people by just looking like a member of his breed. He also had a sense of humour and enjoyed scaring people by running close to them or leaning against visitors and looking fierce until they petted him. I thought Dante would flourish in the wide open spaces during my retreat phase.

I really felt a need to get away from it all after living in a goldfish bowl for so many years. Being in the public eye went with the territory of being a ski racer, now I wanted a private life. Another factor in seeking a lower profile was to downplay the fact that Ann and I were living together. It was easier for my parents, but Mr.and Mrs. Rohmer weren't terribly happy about their daughter living in sin. The impossibility of avoiding close scrutiny in Toronto was demonstrated to us one day when Ann went shopping for some cheese for a small party we were having for a few friends. In the shop the proprietor asked Ann if she was stocking up for her party tonight. He'd read about it in Gary Dunford's column in the *Toronto Sun*.

The house up north had about an acre of grass which grew like weeds and took me a whole day to cut. The basement leaked and I had to get that fixed. Ann had just switched from being co-hostess on Global TV's *That's Life* program to a new job on CTV's *Canada AM* and found the commuting a hassle. We both realized we needed to be closer to where the action was for our careers. Further complications came from our decision to get married and, with all the scurrying to and fro, our place in the country proved to be more trouble than it was worth. In fact, it was worth even less to me in the long run when I lost money on the deal after forking over more cash to make it saleable. Before we left, I was talking to the guy in the gas station near the house. He said the city slickers didn't last as long as he thought we would and we had a good laugh over that.

It was funny and it was a good learning experience. I was quite good at learning from my mistakes on the team, where the attitude was: there's nothing wrong with making a mistake once, but if it happens again people get mad at you. We did things that were wrong all the time as we were learning, and we profited from the experience. However, I didn't want to get into the habit of having to make a mistake to learn anything new. What I did learn from my brief experience as a homeowner was that I don't need it. I don't like to cut the grass and I don't want to have to fix leaky basements or broken dishwashers. I stopped needing to own things when I started getting 20 pairs of skis a year and free cars. I didn't like them any less because I didn't own them. I liked them because they worked, and I really did use 20 pairs of skis a year.

I'm not a conspicuous consumer though I have a few treasures. I have an Italian bike called a Concorde and a Steve Bauer model which I like because they function beautifully for their intended purpose – which is to go fast. I tend to view these things as tools rather than treasures, though I really love the pinball machine in my living-room. We had one at home and my family gave me this one for a recent birthday. It's great fun because it's a game of skill with penalties and rewards. You don't fall and break your neck if you screw up, but you can go down the tube in about ten seconds if you stop concentrating. Come to think of it that sounds a lot like ski racing . . . .

Anyway, Ann and I moved all our stuff back to Toronto to a small house Ann found. It soon became apparent it was too small for Dante, and for me – I was using it as an office. One day I saw an interesting looking place for rent, a very spacious upper duplex, and decided this was the place for me – we moved in and I still live there. With Ann and I so busy, poor old Dante was leading a dog's life and we realized he would have to go. Ann found some people who liked him and I took him away on our last trip together to drop him off to his new owners north of the city.

I gave them his bowl, collar, and lead, showed them how he could heel and all the tricks I'd taught him using hand signals and commands. He was a good dog. I told them to enjoy him and left. I walked down the driveway to my car – then just blew up emotionally. It was one of the saddest days of my life. It didn't matter that Dante would have a good home. The people were dog lovers and had lots of room for him to romp. But now he was gone. Our family always had a dog and Dante had meant so much to me. I knew I could never see him again because if I went to visit him it might confuse him. The depth of my emotion took me by surprise. I drove home bawling my eyes out.

I found an ideal office space in downtown Toronto where I could set up shop and ply my trade, the exact nature of which was still a bit obscure. I knew one of the daughters of the Addison family, who have a large Cadillac dealership in the city, and, when their leasing division moved into a newly renovated townhouse, Boren Consulting Limited took over the top floor. The name of my enterprise started out as a joke back in 1979 when we incorporated a company to look after my business affairs, mainly to manage a blind trust fund so I could remain pure and untainted by money in order to satisfy the Olympic amateur requirements. I regarded the whole thing as a joke and, looking for something innocent and innocuous, I came up with the name Boren, which is as close to "boring" as I could get.

Boren was good for a few laughs and every once in a while I just sit back and giggle about my life. It's partly a survival technique of mine to combat adversity and maintain sanity through comic relief, but much of it really is funny. In skiing people threw motivational war cries at me: "You've got to do it for your team." "It's important that you win because the ski company is behind you." "You've got to do it for your mother and father, your brother, your dog, your province, your country . . . ." I would say to myself, yeah do it for Boren! At a race, when everybody was going nuts with excitement, with thousands of fans packed onto the hill and media people freaking out, I was always able to see the lighter side. Imagine, all this fuss just to watch grown men in skintight suits with long slats on their feet go flashing by for a few seconds . . . this has got to be the most ridiculous sport in the world.

I had tongue in cheek and both feet on the ground when I switched from ski boots to shiny loafers to become the full-time CEO of Boren Consulting Limited. I only saw the tip of the iceberg when I was skiing because, after I negotiated the contracts, I forgot about them and lawyers, accountants, and financial advisers looked after the trust fund. These people still looked after the details so the change from skier to businessman wasn't that dramatic. I just spent less time in a skintight suit and more in a business suit. I used the same approach we had on the team. Skiing was never a war or test of wills. It was me against the mountain and the other guys were the measure. We worked together for the common good and in business that remains my credo.

I hate working *for* people when they *hire* me. That just doesn't fly. We're partners, working together to achieve some goal. I only functioned as a "worker" in a "job" for three days one summer when I was a teenager. I was hired by a metal fabricating plant to punch holes in sheets of metal. The actual labour wasn't too bad, but the atmosphere, the mentality, was very upsetting. I was accustomed to people looking ahead, having dreams and chasing after them. The guys in the plant were content to stay where they were punching holes in metal for a living. They did that day in, day out, for a lifetime, and looked forward to two weeks holiday at the cottage in Muskoka. They were happy, it worked for them, but it just wasn't for me and I quit after three days.

My life was devoted to self-improvement and, when I retired from skiing, this posed difficulties at first. After being the best in the world in my chosen profession, I had to come to grips with the fact that quite likely I would never be the best in the world at anything again. That can be terribly distressing if you dwell on it. And when you get a late start, it seems everybody's better than you are. Well sure they are – they've got several years head start. You can't look back and think, if I'd done this or that ten years ago I'd be where they are today. You just do your best. Every day I tried to do as much as I could and if I made a mistake I fixed it. I didn't waste much time trying to excel in areas that weren't necessary. I learned fast where my strengths lay and capitalized on them. Most of those strengths lay in my track record. Very few people become the best in the world at anything and that distinction is worth something.

It's not my style to just sell my name and let a company run with it. After all, it's *my* name and I really feel it should be associated with something worthwhile and that I should believe in the product and support it properly. Sure, people are trading on my name, but so am I and I have no qualms about that. It doesn't swell my head because I know the name in question is Steve Podborski the ski racer, not the nerd from Don Mills who quit school at 16. The nerd was brought up to have certain principles and he hasn't changed, nor has the ski racer. On the team, I used products I thought performed better. Skiing was believing, in the equipment and in yourself. If something didn't work properly, I didn't use it, and if I didn't believe in it, like tobacco, I didn't want my name associated with it. There's a lot of good stuff out there in the market place and if my name can help promote it, that's a good thing. That's how the world works.

As I became more serious about the business world, I changed Boren to Pod Enterprises and 99 per cent of the company's work is ski-related. The Pod Line with Sun Ice is a major involvement. I helped design it and it's very satisfying to see it doing so well and, with annual sales approaching the two-million-dollar mark, the Pod Enterprises accounting people are happy about the royalties. I help market the line by wearing it myself, appearing on posters and in ad campaigns, and by working in-store at product knowledge sessions with the staff to help familiarize them with the garments. But the biggest thrill for me is seeing people wearing the Pod Line.

The first time I saw one of my jackets walking toward me on the street, I broke into a big, silly grin. I still do.

Dave McPhail and I have put a lot into our ski-boot concept and it could develop into a major project. Ski boots probably evolved from a pair of mukluks worn by some Swede or Norwegian who was running around in the woods on hickory sticks. They needed more edge control, so they were made stiffer, but it's as if the thinking stopped there. If skiing had been invented yesterday, boots would be quite different. Dave McPhail and I took that approach to ski-boot design. We spent several years perfecting our concept by looking closely at the function of the leg and foot in skiing, concentrating on which movements needed to be enhanced, and which ones needed to be restricted. I'm convinced we've got a winner which will give skiing a boot into the 21st century.

It's wonderful to be able to continue my involvement in skiing. So many retired athletes have to turn their backs on their sports careers to make a living. I feel fortunate in being able to promote sport now even more than when I was competing. Besides being a commentator on the CTV network for the 1988 Winter Olympics in Calgary, I'm on the board of directors of the Toronto Ontario Olympic Committee in our bid to get the 1996 games in that city. My *Pod's Perspective* segment on the nationally syndicated TV program *Ski Base* is great fun to do. It offers insights into skiing (all my own ideas) – they just stick me in front of a camera and away I go. I'm also working with Fiberglas Canada, helping to promote the Canadian Freestyle Ski Team. They're some of the best in the world in their sport and not many Canadians know about them – something I know all about. All of this is very public stuff, public relations in the truest sense.

Because skiing is still such a gas for me, my work as Eastern Program Co-ordinator of the Molson Canadian Masters Alpine Series doesn't seem like work at all. My old teammate Dave Murray and Don McQuaid started the concept in B.C. and it's now expanded to a truly national series of ski races that authentically duplicate the atmosphere of World Cup events, minus the serious-ness. People race in age categories from 19 up to you're as old as you feel. The events are held at major ski resorts across the country and there are crowds to watch them, a loud speaker system with music, a commentator who broadcasts biographical information about each competitor, awards ceremonies, and provincial and national finals at the end of the season.

Jim Kirby, a former member of the team as a GS and Slalom specialist, looks after the details of the series in Eastern Canada for me, and part of my job is to make everything run smoothly for the sponsors, suppliers, and individual race organizers. There's great sponsor interest because of the ideal target market it offers them, an affluent group of consumers in several age brackets. People like Xerox supply the computing equipment, Bose does the sound systems, Canadian Airlines flies people to the finals, and a whole bunch of ski-industry companies supply prizes. I hang around the hill at each of my races and just soak up the atmosphere. I try to be impartial and encourage all the competitors, but find I can't be unbiased when it comes to a couple of the entrants whom I know best of all: my mom and dad.

Jeans were my usual off-piste uniform when I was with the team, but John Ritchie used to say if you're going to make a million-dollar deal you've got to look like a million bucks so they'll trust you. I always listened to my coaches and when an endorsement opportunity came along from Alexander Julian menswear, I signed on the dotted line and now look trustworthy enough for people like Best Foods to deal with me. In my first big promotional venture outside the ski industry I'm endorsing Skippy peanut butter for Best. But there's a skiing connection for me: when we were on the team in Europe, we would *kill* for peanut butter.

John Ritchie is now President of Drummond Breweries and Vice President of Marketing of the Principal Group Investment company out west. When John became more involved in the business world, I had to find another agent and chose Brian Cooper of Hollis Marketing. Brian is a very dynamic and aggressive guy who really wants to make his mark in sports marketing. I very much admire him and another of his clients, the bicycle racer Steve Bauer. It's unbelievable what Steve does on a bike. Only skiers can fully appreciate what I've done and I'm sure that's true in Steve Bauer's sport. He's another Canadian racing in Europe in a sport not well known in his country, so I can sympathize with that. But I've done some fairly serious cycling and when I multiply my maximum effort by ten, I'm maybe close to what he does. I'm totally speechless when I think how that guy can ride.

Brian Cooper focused quite a bit of attention on me for the Winter Olympics in Calgary and I regard it as an honour to be a communicator at a major event in the history of Canadian sport. And I see it as a watershed in my career as far as promoting sport is concerned. I honestly feel it's time to pass the torch to others who can fill the role I've been playing for several years. I've been out there working like crazy for sport in Canada and, though I'm very well known for past achievements, I'm no longer performing as an athlete. I'm hoping other winners will come along after the Olympics and do their part. In Europe, there's a much greater turnover in winning ski racers and when you're finished you can go back to a normal life. Apart from Todd Brooker's successes, we haven't had anyone to take over from the original Crazy Canucks as spokesmen and fundraisers. We're happy to do what we can and are pleased we're still high profile enough to help, but it's time for new blood. Another thing I feel strongly about is maintaining the Olympic spirit after the fact by continuing to set goals for yourself and striving for excellence. These simple ideals may sound corny, but they worked for me in ski racing and I still live by them.

Many cynics sneer at jockdom, but some learned people call sport a metaphor for life. Even if you take a middle-ground point of view, it's undeniable that athletes play major roles in society and are an influence on people. The fact that athletes earn their living this way may feed the cynics, but it's also possible to do good works with their celebrity status. In 1980, when Lise Desrochers asked me to do an event with the Ontario Division of the Canadian Paraplegic Association, I said I'll do more than that, I'll become your official spokesman. In the first three years of my involvement, donations to the CPA went from $25,000 to nearly $500,000.

In 1984, the Ontario Minister of Health, Keith Norton, asked me to head a group called the Minister's Advisory Group on Health Promotion, an organization devoted to finding ways to make people more aware of their personal responsibility for their health and well-being. We meet twice a month, for a nominal per diem fee, and my role as chairman is to co-ordinate the talents of a group of experts in several fields: a doctor, a kinesianthropologist, a vice-president from the grocery business, the Dean of Physical Education from York University, an expert in community health, a counsellor on alcohol and drug addiction – a really brilliant group of highly motivated, public-spirited people.

It's been a wonderful experience working with them, but also very frustrating trying to function within the government when you're not part of it. It's two steps forward and one back 90 per cent of the time: the other ten per cent we're putting out fires. But the forward progress gives enough satisfaction and pleasure from our teamwork to make it worthwhile. Part of our mandate is to be a pipeline to the Minister, by going out into the province and taking the pulse of the communities. When we find a problem, we take it right to the top. We've now dealt with four different Health Ministers, a testimony to our impartiality and to our worth.

Nowadays, my date book is as full as it was when I raced, but with a much greater variety of stuff. On the team, I skied for about 200 days a year, took Christmas and New Year off, and trained for the remaining days. One of the things I never realized then was that people in the workaday world usually took weekends off. I sometimes take Sundays off in the summer, but it's nose to the grindstone seven days a week most of the time. Then, in May, I add up all the days I might have rested but didn't and come up with a month of Sundays, which I spend in Hawaii.

Getting my business life organized went surprisingly smoothly, but there was a major setback in my private life after my retirement. I first met Ann Rohmer in 1980 when she was assigned to do a story on me for her new TV program *That's Life*. She came with her crew to the Fitness Institute to film my physiotherapy routine as I recovered from my second knee operation. It was slightly off-putting to see her light up a cigarette, but we had fun doing the interview, with a lot of back and forth repartee – though I was probably the more experienced media person at the time. We made a tentative lunch date for sometime in the future, but I forgot about it until one day that spring as I was sitting in an airport in Japan. We were snowed in and I was flipping through my address book when I saw her name and sent her a postcard. When I got home, I phoned up her studio and left my name. She phoned me back and invited me to come for a drink at her parents' place. I was otherwise engaged and had to decline. I learned later she found this unbelievably shocking because very few people ever said no to her. I could understand that, she's a very attractive and persuasive woman, but I had to take a rain check and she gave me a second chance.

We began to see a lot of each other and, in the spring of 1982, we decided to live together. I first asked her to marry me a year after that. She thought I was kidding, but it got serious the morning after my proposal when she got me up and marched me down to Birks Jewellers to get her engagement ring. We got there at 9 o'clock and had to sit out front with people staring at us until the store opened an hour later. We thought marriage would make our relationship more acceptable to our parents for whom living together was not in the approved category. But actually getting married seemed silly since I was on the road so much and Ann's job took her all over North America. When I finished racing and settled down and her work was centred in Toronto, it seemed the right thing to do. We finally did make it official on May 12, 1984, and much was made of the perfect match between the celebrity athlete and the glamorous media star.

We didn't really enjoy the whole wedding process, which was like a political juggling act with the two families involved. We made some great friends by inviting some people and lost others by not inviting others. I apologize to any who should have been there and were overlooked. We had a big wedding with all the trimmings at the same church in Don Mills where I had gone to Sunday School. The Rohmers were prominent in the church, having donated the carillon bells, and Mr. Rohmer had been instrumental in setting up Thompson House, a church-affiliated seniors' home where my grandmother lives. It was appropriate that we be married there and the wedding was a great success with everyone, including the bride and groom, thinking it would last forever.

Our marriage lasted about a year. There were a number of stressors that interfered with wedded bliss, including our moving house phase, my transition from ski racer to civilian, and Ann's job dissatisfaction. She found the *Canada AM* post unsuitable and it was a very hard time for her. But our biggest problem was the changes brought about by officially tying the knot. When we lived together, we made our own rules. You wash the dishes, I'll vacuum the rug, or we'll get a cleaning lady and split the cost 50-50. We made a deal on everything and it was all up front and talked over.

There was absolutely nothing assumed or taken for granted. I paid for dinner when we went out, Ann bought the groceries. We split the rent. She was a business person with her own career and wanted to contribute equally to our relationship with clearly defined rules. We got along well and she even made an effort to be more health-conscious. Her smoking didn't last very long, since she was really only a social smoker. She only fell off the wagon occasionally when she might have a serious bender with a friend. They'd go off into a corner and giggle together while puffing over cigarettes which I "didn't notice."

Our decision to get married was based on the assumption that everything would continue as before. But the transition from lovers and friends to husband and wife didn't work and we lost what we had before. We became two different people after our wedding. I tried to be a husband like my father and Ann tried to emulate a wife like her mother, at least that's how we perceived our roles. All of a sudden we had to deal with the new personalities we had become and we just staggered around wondering what was going on. It was like a slap in the face. We were confused and bewildered and the pressures of our careers added to our problems.

Ann suggested we see a marriage counsellor and we found a good one, a psychologist, who urged us to make it a team effort. This was fine with me as I was used to being coached, though I'd never let anyone play with my brain before – at least not knowingly. He made a point of being perceived as working fairly for both of us and was always completely realistic. Some of these guys seem as if they're from outer space, but this one had one foot in theory and the other in the nitty-gritty of real life. He was very helpful in advising us on how to handle other problems, like the negative reactions of our families, as well as dealing with the preconceptions, desires, and needs which divided Ann and me. Though he wasn't able to save our marriage, I have great faith in him and still see him occasionally.

Besides the trauma of losing the one who had been so much a part of my life, I had to face up to being a significant failure at something after trying so hard to succeed. Even if only half the blame was mine, it was very hard to come to grips with defeat. I had had major setbacks before, but had always come back; now there was no return. I worried about how we could make a graceful exit from the disaster. Our marriage had been a major media event, which was probably inevitable since we were public figures, but we had tried to keep our private life out of the public domain. As it turned out, the gossip mongers left us alone in our time of trouble and I very much respect the media for that. It could have been front page news, but they showed great consideration which was much appreciated.

Ann and I agreed to try and make the break as painless as possible. We worked out the division of property we'd acquired together and I got her the necessary items, vacuum cleaner, dishes, and so on, to set up her new house. So the classic "irreconcilable differences" ended on a material level after we had shared so much. We're divorced now and still communicate occasionally on the phone. We've both recovered from the trauma and Ann has gone on to great success in her career as a sports announcer on CITY TV, as well as working in other media and as a fitness instructor in Toronto.

It's hard to find anything positive out of such a negative experience, but it helped me learn a lot about myself and, I think, I'm a better person for it. The sessions with the counsellor have given me a greater understanding of others, their perception of me, and my reaction to them. For instance, it was always very annoying when people assumed I was making gazillions of dollars and took it for granted that I would buy them lunch or dinner. I was genuinely upset that people would take advantage of me, yet I felt I should pick up the tab because I was making a fair amount of money, probably more than they were. There were conflicting emotions because of the public perception that I was Steve Podborski, the famous ski racer, while in my own mind I remained Steve Podborski, the nerd from Don Mills. I was getting messed around playing the two roles and had trouble dealing with it. It becomes easier to handle as I learn who and what I am.

I see parallels in a short story by Arthur Miller called *Fame*. The hero, an ultra-successful playwright, has two shows on Broadway and his face is plastered on the front covers of magazines. As he walks down the street, a passerby recognizes him, shakes his hand, and exclaims about meeting the famous celebrity. In a moment of insight, the hero realizes the passerby only sees him as a magazine cover, not as a person. Should he break out of the role in which he is perceived, the public will be terribly disappointed and he risks becoming a nobody. Thus he is only what others want him to be. Other incidents reinforce that feeling, until the hero of the story asks himself, "Who am I?"

Often it seems I'm the guy on the magazine cover. I'm what people perceive me to be and it's hard to live up to that. They want me to be perfect and do everything they imagine somebody like me should do. For my own well-being I have to be two people and strike a balance between the fantasy and the reality. It was easier at first when I was on the team in Europe and just had to be Pod the ski racer; then when I came home I was Steve, the son of Mike and Jackie Podborski – two separate roles that were fairly easy to play. It became harder when I became a winner, and being a former winner hasn't made it much easier.

The circumstances surrounding celebrity make it difficult to sort out the motives of people and to form new friendships, let alone maintain old ones, particularly with women. After my divorce, I was determined to change and make a conscious effort to choose a partner for a long-term relationship very carefully. But I wasn't in any great rush, so it was a pleasant surprise to find Joan.

We met one night in a restaurant and struck up a conversation. She immediately scored points with me when she wondered what my name was. She's beginning a career in modelling and is a very quiet, laid-back person. We get along very well and our relationship is building slowly, though the public/private syndrome sometimes makes it difficult. Recently, I was voted one of the most eligible bachelors in Canada by a magazine. Joan wondered why I didn't tell them about her. I explained that I regard our relationship as totally private, between us and our friends, and the media must have nothing to do with it. My last relationship was very public and I want to change the rules.

14. Pod's Perspective

I won a total of eight World Cup races during my career and a perennial question is why? Why did I become World Cup Downhill Champion? Why did I win more races than my teammates on the Crazy Canucks? Sometimes even they were puzzled by my success. A few years after Jim Hunter had left the team and was racing in a professional series in North America, I met him at the Canadian Championships at Lake Louise. We were chatting away when he took me to one side and asked, "Steve, what's the secret of winning World Cup races?" I replied that there was no secret. He was insistent: "Come on Steve, we were together for years. You can tell me what the secret is." When it became obvious I had no startling revelations to give him, he asked John Ritchie the same question and got the same answer.

There are no *secrets* to winning World Cup races. But there are a lot of factors involved and I'm happy to share them with anyone interested enough to ask. First of all, you've got to be lucky. Jim Hunter was unlucky not to win a race during his career. Sometimes you're victimized by bad weather or a poor start number. It helps to be in the right place at the right time and my time in ski racing coincided with a coming together of circumstances that created opportunities to win races. Seizing those opportunities is part of the game. I was able to gradually build up to success by steadily learning, improving, and maturing. Add good coaching, good equipment, a good ski man, and a good team to back you up and help motivate you, and you have the basic ingredients to be a potential winner.

The Crazy Canucks were famous for going down hills like whirling dervishes – arms windmilling, skis and poles akimbo – seemingly like accidents looking for a place to happen. I looked like this too – whenever I lost control and was trying to prevent an accident. My style was smoother and seemingly more effortless than the others, so much so that, at first, people wondered if I was trying as hard as I could. They thought I didn't look frantic enough to be fast . . . then they checked the stopwatches. Interestingly, though my style was less colourful, people tried to emulate it when I began to win. Recently, I was flattered to hear that Pirmin Zurbriggen, a current Downhill superstar, patterns his style after mine. When my form lapsed into wildness, I tended to slow down. I think the reason I was able to develop this very strong technical ability was because I was stronger. My controlled style was based on the muscular strength I developed from my bust-a-gut training methods.

It helped that I'm built fairly close to the ground and thus able to be more balanced on my skis than taller people. Measurements taken of Downhillers show that I'm a smaller version of Franz Klammer, with relatively short legs. While my low weight was a disadvantage in gliding, my physique was ideal and, when I added power to that physique, it was a distinct advantage. It takes great strength and physical conditioning to just hang on for dear life in the Downhill. Once you have confidence in your ability to survive, you can concentrate on the finer points of going faster.

While racing the Downhill is such a tremendously physical experience, winning it is very much a mental process. After you subtract the practicalities of technique and equipment and the vagaries of luck and circumstance, you're left with the mind of the skier. What you have in your head before the start plays a vital role in establishing your time at the finish, or whether you finish at all.

I believe there are three ways to approach Downhill racing: skiing on the fringe, skiing safely within your limits, and finally, not knowing your limits and being worried about it. This last way is the slow way and that's the way the rank and file race until they learn better, though many of them never do. These guys ski with question marks in their heads. They're erratic, alternating between fast and slow, because they're unable to arrive at a balance. They don't know what's going to happen at the next turn on the course and, when something goes wrong, they don't know why and are unable to improve. Their problems can stem from timidity, stupidity, bullheadedness, insensitivity, lack of sympathy for the requirements of the sport, or a combination of these failings. Most skiers go through this stage, I certainly did, but experience is not always the best teacher for some and they remain at the bottom of the results.

There's no substitute for practical experience and you need the ability to absorb the lessons that fly in your face as you ski down a hill at 90 miles an hour. With the wind screaming like a banshee in your helmet, the scenery flying by in a blur, there's a natural tendency to just concentrate on saving your life. It takes great presence of mind (though some might say absence of it) to keep your wits about you enough to establish such truths as the fact that merely inclining your helmet a fraction to either side will dramatically change your direction.

The middle-of-the-road skiers usually finish that way in the results. They're the guys who know what their limits are and stay safely within them. They make their turns and hold their lines and they might finish sixth or tenth – quite respectable results when you consider they're better than all but a handful of skiers in the world. Sometimes, when everybody else makes mistakes, this type of skier pulls a win out of the hat. But they don't win consistently because they've got a built-in mental governor that holds them back from making that extra effort. Even those with a winning mindset can succumb to this kind of thinking on a given day, and I have some top ten finishes that show what can happen when I applied the mental brakes.

As a Crazy Canuck I tended to ski on the fringe. I was never doubtful or hesitant at the start of a race. I *knew* I was going to make it. I was going to run this race come hell or high water and 99 per cent of the time my conviction proved to be correct. It was something of an act of faith but similar, in a way, to getting into your car to drive to work. It becomes routine, you know the route by heart, where the stop signs and traffic lights are, and you have a clear idea of how long the journey will take. You don't worry about an accident until it happens; then you deal with it as best you can. If you dwell on all the potential hazards, you'll be late for work. Carried to the extreme, this state of mind can make you paralyzed with fear and you'll never leave the safety of your home or bed.

Overcoming fear is a fascinating aspect of Downhill racing. You have to program your brain so that fear doesn't become dominant. When you're rocketing down a hill, your body doesn't like what it sees and hears and the natural reaction is to want to retreat from the precipice and put a halt to the howling of the wind. A friend of mine demonstrated this one time by betting another guy he couldn't walk closer than three feet to the edge of a cliff on a mountainside. The would-be brave one accepted the bet, approached the 1000-foot drop, and came to an immediate halt at the three-foot mark. My friend won the bet because as soon as the other guy's eyes saw further down than his brain approved of, he had to stop. Ski racing is like that: you have to constantly perform feats contrary to all your instincts of self-preservation. Your brain has to dominate your senses and overrule their reluctance to venture into dangerous situations. But your body is the vehicle for your descent, so your muscles have a very large say in the matter. So the difference between go and no go in the Downhill involves striking a delicate balance between brain and muscle power.

You push yourself to the limit, looking for that edge beyond the horizon. This approach leaves no room for error, no safety margin and you have to be prepared to take the painful consequences. John Ritchie frequently told the press that I was completely fearless. Though I was never actually afraid, I was often concerned. The first time down Kitzbühel, after coming back from my first knee injury, was cause for concern. I really wondered about making the turn where I'd fallen, and the situation was made worse when a late start number prolonged the agony of waiting. I banished negative thoughts by concentrating on the fact that my rivals, whom I was convinced I could beat, had made it down safely. I always felt confident my skiing abilities could handle whatever was thrown at me. I was worried about racing in poor visibility because travelling at 60 to 80 miles an hour, when you can only see 30 feet ahead, cuts into the time you have to react to obstacles like trees approaching at full speed. You need time to anticipate, and fog or a snowstorm are disorienting because the feedback from such course conditions is naturally restricted. But most of the time I was afraid of falling only because it would ruin my run. When I did lose it completely and went flipping ass over teakettle, I wasn't worried about wrecking my knee, bashing my head or, even worse, breaking my skis. I would think: "Damn! there goes my run."

That was the prevailing attitude on the team and this apparent disregard for our safety contributed to the legend of the Crazy Canucks. We probed the outer limits of Downhill racing and in so doing went further than most. We got badly crunched, but we won races. We didn't have the preconceptions of the European teams who were steeped in the tradition of accepted form. We pushed, made mistakes and crashed, got up, dusted ourselves off, and tried it again, having learned how far we could go. Our headlong approach was ideal for Downhill at that time and we changed the face of the sport.

There are several shades of meaning to the word "crazy": besides mad or demented, it can mean full of flaws, unsound and shaky. It can refer to irregular pieces fitted together without pattern, as in crazy quilt, and it can mean extremely eager. I suppose most of these definitions applied to the Crazy Canucks. We weren't bound by the perceived sane limits of the sport that confined the Europeans. We took wild chances on the courses because we didn't know any better. We had no preconceptions and convictions to hold us back and we were able to break new ground because of this. We tucked where others had feared to tread and flew to new heights because we wouldn't back off. It might have been mad, but it was also very fast, which tended to make our mistakes spectacular. We were a team of disparate personalities bound together in a common cause and we were keen as hell. We used the "crazy" approach to create a momentum, a driving force that's necessary to conquer a hill like Kitzbühel.

All the right physical attributes, bravery, and all the skill in the world won't make you a winner unless you have the proper attitude and motivation. You've got to *want* to win and not be content with anything less. Our goal was always to *win* races, not just be on the World Cup tour and ski in the same races as the great Klammer. We were there to win and felt that collectively as a team. And as an individual I worked on the premise that I had to beat myself to win. I didn't leave the starting gate with the idea of beating Klammer or Weirather. If I keyed on them and finished ninth while they were tenth and 11th, I might have been content with that. Instead, I wanted to do my best and I figured if I bettered myself, stretched myself, pushed myself, I'd finish up beating the other guys. After you've done that and won a few races, the fear of failing is another great motivator. You want to preserve your reputation as a winner and thinking about this helps keep you in a winning frame of mind.

In this same vein, setbacks can act as a motivator. I came back from my knee injuries hungrier than ever for success. The Pavlovian theory of conditioned reflexes works the same for a ski racer as it did for Pavlov's dog. Teach the dog that he gets a bone when he rings the bell and he'll ding it like crazy thereafter. Give the hungry ski racer a good year, then take it away, and he'll ski like crazy to try and come back to savour that taste of victory again.

Non-winning phases and the unfairness of our situation and circumstances were helpful in continuing our early success in Europe. It was unfair that we were still second-class citizens after our first wins, getting only a small percentage of the recognition and the money that the establishment teams received. It was unfair that we had inferior skis and suits. You either give up or you persevere and ride through the rough stuff. We had nowhere to go but up when we started and after we got up and were knocked down again, we came back for more. We were out to avenge our grievances and winning was the best revenge.

To overcome adversity it helps to be really stupidly stubborn. As ski racers we'd spend hours sitting on a plane crossing the Atlantic, land disoriented with our eyeballs spinning from jetlag, hop into a car, drive our buns off for hours while half asleep, arrive at a hotel where people blabbed away at us in languages we couldn't understand, and get up on a hill with people stepping on our skis and poking us with their poles – then go rocketing down a slope at 70 miles an hour. If you blow your run and get hurt, they send you home in a bag. If you avoid that, you stay in Europe and your girlfriend dumps you a few weeks after you've left Canada, a new Prime Minister is elected, and you don't hear about it. When you go back for a visit, you're a stranger to your own family and the dog bites you and your friends are talking about current events like the Mackenzie Brothers and "hosers" and you haven't a clue what's going on. You're a displaced person, a misunderstood person, and that's scary. The only place you belong is on the ski team and that's a very small world of no more than ten people whose only common interest is ski racing.

You stay on the team partly because you don't know any alternative and hopefully because you have some success. You stay because you love to ski and it's the most amazing thing in your world to be able to ski with the best in the world and then improve to become the best of all. You're opening up new horizons, setting new records, winning races, and people are investing in you to make you go faster and you feel great. You believe you're doing something very significant and important and skiing opens the door to other experiences that make it all worthwhile.

You go out in the darkness of early morning on a training run in Switzerland with Venus and Mars and all the stars shining brilliantly in the black sky. The only sound is your breathing and the snow crunching underfoot and it's beautiful. You're skiing in brilliant sunshine on a glacier high up in the Andes in Chile and a condor soars by, its wings whistling in the wind. It's a magnificent spectacle and you're happy to be alive.

One of my favourite World Cup memories comes from a late afternoon jogging session on the narrow footpaths on the Alps above Wengen. It was in the days before I wrecked my knees and could still run and I was out and about in a winter wonderland. It was so spectacularly beautiful that I sat down for awhile and just took it all in. The Jungfrau, Monch, and Eiger peaks loomed overhead and across the Lauterbrunnen valley from Wengen lay the village of Murren huddled on top of a 3000-foot precipice. When they play tennis on the courts in Murren, a volley that goes over the fence is never seen again. It was warm where I sat and the sun was casting purple shadows on the snowy panorama beneath. At the far end of the valley, the glaciers were a marvellous greenish blue and the hills above the treeline were dotted with snowed-in wooden chalets where the Swiss farmers keep their cattle in summer. Down in quaint and charming Wengen, one of the toy trains of the Bernese Oberland cog railway pulled into the station, and everywhere I looked seemed like a scene from a picture postcard.

Those moments of spiritual enlightenment were good for the soul and helped keep me motivated and on my chosen path. Still, I was often homesick and lonely. The others on the team probably felt that way too, but no one showed it because it was felt that it might undermine the confidence of the team. We tried to keep everything upbeat and give each other positive reinforcement – not always easy when we were exposed to each other 24 hours a day in close confinement. When I felt in need of private time, I retreated to the bathroom with a book and shut the door on the rest of the world. I'd disappear in there for half an hour to 45 minutes and it became a team joke. Todd Brooker made a lot of hay out of my "toilet-reading" at my retirement dinner and everybody had a good laugh.

There were often lighter moments on the team to help keep up morale. We made sport of Dave Murray's habit of lying nude on his bed while reading. After a few pages he tended to fall asleep this way and would lie there in his birthday suit with the book on his chest. I called it "chest reading" and, one New Year's Day at our hotel in St. Moritz, he had an unexpected audience for his performance. We had the day off and were invited out for some schnapps. I was rooming with Mur and he came back to the hotel before me. On my return, I came upstairs to find two chambermaids absent-mindedly vacuuming the rug in the hall while staring intently through the open door of our room. Sure enough, good old Mur was sound asleep stark naked doing his chest-reading act.

Motivational books say that success is its own reward, but success can also breed failure. Up to the point of actually winning, all I ever thought about was skiing faster. Winning brought many new pressures that had to be dealt with. I had to learn how to handle the pressures of the media and the public. I had to become even more self-centred – sometimes to the point of being nasty, which doesn't come naturally to me – in order to keep my focus on skiing. Then I had to contend with other distractions like the demands of the team suppliers which cut into my training time. They had a big investment in me and part of the deal called for me to spend time promoting their equipment. If I had dwelled on all the negatives, I might have decided winning wasn't worth it and rested on my laurels. This is another reason why most Downhillers win only one race during their careers.

Turning negatives into positives is a very important aspect of successful thinking. Optimists win races, pessimists are also-rans. While winning meant I had less control of my circumstances outside of skiing, I was still in charge of my own destiny in a race, and even better equipped to influence my fate. Success had bred success in that my performance potential improved. I was surrounded with all the trappings of success, the best people were on my side and I had the best equipment to do the job. A lot of people had a lot riding on me and that pressure could easily have been negative. I looked at the bright side: all these people were behind me all the way. With this kind of support how could I possibly go wrong? This attitude gave me an even greater clarity of purpose and cleared my mental decks for the supreme pleasure in my life: racing Downhill.

If all that sounds too pat and perfect, it was. I sometimes fell from a state of mental grace and grovelled around like a shrub. One of those times was at Kitzbühel, always an emotional place whether you're first or one hundred and first. Following the first race of the doubleheader in 1983, where I finished second and ninth, I misplaced my helmet and was rushing around looking for it and worrying about being late for another engagement. I must have been making a noticeable spectacle of myself because somebody stuck his head out a nearby window and asked what was wrong. I told him I'd lost my helmet and he laughed at my predicament. I flew into a comprehensive rage and was all set to go up there and beat the shit out of him. There I was trying to win World Cup races and this jerk was laughing because I was upset. I was ready to commit bodily harm but the others held me back. Besides, I had my ski boots on and couldn't have clumped after the culprit with any dignity. The helmet turned out to be behind the seat in the equipment van.

After this flipping out episode, I gave myself a little pep talk, something like: "Steve, get it together. You're letting little things throw you when there are much more important things to worry about." To keep things in perspective I found it useful to reduce ski racing to its essence: the contestants are grown men wearing bizarre suits so indecently skintight they would surely be arrested anywhere else. They've got funny helmets on their heads, carry bent sticks in their hands, and their weird boots (which look as though they might be fashionable on Mars) are tied to long, skinny fibreglass slats. Thus attired, the players stand around in the cold waiting their turn to play a game which lasts not much longer than two minutes. The object of the exercise is to see who can fall off a mountain the fastest.

It's a ridiculous sport really, though probably no more silly than men in short pants chasing a small chunk of black rubber around a sheet of frozen water. The point is, to help keep your feet on the ground, you need to season seriousness with a grain or two of salt.

And, since most of humankind's endeavours are ultimately ridiculous and futile, you might as well have as much fun as you can along the way. No matter how carried away I got by the course of events, I was always able to come back to earth by remembering where I came from, though I was often unsure of where I was going.

I saw and did things that were amazing to me at the time, and still are. When I first went to Japan, I found the countryside in the ski areas around Furano and Sapporo looked like Northern Quebec, except there were Coke machines beside the road. The cultural differences went further than I had imagined. One night after a race, the Descente ski-wear people invited us to a dinner. We were the guests of honour, hotshot Downhill racers from across the big water. One of those who served us was a young Japanese girl who'd never even *seen* a caucasian before. The round eyes were a source of wonder to her and we fell over ourselves trying to keep pace with the incredibly polite Japanese. One of the guests was a restaurant owner from Tokyo who befriended us and helped us with translations. We casually mentioned that we might like to see his restaurant in Tokyo, then forgot about it.

A few days later, at our hotel in Tokyo, we were all starving and dove into the best buffet dinner I'd ever seen in my life. The round eyes wolfed down everything in sight. We finished up with absolutely delicious marinated strawberries and I was so stuffed I could feel them sitting there at the top of my throat. Having been the first in line, I was the first one out and was met in the lobby by our friend the restaurant owner. "Good evening Steve-san. Are you and the others ready to go to dinner now?" There was no way I could refuse his offer of hospitality, we'd just have to bite the bullet, or the sushi. So I said, "Of course, just give us ten minutes and we'll be ready." After I'd accepted his invitation, it occurred to me he must have seen us at the buffet with food flying around all over the place and that he was being polite, as he had to be, in the Japanese tradition. Anyway, I collected the other guys and we went to his restaurant and had another enormous meal which left us in physical pain.

I left Don Mills with a blank sheet of paper and filled it with experiences in other lands. Travelling with the team, we learned to communicate in other languages, operate in other cultures, and become more cosmopolitan in our outlook. We used to joke about being "citizens of the world" living in the global village . . . Austria today, Japan tomorrow, and who knows where the day after. We went to a kind of international school of public relations and, I think, we're all the better for it. For a while, I seriously considered living permanently in Europe, then realized I could never be completely at ease there because the language and cultural differences would prevent me from settling in completely. But living and learning abroad enriched my life and made me a much better Canadian.

Today, when parents ask me if their kids should leave school to go skiing, I say sure, let them take some time off from school to learn about other aspects of life from experience instead of books. If I had stayed home and gone to university, I would have had a much narrower outlook on life and a more limited understanding of the differences in people. I remember when our football team in junior high school played a team from a technical school where the students were learning a trade. I couldn't figure out why they wanted to become skilled workers in sheet metal or carpentry. Left unchecked, that kind of thinking leads to bigotry and prejudice and looking down on people who are different from you. This attitude can work in reverse when you become envious, jealous or spiteful about those who have more than you do. Sampling slices of life outside your own milieu is the best cure for that.

Travel broadens the mind and I soon learned to understand, appreciate, and enjoy people who are different from me. To be a winner, I'm convinced it helps if you're a well-rounded, tolerant, and understanding person. Meeting so many people from different walks of life gave me valuable social confidence. I learned a lot of the social graces by trial and error and can now deal with royalty as easily as the guy next door (who seems to be a lot more fun to talk to in most cases), so I'm never totally out of my depth.

Another key to my success was learning how to learn, and serving time in the University of Life extends that concept beyond the borders of conventional education. Experience is the best teacher and the quest for knowledge is only successful when you're able to ask questions and recognize the answers when you see them. On the team, we had to learn fast. We weren't afraid to make mistakes, provided we learned from them. We also learned to believe in the old cliché that there's no substitute for hard work. It really *does* work. You just keep your nose to the grindstone until you succeed.

Success can be measured in many ways. I guess I always try to make a game of life and seeking success is an enjoyable part of the game. I take great pleasure in riding my bike with the Queen City Club and winning a Thursday night sprint. That doesn't mean a thing to anyone besides the other guys in the club and even they forget about it a few minutes later. I don't because I'm not a real bike racer and it's fun to try hard, to plan my race, to push myself, and maybe win.

Hard-earned success gives you valuable inner confidence and self-assurance to better handle whatever life throws at you. It helps you to plow ahead through each day without being plagued by self-doubt . . . at least not too much! Many people go through life wondering if they're doing the right thing, not knowing if they're in the right job, or even if they're having fun. My response would be, "Are you being the best you can be?" That's what really counts. That's the bottom line.

Becoming the best Downhill racer in the world completely changed my life. But *trying* to succeed, putting all that effort into it, changed it more because it made me stronger. Fighting against the odds and the unfairness, coming back from the injuries and the defeats were more important than winning the World Cup Downhill Championship. Many people have tragedies and setbacks that affect them adversely for the rest of their lives. I was very, very lucky to be able to scramble back from failures and I was fortunate to have had wonderful people around to help me make a go of it again.

I keep my World Cup in the basement of my office and seldom look at it, but many of my trophies and assorted items of skiing memorabilia are at our chalet in Craigleith. The place is like a museum and my mom is the custodian. The medals and ribbons and cups are mostly just symbols of races to me and receiving them was simply a token of recognition from others at the time. What really matters to me now is the memories they bring back.

There's a picture of me on skis, aged five or six, with a primitive little ski suit on, and I'm wearing a little headband and have a brushcut. It's quite hilarious! One poster shows me in South America wearing the frayed old Downhill suit my mother sewed for me that first year I was on the team. Beside it is another poster, produced by the federal government to promote Canada in Europe, with an image of me as the World Cup Downhill Champion skiing down a hill kicking up a dust of stylized maple leaves. I've got the binding that snapped in one of my big wipeouts, at Val Gardena in 1978 . . . maybe I should get that bronzed.

All I've got to show from the 1976 Winter Olympics, when I sat miserably at home with my leg in a cast, is a funny poster my mom brought back from Innsbruck. She got it as a souvenir for her wounded son, not realizing it was a cartoon of a skier taking a pee. It hangs in our bathroom. There's a whole collection of badges like *Go Podborski Go* and *We Ski Like Podborski* – something which was very tough to do, especially for Podborski.

Downstairs I've got my Fischer ski bag with my name on it. My old G-1's are in there, my favourite pair which won me five or six races. Those skis went to war with me and they're battered and worn after all that rattling and shaking in so many mountain battles. They're taped up around the tips because they were broken so often, including the time I took them on that wild ride through the fence at Kitzbühel. When I run my fingers along what's left of the metal edges, I remember all the work my ski man Hans Ramelmuller put into them. They're filed away to almost nothing and the bases are full of gouges where I hit rocks. Hans would flip out if he saw me handling them because even the natural oil in your fingers gets into the bases and slows you down.

Just seeing those skis makes my heart pound. And sometimes, so I'm told, when I'm lying in bed asleep and dreaming with a smile on my face, I sit up and say, "It's a great day for the race!"

. . . And it always will be for the kid from Don Mills who could ski fast.

15. Statistics

Born: 25 July, 1957, Don Mills, Ontario

1973-74: Raced on Canadian Team in CAN AM series; won Downhill at Whistler, B.C.

1974-75: Raced on Canadian World Cup Team; won North American Junior Downhill, Whitefish, Montana.

1975-76: Badly injured right knee in fall at Kitzbühel.

1976-77: North American Junior Downhill Champion and Canadian Slalom Champion; ranked 25th in World Cup Downhill.

1977-78: Seventh in the World Championships at Garmisch-Partenkirchen; ranked 15th in the World Cup Downhill.

1978-79: Won first World Cup Downhill, at Morzine.

1979-80: Won Bronze Medal in the Winter Olympics at Lake Placid (the first Canadian male skier to win an Olympic medal); named Ontario Athlete of the Year 1980; re-injured right knee in fall in training run; ranked ninth in Downhill.

1980-81: Won World Cup Downhill Races at St. Moritz, Garmisch-Partenkirchen, and Kitzbühel; won CP Air Award as Sports Federation Athlete of the Month for December, 1980 and January, 1981; Ontario Amateur Athlete of the Year 1981; winner of John Semmelink Award from the Canadian Ski Association; winner of Norton Crowe Award as Male Athlete of the Year 1981; named *Ski Racing*'s 1981 Canadian Alpine Skier of the Year; finished second in Downhill points; ranked first in International Ski Federation Downhill.

1981-82: Won World Cup Downhill races at Crans-Montana, Kitzbühel, and Garmisch-Partenkirchen; named World Cup
Downhill Champion (the first non-European winner); winner
of the Norton Crowe Award as Male Athlete of the Year 1982;
winner of World Champion Award from the Government of
Canada; named *Ski Racing*'s 1982 Canadian Alpine Skier of
the Year; ranked first in Downhill.

1982-83: Winner of Excellence Award from the Government of
Ontario in January, 1983; injured left knee in fall at Aspen,
February, 1983; made an Officer of the Order of Canada;
ranked 11th in Downhill.

1983-84: Won eighth and final World Cup Downhill race at Garmisch-Partenkirchen; 1984 Canadian National Alpine Champion; named 1984 *Ski Racing*'s Canadian Male Alpine Skier of
the Year; ranked fifth in Downhill; retired in March of 1984.

1985: Inducted into the Canadian Amateur Sports Hall of Fame.

1987: Inducted into the Canadian Sports Hall of Fame.

THE MEN'S WORLD CUP DOWNHILL RESULTS
DURING THE CRAZY CANUCK ERA

Note: World Cup points are awarded on the basis of 25 for first
place in a race, 20 for second, 15 for third, and so on down to 1
point for 15th place, with a competitor's best five races to count at
the end of the season. (N.B. Certain finishing times were unavailable
in following statistics.)

1974-75

CANADIAN WORLD CUP SQUAD: Gary Aiken, Yvon Blackburn, Alain
Cousineau, Russell Goodman, Phil Graves, Jim Hunter, Dave
Irwin, Bob Miller, David Murray, STEVE PODBORSKI, Ken Read,
Rob Safrata.

CAN-AM SQUAD: Jeff Armstrong, Jean Beaulieu, Daniel Bergeron,
Yves Blackburn, Steve Hamilton, John Hilland, Terry Howe,

Keith Humfrey, Tom Irwin, Dave Lambert, Joey Lavigne, Tom Prochazka, Sean Russell.

TALENT SQUAD: Germain Barrette, Steve Gilmour, Doug Hardman, Peter Monod, Phil Monod, Kim Pearce, Craig Podborski, Michel Pratte, Raymond Pratte.

Val d'Isère, France: 8 December, 1974

1.	Franz Klammer, Austria	2:03.19
2.	Werner Grissmann, Austria	2:04.01
3.	Michael Veith, West Germany	2:04.09
23.	Dave Murray, Canada	2:07.70
28.	Jim Hunter, Canada	2:08.51
30.	Ken Read, Canada	2:08.67
31.	Dave Irwin, Canada	2:09.11
31.	STEVE PODBORSKI, Canada	2:09.11
37.	Gary Aiken, Canada	2:09.57

St. Moritz, Switzerland: 15 December, 1974

1.	Franz Klammer, Austria	1:54.72
2.	Herbert Plank, Italy	1:56.08
3.	Werner Grissmann, Austria	1:56.60
12.	Jim Hunter, Canada	1:58.54
23.	STEVE PODBORSKI, Canada	1:59.57
24.	Gary Aiken, Canada	1:59.87
26.	Ken Read, Canada	2:00.24
47.	Dave Irwin, Canada	2:03.65
DSQ:	Dave Murray, Canada	

Garmisch-Partenkirchen, West Germany: 5 January, 1975

1.	Franz Klammer, Austria	1:43.31
2.	Werner Grissmann, Austria	1:44.70
3.	Josef Walcher, Austria	1:44.96
17.	Gary Aiken, Canada	1:46.73
23.	Dave Irwin, Canada	1:47.13
25.	Jim Hunter, Canada	1:47.27
29.	Ken Read, Canada	1:47.40

42. Dave Murray, Canada 1:48.67

Wengen, Switzerland: 11 January, 1975
1. Franz Klammer, Austria 2:35.19
2. Herbert Plank, Italy 2:38.73
3. Erik Haker, Norway 2:38.85

16. Jim Hunter, Canada 2:41.71
17. Dave Murray, Canada 2:41.91
31. Dave Irwin, Canada 2:44.21
36. Gary Aiken, Canada 2:44.79
DNS: STEVE PODBORSKI

Kitzbühel, Austria: 18 January, 1975
1. Franz Klammer, Austria 2:03.22
2. Gustavo Thoeni, Italy 2:03.23
3. Werner Grissmann, Austria 2:03.30

14. Dave Murray, Canada 2:06.00
15. Dave Irwin, Canada 2:06.15
19. Ken Read, Canada 2:06.67
21. Jim Hunter, Canada 2:06.73
34. Gary Aiken, Canada 2:09.46
36. STEVE PODBORSKI, Canada 2:10.15

Innsbruck, Austria: 26 January, 1975
1. Franz Klammer, Austria 1:55.78
2. Bernhard Russi, Switzerland 1:56.27
3. Herbert Plank, Italy 1:56.61

6. Dave Irwin, Canada 1:57.38
10. Jim Hunter, Canada 1:57.90
16. Ken Read, Canada 1:59.05
19. STEVE PODBORSKI, Canada 1:59.20
22. Dave Murray, Canada 1:59.31

Chamonix, France, 1 February, 1975
1. Walter Vesti, Switzerland 2:03.11
2. Rene Berthod, Switzerland 2:03.18

3. Philippe Roux, Switzerland 2:03.79

8. Ken Read, Canada 2:06.14
11. Dave Murray, Canada 2:07.02
12. Jim Hunter, Canada 2:07.19
15. STEVE PODBORSKI, Canada 2:07.67
31. Dave Irwin, Canada 2:09.62
37. Gary Aiken, Canada 2:10.83

Jackson Hole, Wyoming, USA: 9 March, 1975
1. Franz Klammer, Austria 1:55.64
2. Michael Veith, West Germany 1:57.82
3. Rene Berthod, Switzerland 1:57.84

11. Jim Hunter, Canada 1:59.22
18. STEVE PODBORSKI, Canada 2:00.84
19. Gary Aiken, Canada 2:01.10
21. Bob Miller, Canada 2:01.74
23. Dave Murray, Canada 2:02.50
26. Dave Irwin, Canada 2:02.89
30. Rob Safrata, Canada 2:03.83
33. Yvon Blackburn, Canada 2:04.92
36. Kim Pearce, Canada 2:06.66

Val Gardena, Italy: 21 March, 1975
1. Franz Klammer, Austria 2:01.22
2. Erik Haker, Norway 2:01.84
3. Bernhard Russi, Switzerland 2:02.27

1974-75
World Cup Downhill Final Point Standings
1. Franz Klammer, Austria 125
2. Werner Grissmann, Austria 81
3. Herbert Plank, Italy 71

1975-76

CANADIAN WORLD CUP SQUAD: Jim Hunter, Dave Irwin, Bob Miller, Dave Murray, STEVE PODBORSKI, Ken Read.

EUROPA CUP SQUAD: Yvon Blackburn, John Hilland, Keith Humfrey, Rob Safrata.

CAN AM SQUAD: Germaine Barrette, Jean Beaulieu, Joey Lavigne, Jack Woods.

TRAINING SQUAD: Peter Monod, Phil Monod, Raymond Pratte.

Val d'Isère, France: 7 December, 1975

1. Ken Read, Canada 2:04.97
2. Herbert Plank, Italy 2:05.58
3. Bernhard Russi, Switzerland 2:05.62

4. Dave Irwin, Canada 2:05.78
9. Jim Hunter, Canada 2:07.11
10. STEVE PODBORSKI, Canada 2:07.28
13. Dave Murray, Canada 2:07.86

Madonna di Campiglio, Italy: 12 December, 1975

1. Franz Klammer, Austria 1:39.95
2. Philippe Roux, Switzerland 1:40.89
3. Erik Haker, Norway 1:40.92

4. Dave Irwin, Canada 1:41.21
11. Ken Read, Canada 1:42.22
15. Dave Murray, Canada 1:42.66
16. STEVE PODBORSKI, Canada 1:42.85
17. Jim Hunter, Canada 1:42.89

Schladming, Austria: 20 December, 1975

1. Dave Irwin, Canada 2:00.84
2. Klaus Eberhard, Austria 2:02.45
3. Herbert Plank, Austria 2:02.51

7. Dave Murray, Canada 2:03.49
15. Jim Hunter, Canada 2:04.26
17. Ken Read, Canada 2:04.32
26. STEVE PODBORSKI, Canada 2:05.37

Wengen(1), Switzerland (Garmisch replacement): 9 January, 1976

1. Herbert Plank, Italy 2:08.48
2. Franz Klammer, Austria 2:08.68
3. Bernhard Russi, Switzerland 2:08.72

6. Jim Hunter, Canada 2:09.74
10. Dave Murray, Canada 2:10.24
11. STEVE PODBORSKI, Canada 2:10.38
12. Ken Read, Canada 2:10.46
18. Dave Irwin, Canada 2:11.51
19. Dave Currier, Canada 2:11.52

Wengen(2), Switzerland: 10 January, 1976

1. Franz Klammer, Austria 2:40.36
2. Philippe Roux, Switzerland 2:42.58
3. Jim Hunter, Canada 2:42.68

7. Dave Murray, Canada 2:44.72
8. STEVE PODBORSKI, Canada 2:44.87

Morzine-Avoriaz, France: 17 January, 1976

1. Franz Klammer, Austria 1:54.24
2. Bernhard Russi, Switzerland 1:54.33
3. Anton Steiner, Austria 1:54.88

13. Jim Hunter, Canada 1:56.93
15. Ken Read, Canada 1:57.19
20. STEVE PODBORSKI, Canada 1:57.27
31. Dave Murray, Canada 1:59.01
39. Rob Safrata, Canada 2:01.12
44. Yvon Blackburn, Canada 2:02.93

Kitzbühel, Austria: 25 January, 1976

1. Franz Klammer, Austria 2:03.79
2. Erik Haker, Norway 2:05.85
3. Josef Walcher, Austria 2:06.47

7. Jim Hunter, Canada 2:06.75
8. Dave Murray, Canada 2:06.77
11. Ken Read, Canada 2:07.25

47. Yvon Blackburn, Canada 2:15.07

Aspen, Colorado, USA: 12 March, 1976

1. Franz Klammer, Austria 1:54.12
2. Rene Berthod, Switzerland 1:54.24
3. Ernst Winkler, Austria 1:55.14

8. Ken Read, Canada 1:55.59
16. Dave Irwin, Canada 1:57.19
25. Rob Safrata, Canada 1:58.96
31. Dave Murray, Canada 1:59.88
35. Jim Hunter, Canada 2:00.73
43. Jean Beaulieu, Canada 2:02.94
45. Keith Humfrey, Canada 2:04.47

1975-76
World Cup Downhill Final Point Standings

1. Franz Klammer, Austria 125
2. Herbert Plank, Italy   77
3. Bernhard Russi, Switzerland   66

5. Dave Irwin, Canada   47

THE OLYMPIC GAMES, Innsbruck, Austria:
5 February, 1976

1. Franz Klammer, Austria 1:45.73
2. Bernhard Russi, Switzerland 1:46.06
3. Herbert Plank, Italy 1:46.59

5. Ken Read, Canada 1:46.83
8. Dave Irwin, Canada 1:47.41
10. Jim Hunter, Canada 1:47.52
18. Dave Murray, Canada 1:48.43

1976-77

CANADIAN DOWNHILL "A" TEAM: Jim Hunter, Dave Irwin, Dave
   Murray, STEVE PODBORSKI, Ken Read
"C" TEAM: Germaine Barrette, Jean Beaulieu, Yvon Blackburn, Keith

Humfrey, Peter Monod, Philip Monod, Raymond Pratte, Rob
Safrata.

Val Gardena(1), Italy: 17 December, 1976

1. Franz Klammer, Austria 2:03.83
2. Herbert Plank, Italy 2:04.91
3. Erik Haker, Norway 2:05.07

14. Dave Irwin, Canada 2:07.53
17. Ken Read, Canada 2:08.29
18. STEVE PODBORSKI, Canada 2:08.37
29. Dave Murray, Canada 2:10.71
34. Jim Hunter, Canada 2:11.72

Val Gardena(2), Italy: 18 December, 1976

1. Franz Klammer, Austria 2:05.71
2. Josef Walcher, Austria 2:06.66
3. Bernhard Russi, Switzerland 2:07.30

22. Dave Irwin, Canada 2:11.04
24. Ken Read, Canada 2:11.58
27. STEVE PODBORSKI, Canada 2:12.48
37. Dave Murray, Canada 2:15.99
38. Jim Hunter, Canada 2:16.26

Garmisch-Partenkirchen, West Germany: 8 January, 1977

1. Franz Klammer, Austria 2:02.63
2. Ernst Winkler, Austria 2:03.38
3. Peter Wirnsberger, Austria 2:04.13

39. Dave Murray, Canada 2:08.66
42. STEVE PODBORSKI, Canada 2:09.14
43. Dave Irwin, Canada 2:09.16
46. Jim Hunter, Canada 2:09.20
49. Ken Read, Canada 2:09.52

Kitzbühel, Austria: 15 January, 1977

1. Franz Klammer, Austria 2:09.71
2. Rene Berthod, Switzerland 2:10.64

3. Bernhard Russi, Switzerland 2:10.81

27. Dave Irwin, Canada 2:16.54
32. STEVE PODBORSKI, Canada 2:17.53
33. Ken Read, Canada 2:17.79
35. Dave Murray, Canada 2:18.56
42. Jim Hunter, Canada 2:20.74

Wengen, Switzerland: 22 January, 1977
1. Franz Klammer, Austria 2:35.66
2. Sepp Ferstl, West Germany 2:36.65
3. Bernhard Russi, Switzerland 2:36.78

27. Ken Read, Canada 2:40.65
29. Dave Murray, Canada 2:40.78
31. STEVE PODBORSKI, Canada 2:41.66
38. Dave Irwin, Canada 2:42.92

Morzine-Avoriaz(1), France: 30 January, 1977
1. Bernhard Russi, Switzerland 1:45.57
2. Josef Walcher, Austria 1:46.16
3. Ernst Winkler, Austria 1:46.18

27. Dave Murray, Canada 1:50.05
31. STEVE PODBORSKI, Canada 1:50.32
DNF: Ken Read, Canada

Morzine-Avoriaz(2), France: 31 January, 1977
1. Josef Walcher, Austria 1:43.61
2. Herbert Plank, Italy 1:43.70
3. Bernhard Russi, Switzerland 1:43.82

17. Ken Read, Canada 1:46.63
25. Dave Murray, Canada 1:47.56
DNF: STEVE PODBORSKI, Canada

Laax, Switzerland: 18 February, 1977
1. Franz Klammer, Austria 1:59.10
2. Sepp Ferstl, West Germany 1:59.51
3. Bernhard Russi, Switzerland 1:59.54

14. Ken Read, Canada 1:61.48

Heavenly Valley(1), California, USA: 12 March, 1977
1. Josef Walcher, Austria 1:36.44
2. Werner Grissmann, Austria 1:37.14
3. Bernhard Russi, Switzerland 1:37.20

13. STEVE PODBORSKI, Canada 1:39.94
25. Dave Murray, Canada 1:41.37
34. Raymond Pratte, Canada 1:42.85
36. Keith Humfrey, Canada 1:43.47
41. Jean Beaulieu, Canada 1:45.43
DNF: Ken Read, Canada

Heavenly Valley(2), California, USA: 13 March, 1977
1. Bartl Gensbichler, Austria 1:46.91
2. Ernst Winkler, Austria 1:47.13
3. Peter Fischer, West Germany 1:47.52

25. Ken Read,Canada 1:53.66
26. Jean Beaulieu, Canada 1:53.91
34. Raymond Pratte, Canada 1:57.87
35. Dave Murray, Canada 1:57.88
36. STEVE PODBORSKI, Canada 1:58.21
39. Keith Humfrey, Canada 2:02.41

1976-77
World Cup Downhill Final Point Standings
1. Franz Klammer, Austria   125
2. Josef Walcher, Austria   101
3. Bernhard Russi, Switzerland   85

1977-78

CANADIAN DOWNHILL "A" TEAM: STEVE PODBORSKI, Ken Read
"B" TEAM: Dave Irwin, Dave Murray
"C" TEAM: Rob Safrata, Tim Gilhooly
TRAINING SQUAD: Mike Irwin, Robin McLeish, Bob Miller, Sylvain
     Roussille, Jay McKim, Todd Brooker
DEVELOPMENT SQUAD: Bob Allison

Val d'Isère, France: 11 December, 1977

1. Franz Klammer, Austria 2:07.61
2. Herbert Plank, Italy 2:07.89
3. Joself Walcher, Austria 2:07.95

4. Ken Read, Canada 2:08.09
21. STEVE PODBORSKI, Canada 2:10.51
41. Bob Miller, Canada 2:14.26
63. Tom Gilhooly, Canada 2:33.52

Val Gardena, Italy: 18 December, 1977

1. Herbert Plank, Italy 2:01.47
2. Peter Wirnsberger, Austria 2:02.60
3. Franz Klammer, Austria 2:03.32

14. STEVE PODBORSKI, Canada 2:05.26
32. Tim Gilhooly, Canada 2:08.55
35. Bob Miller, Canada 2:09.90
37. Sylvain Roussille, Canada 2:10.13
DNF: Ken Read, Canada

Cortina d'Ampezzo, Italy: 22 December, 1977

1. Herbert Plank, Italy 1:50.99
2. Bernhard Russi, Switzerland 1:51.13
3. Peter Wirnsberger, Austria 1:51.24

9. Ken Read, Canada 1:52.21
19. STEVE PODBORSKI, Canada 1:53.15

Kitzbühel(1), Austria: 20 January, 1978

1. Josef Walcher, Austria 2:06.90
2. Walter Vesti, Switzerland 2:06.97
3. Renato Anatonioli, Italy 2:07.05

10. STEVE PODBORSKI, Canada 2:07.81
12. Ken Read, Canada 2:07.88

Kitzbühel(2), Austria: 21 January, 1978

1. Sepp Ferstl, West Germany 2:07.81
2. Josef Walcher, Austria 2:07.81
3. Michael Veith, West Germany 2:07.85

8. Ken Read, Canada 2:08.82
14. STEVE PODBORSKI, Canada 2:09.43
21. Dave Murray, Canada 2:10.72
29. Bob Miller, Canada ....

Les Houches, France: 11 February, 1978
1. Ken Read, Canada 2:08.11
2. Dave Murray, Canada 2:08.27
3. Michael Veith, West Germany 2:08.46

20. STEVE PODBORSKI, Canada 2:10.72
42. Robin McLeish, Canada 2:14.10
45. Mike Irwin, Canada 2:14.37
51. Todd Brooker, Canada 2:15.74
52. Jay McKim, Canada 2:16.27

Laax(1), Switzerland: 10 March, 1978
1. Ulrich Speiss, Austria 1:57.96
2. Franz Klammer, Austria 1:58.18
3. Erik Haker, Norway 1:58.55

4. STEVE PODBORSKI, Canada 1:58.71
6. Ken Read, Canada 1:58.82
27. Dave Murray, Canada 2:01.11

Laax(2), Switzerland: 11 March, 1978
1. Franz Klammer, Austria 1:55.76
2. Erik Haker, Norway 1:55.79
3. Ulrich Speiss, Austria 1:56.16

4. Ken Read, Canada 1:56.63
6. STEVE PODBORSKI, Canada 1:57.07
20. Dave Murray, Canada 2:00.35

1977-78
World Cup Downhill Final Point Standings
1. Franz Klammer, Austria   96
2. Josef Walcher, Austria   74
3. Herbert Plank, Italy   73

4. Ken Read, Canada   56

12. Dave Murray, Canada 20
15. STEVE PODBORSKI, Canada 18

Men's Downhill World Championships
Garmisch-Partenkirchen, West Germany:
29 January, 1978

1. Josef Walcher, Austria 2:04.12
2. Michael Veith, West Germany 2:04.19
3. Werner Grissmann, Austria 2:04.46

7. STEVE PODBORSKI, Canada 2:04.98
18. Dave Murray, Canada 2:07.50
22. Ken Read, Canada 2:08.01

1978-79

CANADIAN DOWNHILL "A" TEAM: Dave Murray, STEVE PODBORSKI, Ken Read
"B" TEAM: Dave Irwin
"C" TEAM: Todd Brooker, Tim Gilhooly, Robin McLeish, Sylvain Roussille
TRAINING SQUAD: Mike Irwin
DEVELOPMENT TEAM: Gary Athans, Scott Hutcheson, Bob Styan

Schladming, Austria: 10 December, 1978

1. Ken Read, Canada 1:32.11
2. Dave Murray, Canada 1:32.17
3. Vladimir Makeev, USSR 1:32.24

7. Dave Irwin, Canada 1:32.71
9. STEVE PODBORSKI, Canada 1:32.75
40. Mike Irwin, Canada 1:35.43
52. Sylvain Roussille, Canada 1:36.71
DNF: Tim Gilhooly, Todd Brooker

Val Gardena(1), Italy: 16 December, 1978

1. Josef Walcher, Austria 2:11.86
2. Peter Mueller, Switzerland 2:12.16
3. Walter Vesti, Switzerland 2:12.91

10. STEVE PODBORSKI, Canada 2:13.73
11. Ken Read, Canada 2:13.75
19. Dave Murray, Canada 2:15.24
DNF: Tim Gilhooly, Robin McLeish   DNS: Todd Brooker

Val Gardena(2), Italy: 17 December, 1978
1. Erik Haker, Norway 2:06.37
2. Peter Mueller, Switzerland 2:07.63
3. Ken Read, Canada 2:08.45

8. Dave Murray, Canada 2:09.36
36. Robin McLeish, Canada 2:13.38
41. Todd Brooker, Canada 2:14.54

Morzine-Avoriaz, France: 6 January, 1979
1. STEVE PODBORSKI, Canada 1:43.97
2. Herbert Plank, Italy 1:44.41
3. Ulrich Speiss, Austria 1:44.60

42. Robin McLeish, Canada 1:48.46
47. Mike Irwin, Canada 1:50.01
DSQ: Ken Read, Dave Murray

Crans-Montana, Switzerland: 14 January, 1979
1. Toni Buergler, Switzerland 1:58.19
2. Peter Mueller, Switzerland 1:58.43
3. Ken Read, Canada 1:59.10

7. STEVE PODBORSKI, Canada 2:00.24
9. Dave Murray, Canada 2:00.60
15. Mike Irwin, Canada 2:00.97
    Tim Gilhooly, Canada 2:00.97
17. Robin McLeish, Canada 2:01.05
23. Dave Irwin, Canada 2:01.30

Kitzbühel, Austria: 20 January, 1979
1. Sepp Firstl, West Germany 2:04.48
2. Peter Wirnsberger, Austria 2:04.68
3. Ulrich Speiss, Austria 2:05.45

8. STEVE PODBORSKI, Canada 2:06.01

| 10. | Ken Read, Canada | 2:06.15 |
| 22. | Dave Murray, Canada | 2:08.62 |

Garmisch-Partenkirchen, West Germany: 27 January, 1979

1.	Peter Wirnsberger, Austria	1:57.44
2.	Ulrich Speiss, Austria	1:57.82
3.	Herbert Plank, Italy	1:57.85
13.	Ken Read, Canada	1:58.83
17.	Dave Irwin, Canada	1:59.25

Villars, Switzerland: 1 February, 1979

1.	Peter Mueller, Switzerland	1:45.97
2.	Leonhard Stock, Austria	1:46.19
3.	Werner Grissmann, Austria	1:46.20
22.	Dave Murray, Canada	1:47.89
30.	Ken Read, Canada	1:48.48
34.	Dave Irwin, Canada	1:48.61
38.	STEVE PODBORSKI, Canada	1:48.87

Lake Placid, N.Y., USA: 3 March, 1979

1.	Peter Wirnsberger, Austria	1:42.88
2.	Peter Mueller, Switzerland	1:42.91
3.	Dave Murray, Canada	1:42.99
7.	Ken Read, Canada	1:44.13
8.	STEVE PODBORSKI, Canada	1:44.17
20.	Dave Irwin, Canada	1:45.50
41.	Mike Irwin, Canada	1:48.13
47.	Bob Styan, Canada	1:48.77
48.	Robin McLeish, Canada	1:48.90
49.	Germain Barrette, Canada	1:48.98
51.	Todd Brooker, Canada	1:49.19
53.	Chris Kent, Canada	1:49.31

1978-79
World Cup Downhill Final Point Standings

1. Peter Mueller, Switzerland 109
2. Peter Wirnsberger, Austria 89
3. Toni Buergler, Switzerland 80

4. Ken Read, Canada 75
10. STEVE PODBORSKI, Canada 52
    Dave Murray, Canada 52
33. Dave Irwin, Canada 10

1979-80

CANADIAN DOWNHILL "A" TEAM: Dave Irwin, Dave Murray, STEVE PODBORSKI, Ken Read
"C" TEAM: Todd Brooker, Tim Gilhooly, Mike Irwin, Robin McLeish, Sylvain Roussille

Val d'Isère, France: 7 December, 1979

1. Peter Wirnsberger, Austria 2:01.83
2. Herbert Plank, Italy 2:02.13
3. Erik Haker,Norway 2:02.37

9. Dave Murray, Canada 2:03.76
14. Dave Irwin, Canada 2:03.96
27. Chris Kent, Canada 2:05.48
51. Mike Irwin, Canada 2:07.54
60. Craig Podborski, Canada 2:08.58
DNF: Ken Read, STEVE PODBORSKI, Robin McLeish, Tim Gilhooly, Bob Styan

Val Gardena, Italy: 16 December, 1979

1. Peter Mueller, Switzerland 2:03.94
2. Erik Haker, Norway 2:04.72
3. Werner Grissmann, Austria 2:04.84

7. Ken Read, Canada 2:05.96
8. Tim Gilhooly, Canada 2.06.28
11. Dave Murray, Canada 2:06.45
17. Robin McLeish, Canada 2:06.74

25.	Mike Irwin, Canada	2:07.52
40.	Chris Kent, Canada	2:08.56
45.	STEVE PODBORSKI, Canada	2:08.69
47.	Bob Styan, Canada	2:08.82
56.	Dave Irwin, Canada	2:09.39
58.	Craig Podborski, Canada	2:09.48

Pra-Loup, France: 6 January, 1980

1.	Peter Mueller, Switzerland	1:53.56
2.	Herbert Plank, Italy	1:54.37
3.	Erik Haker, Norway	1:54.44

14.	Ken Read, Canada	1:55.60
15.	Dave Murray, Canada	1:55.64
19.	Robin McLeish, Canada	1:56.16
24.	Tim Gilhooly, Canada	1:56.35
30.	Dave Irwin, Canada	1:56.67
40.	Chris Kent, Canada	
42.	Bob Styan, Canada	
56.	Mike Irwin, Canada	1:58.60
61.	Craig Podborski, Canada	1:59.20

DNF: STEVE PODBORSKI

Kitzbühel, Austria: 12 January, 1980

1.	Ken Read, Canada	2:04.93
2.	Harti Weirather, Austria	2:05.51
3.	Herbert Plank, Italy	2:05.61

5.	Dave Irwin, Canada	2:05.89
17.	Dave Murray, Canada	2:07.32
27.	Mike Irwin, Canada	2:08.59
51.	Robin McLeish, Canada	2:12.34

DNF: STEVE PODBORSKI

Wengen(1), Switzerland: 18 January, 1980

1.	Ken Read, Canada	2:31.31
2.	Josef Walcher, Austria	2:31.34
3.	Peter Wirnsberger, Austria	2:31.58

| 8. | STEVE PODBORSKI, Canada | 2:32.20 |

25. Dave Murray, Canada 2:34.67
36. Mike Irwin, Canada 2:36.57
48. Robin McLeish, Canada 2:39.62
DNF: Dave Irwin

Wengen(2), Switzerland: 19 January, 1980
1. Peter Mueller, Switzerland 2:30.56
2. Ken Read, Canada 2:30.58
3. STEVE PODBORSKI, Canada 2:30.66

19. Dave Murray, Canada 2:33.56
DSQ: Mike Irwin, Robin McLeish

Lake Louise, Alberta, Canada, 4 March, 1980
1. Herbert Plank, Italy 1:50.47
2. Harti Weirather, Austria 1:51.24
3. Werner Grissmann, Austria 1:51.47

4. STEVE PODBORSKI, Canada 1:51.76
8. Ken Read, Canada 1:52.39
12. Dave Irwin, Canada 1:52.89
21. Dave Murray, Canada ....
31. Mike Irwin, Canada ....
39. Gary Athans, Canada ....
40. Scott Hutcheson, Canada ....
41. Greg Hann, Canada ....
44. Germain Barrette, Canada ....
49. Craig Podborski, Canada ....
52. Chris Kent, Canada ....
56. David Roth, Canada ....
DNF: Robin McLeish

1979-80
World Cup Downhill Final Point Standings
1. Peter Mueller. Switzerland 96
2. Ken Read, Canada 87
3. Herbert Plank, Italy 81

9. STEVE PODBORSKI, Canada 35
17. Dave Irwin, Canada 17

24. Tim Gilhooly, Canada 8

**THE OLYMPIC GAMES: Lake Placid, N.Y., USA:
14 February, 1980**

1. Leonhard Stock, Austria 1:45.50
2. Peter Wirnsberger. Austria 1:46.12
3. STEVE PODBORSKI, Canada 1:46.62

10. Dave Murray, Canada 1:47.95
11. Dave Irwin, Canada 1:48.12
DNF: Ken Read

1980-81

CANADIAN DOWNHILL "A" TEAM: Dave Irwin, Dave Murray, STEVE
  PODBORSKI, Ken Read
"B" TEAM: Tim Gilhooly, Robin McLeish
"C" TEAM: Todd Brooker, Chris Kent, Doug Kerr, Brian O'Rourke,
  Bob Styan

Val d'Isère, France: 7 December, 1980

1. Uli Speiss, Austria 2:00.15
2. Ken Read, Canada 2:00.52
3. STEVE PODBORSKI, Canada 2:00.71

4. Chris Kent, Canada 2:01.24
5. Dave Irwin, Canada 2:01.33
7. Dave Murray, Canada 2:01.48
17. Tim Gilhooly, Canada ....
26. Robin McLeish, Canada ....
31. Brian O'Rourke, Canada ....
38. Bob Styan, Canada ....
50. Doug Kerr, Canada ....

Val Gardena(1), Italy: 14 December, 1980

1. Peter Mueller, Switzerland 2:01.24
2. Harti Weirather, Austria 2:01.59
3. STEVE PODBORSKI, Canada 2:02.00

11. Ken Read, Canada 2:03.13

14. Dave Murray, Canada 2:03.33
27. Dave Irwin, Canada 2:04.11
42. Robin McLeish, Canada 2:05.59
DNF: Chris Kent

Val Gardena(2), Italy: 15 December, 1980

1. Harti Weirather, Austria 1:52.96
2. Uli Speiss, Austria 1:53.09
3. Peter Mueller, Switzerland 1:53.36

6. Ken Read, Canada 1:53.90
10. STEVE PODBORSKI, Canada 1:54.26
11. Dave Murray, Canada 1:54.30
31. Robin McLeish, Canada 1:55.64
48. Tim Gilhooly, Canada 1:56.98
DNS: Dave Irwin

St. Moritz, Switzerland: 21 December, 1980

1. STEVE PODBORSKI, Canada 1:54.31
2. Peter Wirnsberger, Austria 1:54.51
3. Peter Mueller, Switzerland 1:54.88

9. Ken Read, Canada 1:55.36
11. Dave Irwin, Canada 1:55.56
14. Dave Murray, Canada 1:55.92
21. Robin McLeish, Canada ....
DNF: Tim Gilhooly

Garmisch, West Germany: 10 January, 1981

1. STEVE PODBORSKI, Canada 1:55.48
2. Peter Mueller, Switzerland 1:56.05
3. Harti Weirather, Austria 1:56.31

12. Dave Irwin, Canada 1:58.32
14. Dave Murray, Canada 1:58.35
28. Robin McLeish, Canada ....
31. Tim Gilhooly, Canada 1:59.58
DNF: Ken Read

Kitzbühel, Austria: 17 January, 1981

1. STEVE PODBORSKI, Canada 2:03.76
2. Peter Mueller, Switzerland 2:04.16
3. Peter Wirnsberger, Austria 2:04.74

23. Dave Murray, Canada ....
29. Robin McLeish, Canada ....
DNF: Tim Gilhooly, Dave Irwin

Wengen, Switzerland: 24 January, 1981

1. Toni Buergler, Switzerland 2:27.91
2. Harti Weirather, Austria 2:28.27
3. STEVE PODBORSKI, Canada 2:28.46

25. Dave Irwin, Canada ....
27. Dave Murray, Canada ....
37. Tim Gilhooly, Canada ....
38. Robin McLeish, Canada ....

St. Anton, Austria: 31 January, 1981

1. Harti Weirather, Austria 1:59.67
2. Peter Wirnsberger, Austria 1:59.73
3. STEVE PODBORSKI, Canada 2:00.15

22. Todd Brooker, Canada 2:02.29
    Tim Gilhooly, Canada 2:02.29
26. Dave Irwin, Canada 2:02.58
30. Robin McLeish, Canada 2:02.89
37. Brian O'Rourke, Canada 2:02.23
49. Bob Styan, Canada 2:04.58
50. Doug Kerr, Canada 2:04.77

Aspen(1), Colorado, USA: 5 March, 1981

1. Valeri Tsyganov, USSR 1:52.95
2. Harti Weirather, Austria 1:53.11
3. G. Pfaffenbichler, Austria 1:53.18

10. STEVE PODBORSKI, Canada 1:54.35
13. Dave Irwin, Canada 1:54.57
27. Robin McLeish, Canada ....
30. Brian O'Rourke, Canada ....

31. Gary Athans, Canada ....
32. Bob Styan, Canada ....
34. Doug Kerr, Canada ....
37. Bill Irwin, Canada ....
DNF: Todd Brooker, Dave Murray

Aspen(2), Colorado, USA: 6 March, 1981
1. Harti Weirather, Austria 1:52.21
2. STEVE PODBORSKI, Canada 1:52.49
3. Franz Heinzer, Switzerland 1:52.59

21. Dave Murray, Canada ....
23. Dave Irwin, Canada ....
34. Robin McLeish, Canada ....
36. Brian O'Rourke, Canada ....
38. Todd Brooker, Canada ....
40. Gary Athans, Canada ....
43. Bob Styan, Canada ....

1980-81
World Cup Downhill Final Points Standing
1. Harti Weirather, Austria 115
2. STEVE PODBORSKI, Canada 110
3. Peter Mueller, Switzerland 95

12. Ken Read, Canada 42
20. Dave Irwin, Canada 23
22. Dave Murray, Canada 20
27. Chris Kent, Canada 12

1981-82

CANADIAN DOWNHILL "A" TEAM: Dave Irwin, Robin McLeish, Dave Murray, STEVE PODBORSKI, Ken Read
"C" TEAM: Gary Athans, Todd Brooker, Chris Kent, Doug Kerr, Brian O'Rourke, Bob Styan
TRAINING SQUAD: Felix Belczyk

Val d'Isère, **France: 6 December, 1981**

1. Franz Klammer, Austria 2:05.22
2. Peter Mueller, Switzerland 2:05.48
3. Toni Buergler, Switzerland 2:05.63

4. STEVE PODBORSKI, Canada 2:05.70
5. Ken Read, Canada 2:06.09
21. Todd Brooker, Canada 2:08.60
22. Dave Murray, Canada 2:08.61
24. Dave Irwin, Canada 2:08.66
29. Robin McLeish, Canada 2:09.24
41. Doug Kerr, Canada ....
56. Brian O'Rourke, Canada ....
58. Bob Styan, Canada ....
DNF: Chris Kent

Val Gardena, **Italy: 13 December, 1981**

1. Erwin Resch, Austria 2:07.41
2. Konrad Bartelski, UK 2:07.52
3. Leonhard Stock, Austria 2:07.81

4. STEVE PODBORSKI, Canada 2:07.91
14. Todd Brooker, Canada 2:09.34
16. Dave Murray, Canada 2:09.52
24. Robin McLeish, Canada 2:09.93
    Ken Read, Canada 2:09.93
35. Chris Kent, Canada 2:10.90

Crans-Montana, **Switzerland: 21 December, 1981**

1. STEVE PODBORSKI, Canada 2.09.22
2. Peter Mueller, Switzerland 2:09.37
3. Ken Read, Canada 2:09.83

14. Todd Brooker, Canada 2:11.17
30. Chris Kent, Canada 2:12.72
32. Dave Murray, Canada 2:12.97

35. Robin McLeish, Canada 2:13.07

Kitzbühel(1), Austria: 15 January, 1982

1. Harti Weirather, Austria 1:57.20
2. STEVE PODBORSKI, Canada 1:57.89
3. Ken Read, Canada 1:57.97

13. Todd Brooker, Canada 1:59.20
21. Dave Murray, Canada ....
26. Dave Irwin, Canada ....
30. Chris Kent, Canada ....
42. Robin McLeish, Canada ....
47. Doug Kerr, Canada ....

Kitzbühel(2), Austria: 16 January, 1982

1. STEVE PODBORSKI, Canada 1:57.24
2. Franz Klammer, Austria 1:57.78
3. Ken Read, Canada 1:57.90

11. Dave Murray, Canada 1:58.68
20. Todd Brooker, Canada 1:59.76
23. Dave Irwin, Canada 2:00.44
29. Chris Kent, Canada 2:00.79
33. Robin McLeish, Canada 2:01.11
DNF: Doug Kerr

Wengen, Switzerland: 24 January, 1982

1. Harti Weirather, Austria 2:04.43
2. Erwin Resch, Austria 2:04.93
3. Peter Wirnsberger, Austria 2:04.96

11. STEVE PODBORSKI, Canada 2:06.43
23. Ken Read, Canada ....
27. Chris Kent, Canada ....
35. Dave Murray, Canada ....
38. Dave Irwin, Canada ....
47. Robin McLeish, Canada ....
49. Todd Brooker, Canada ....
62. Doug Kerr, Canada ....

Garmisch-Partenkirchen, West Germany: 13 February, 1982

1. STEVE PODBORSKI, Canada 1:50.52
2. Conrad Cathomen, Switzerland 1:50.81
3. Harti Weirather, Austria 1:50.94

15. Todd Brooker, Canada 1:52.25
19. Dave Murray, Canada 1:52.75
20. Ken Read, Canada 1:52.98
26. Robin McLeish, Canada 1:53.32
34. Dave Irwin, Canada 1:54.21
39. Chris Kent, Canada 1:54.76

Whistler, B.C., Canada: 27 February, 1982

1. Peter Mueller, Switzerland 2:14.38
2. STEVE PODBORSKI, Canada 2:15.53
3. Dave Irwin, Canada 2:15.73

5. Todd Brooker, Canada 2:16.37
7. Ken Read, Canada 2:16.62
13. Bob Styan, Canada 2:17.85
23. Chris Kent, Canada 2:19.09
30. Doug Kerr, Canada 2:19.52
34. Robin McLeish, Canada 2:19.83
36. Dave Murray, Canada 2:19.99
37. Felix Belczyk, Canada 2:20.04
43. Paul Boivin, Canada 2:20.66
44. Jeff MacInnis, Canada 2:20.68
47. Gary Athans, Canada 2:21.52
51. Brian Fry, Canada 2:22.08
52. Derek Trussler, Canada 2:22.73
DNF: Bob Talbot

Aspen(1), Colorado, USA: 5 March, 1982

1. Peter Mueller, Switzerland 1:47.17
2. Harti Weirather, Austria 1:47.28
3. Conrad Cathomen, Switzerland 1:47.55

8. Ken Read, Canada 1:48.03
9. Todd Brooker, Canada 1:48.06

13.	Dave Irwin, Canada	1:48.51
14.	STEVE PODBORSKI, Canada	1:48.84
26.	Dave Murray, Canada	1:49.88
34.	Robin McLeish, Canada	1:50.56
43.	Gary Athans, Canada	1:51.70
44.	Chris Kent, Canada	1:51.79
45.	Felix Belczyk, Canada	1:51.83
48.	Doug Kerr, Canada	1:52.12

Aspen(2), Colorado, USA: 6 March, 1982

1.	Peter Mueller, Switzerland	1:46.50
2.	Todd Brooker, Canada	1:47.18
3.	Helmut Hoeflehner, Austria	1:47.31
7.	Dave Irwin, Canada	1:47.90
14.	STEVE PODBORSKI, Canada	1:48.67
20.	Bob Styan, Canada	1:49.51
26.	Robin McLeish, Canada	1:49.91
35.	Dave Murray, Canada	1:50.44
40.	Gary Athans, Canada	1:50.67
44.	Jeff MacInnis, Canada	1:51.43
45.	Paul Boivin, Canada	1:51.86

1981-82
World Cup Downhill Final Point Standings

1.	STEVE PODBORSKI, Canada	115
2.	Peter Mueller, Switzerland	115
3.	Harti Weirather, Austria	97
6.	Ken Read, Canada, Canada	65
14.	Todd Brooker, Canada	43
16.	Dave Irwin, Canada	27
31.	Dave Murray, Canada	5
33.	Bob Styan, Canada	3

Men's Downhill World Championships
Schladming, Austria: 6 February, 1982

1.	Harti Weirather, Austria	1:55.10
2.	Conrad Cathomen, Switzerland	1:55.58
3.	Erwin Resch, Austria	1:55.73

9.	STEVE PODBORSKI, Canada	1:56.78
11.	Dave Murray, Canada	1:56.94
13.	Todd Brooker, Canada	1:57.16
14.	Ken Read, Canada	1:57.18

1982-83

CANADIAN DOWNHILL "A" TEAM: Todd Brooker, Robin McLeish, STEVE PODBORSKI, Ken Read
"B" TEAM: Bob Styan
"C" TEAM: Doug Kerr, Chris Kent, Brian O'Rourke, Gary Athans, Felix Belczyk
TRAINING SQUAD: Bob Talbot, Scott Shaver, Chris McIver, Derek Trussler, Paul Boivin, Brian Fry, Stan Hanson, Jeff MacInnis

Pontresina, Switzerland: 5 December, 1982

1.	Harti Weirather, Austria	1:42.13
2.	Franz Klammer, Austria	1:43.15
3.	Peter Mueller, Switzerland	1:43.21
6.	Ken Read, Canada	1:43.44
12.	STEVE PODBORSKI, Canada	1:44.12
36.	Todd Brooker, Canada	1:45.45
41.	Felix Belczyk, Canada	1:45.58
46.	Robin McLeish, Canada	1:45.95
49.	Chris Kent, Canada	1:46.26
50.	Gary Athans, Canada	1:46.34
56.	Bob Styan, Canada	1:46.57
60.	Brian O'Rourke, Canada	1:47.13
64.	Doug Kerr, Canada	1:47.49

Val Gardena(1), Italy: 19 December, 1982

1.	Conrad Cathomen, Switzerland	2:09.54
2.	Erwin Resch, Austria	2:09.87
3.	Franz Klammer, Austria	2:10.09
5.	Ken Read, Canada	2:10.39
11.	Todd Brooker, Canada	2:11.35
24.	STEVE PODBORSKI, Canada	2:12.81
31.	Chris Kent, Canada	2:13.09

37. Bob Styan, Canada 2:13.46
41. Robin McLeish, Canada 2:13.85
60. Doug Kerr, Canada 2:14.80

Val Gardena(2), Italy: 20 December, 1982
1. Franz Klammer, Austria 2:08.91
2. Peter Mueller, Switzerland 2:09.39
3. Urs Raeber, Switzerland 2:09.61

6. Todd Brooker, Canada 2:10.58
7. Ken Read, Canada 2:10.61
17. STEVE PODBORSKI, Canada 2:12.21
37. Robin McLeish, Canada 2:14.09

Val d'Isère(1), France: 9 January, 1983
1. Erwin Resch, Austria 1:59.26
2. Peter Luescher, Switzerland 1:59.44
3. Conrad Cathomen. Switzerland 1:59.56

4. Ken Read, Canada 1:59.57
27. Paul Boivin, Canada ....
31. Felix Belczyk, Canada ....
35. Gary Athans, Canada ....
37. Robin McLeish, Canada ....
44. Doug Kerr, Canada ....
46. Chris Kent, Canada ....
51. Bob Styan, Canada ....
DNF: Todd Brooker, STEVE PODBORSKI

Val d'Isère(2), France: 10 January, 1983
1. Conrad Cathomen, Switzerland 1:59.20
2. Ken Read, Canada 1:59.32
3. Danilo Sbardellotto, Italy 1:59.66

20. Robin McLeish, Canada ....
27. Felix Belczyk, Canada ....
34. STEVE PODBORSKI, Canada ....
44. Bob Styan, Canada ....
46. Gary Athans, Canada ....
47. Chris Kent, Canada ....

49. Doug Kerr, Canada ....

Kitzbühel(1), Austria: 21 January, 1983
1. Bruno Kernen, Switzerland 2:06.68
2. STEVE PODBORSKI, Canada 2:06.79
3. Urs Raeber, Switzerland 2:07.19

13. Robin McLeish, Canada 2:08.41
    Ken Read, Canada 2:08.41
17. Todd Brooker, Canada ....
26. Chris Kent, Canada ....
27. Doug Kerr, Canada ....
35. Felix Belczyk, Canada ....
45. Paul Boivin, Canada ....

Kitzbühel(2), Austria: 22 January, 1983
1. Todd Brooker, Canada 2:01.96
2. Urs Raeber, Switzerland 2:02.19
3. Ken Read, Canada 2:02.47

9. STEVE PODBORSKI, Canada 2:03.20
20. Robin McLeish, Canada ....
27. Chris Kent, Canada ....
30. Felix Belczyk, Canada ....
38. Doug Kerr, Canada ....
DNF: Paul Boivin, Canada

Sarajevo, Jugoslavia: 28 January, 1983
1. G. Pfaffenbichler, Austria 1:48.81
2. STEVE PODBORSKI, Canada 1:49.02
3. Franz Klammer, Austria 1:49.07

5. Ken Read, Canada 1:49.76
14. Todd Brooker, Canada 1:50.94
32. Chris Kent, Canada 1:53.42
DNF: Robin McLeish, Doug Kerr

St. Anton, Austria: 5 February, 1983
1. Peter Luescher, Switzerland 2:04.22
2. Silvano Meli, Switzerland 2:04.82

231

3. Harti Weirather, Austria 2:05.00

4. STEVE PODBORSKI, Canada 2:05.08
15. Todd Brooker, Canada 2:06.40
24. Felix Belczyk, Canada ....
25. Robin McLeish, Canada ....
31. Doug Kerr, Canada ....
52. Chris Kent, Canada ....
DNF: Ken Read

Aspen, Colorado, USA: 6 March, 1983
1. Todd Brooker, Canada 1:47.97
2. Michael Mair, Italy 1:48.24
3. Helmut Hoeflehner, Austria 1:48.54

11. Ken Read, Canada 1:49.30
20. Robin McLeish, Canada 1:50.08
39. Paul Boivin, Canada 1:51.15
45. Bob Styan, Canada 1:51.72
47. Doug Kerr, Canada 1:51.88
50. Donald Stevens, Canada 1:52.22
51. Felix Belczyk, Canada 1:52.61

Lake Louise, Alberta, Canada: 12 March, 1983
1. Helmut Hoeflehner, Austria 1:40.52
2. Franz Klammer, Austria 1:40.74
3. Conrad Cathomen, Switzerland 1:40.77

15. Robin McLeish, Canada 1:41.68
30. Bob Styan, Canada 1:43.13
32. Felix Belczyk, Canada 1:43.18
39. Scott Shaver, Canada 1:44.24
40. Gary Athans, Canada 1:44.35
41. Doug Kerr, Canada 1:44.37
42. Paul Boivin, Canada 1:44.38
45. Chris Kent, Canada 1:44.70
48. Brian O'Rourke, Canada 1:45.08
49. Donald Stevens, Canada 1:45.54
51. Chris McIver, Canada 1:45.66
53. Jeff MacInnis, Canada 1:46.02

54. Stan Hanson, Canada 1:46.15
DNF: Todd Brooker, Ken Read

1982-83
World Cup Downhill Final Point Standings

1. Franz Klammer, Austria 95
2. Conrad Cathomen, Switzerland 92
3. Harti Weirather, Austria 74

8. Ken Read, Canada 69
11. STEVE PODBORSKI, Canada 63
33. Robin McLeish, Canada 4

1983-84

CANADIAN DOWNHILL "A" TEAM: Todd Brooker, STEVE PODBORSKI
"B" TEAM: Robin McLeish, Felix Belczyk, Paul Boivin
"C" TEAM: Gary Athans, Chris Kent

Schladming, Austria: 4 December, 1983

1. Erwin Resch, Austria 1:58.50
2. Harti Weirather, Austria 1:58.89
3. STEVE PODBORSKI, Canada 1:58.90

6. Todd Brooker, Canada 1:59.16
37. Scott Shaver, Canada 2:02.50
45. Gary Athans, Canada 2:02.98
47. Chris Kent, Canada 2:03.12
59. Paul Boivin, Canada 2:03.53
60. Stan Hanson, Canada 2:03.57
68. Chris McIver, Canada 2:04.24
DNF: Felix Belczyk

Val d'Isère, France: 9 December, 1983

1. Franz Heinzer, Switzerland 2:01.56
2. Todd Brooker, Canada 2:01.57
3. Harti Weirather, Austria 2:01.62

7. STEVE PODBORSKI, Canada 2:02.14
31. Paul Boivin, Canada 2:04.27

36. Chris Kent, Canada 2:04.56
42. Gary Athans, Canada 2:05.26
55. Scott Shaver, Canada 2:07.03
59. Chris McIver, Canada 2:07.41
66. Donald Stevens, Canada 2:08.27
DNF: Stan Hanson

Val Gardena, Italy: 18 December, 1983
1. Urs Raeber, Switzerland 1:56.80
2. Todd Brooker, Canada 1:57.41
3. STEVE PODBORSKI, Canada 1:57.69

9. Paul Boivin, Canada 1:58.67
15. Gary Athans, Canada 1:58.92
18. Chris Kent, Canada ....

Laax, Switzerland: 7 January, 1984
1. Urs Raeber, Switzerland 1:56.75
2. Franz Klammer, Austria 1:56.86
3. Michael Mair, Italy 1:57.30

17. STEVE PODBORSKI, Canada 1:58.40
38. Gary Athans, Canada 2:00.23
40. Chris Kent, Canada 2:00.38
49. Robin McLeish, Canada 2:01.41
56. Scott Shaver, Canada 2:01.76
59. Donald Stevens, Canada 2:02.12
DNF: Chris McIver, Todd Brooker, Paul Boivin

Wengen, Switzerland: 15 January, 1984
1. Bill Johnson, USA 2:10.89
2. Anton Steiner, Austria 2:11.00
3. Erwin Resch, Austria 2:11.06

5. Gary Athans, Canada 2:11.52
20. STEVE PODBORSKI, Canada 2:12.56
21. Todd Brooker, Canada 2:12.69
28. Paul Boivin, Canada 2:13.05
36. Chris Kent, Canada 2:13.59
54. Scott Shaver, Canada 2:14.46

Robin McLeish, Canada 2:14.46
57. Chris McIver, Canada 2:14.65
69. Don Stevens, Canada 2:15.76

Kitzbühel, Austria: 21 January, 1984
1. Franz Klammer, Austria 2:02.82
2. Erwin Resch, Austria 2:03.39
3. Anton Steiner, Austria 2:03.43

20. STEVE PODBORSKI, Canada 2:04.52
34. Gary Athans, Canada 2:05.94
36. Chris Kent, Canada 2:05.98
40. Paul Boivin, Canada 2:06.46
55. Robin McLeish, Canada 2:08.16
DNF: Todd Brooker

Garmisch-Partenkirchen, West Germany: 28 January, 1984
1. STEVE PODBORSKI, Canada 1:56.95
2. Erwin Resch, Austria 1:57.20
3. Franz Klammer, Austria 1:57.44

45. Gary Athans, Canada 2:01.65
48. Chris Kent, Canada 2:01.93

Cortina, Italy: 2 February, 1984
1. Helmut Hoeflehner, Austria 1:51.81
2. Urs Raeber, Switzerland 1:53.05
3. Conrad Cathomen, Switzerland 1:53.05

6. STEVE PODBORSKI, Canada 1:53.59
33. Gary Athans, Canada 1:55.75
44. Paul Boivin, Canada 1:57.96

Aspen, Colorado, USA: 4 March, 1984
1. Bill Johnson, USA 1:49.60
2. Helmut Hoeflehner, Austria 1:49.85
3. Anton Steiner, Austria 1:49.85

8. STEVE PODBORSKI, Canada 1:50.31
11. Gary Athans, Canada 1:50.60

14.	Todd Brooker, Canada	1:50.88
27.	Paul Boivin, Canada	1:51.91
28.	Robin McLeish, Canada	1:52.05
35.	Chris Kent, Canada	1:52.37
41.	Scott Shaver, Canada	1:52.64
42.	Felix Belczyk, Canada	1:52.88
48.	Chris McIver, Canada	1:53.20
54.	Donald Stevens, Canada	1:54.20

Whistler B.C., Canada: 11 March, 1984

1.	Bill Johnson, USA	2:02.85
2.	Helmut Hoeflehner, Austria	2:03.17
3.	Pirmin Zurbriggen, Switzerland	2:03.18
4.	Todd Brooker, Canada	2:03.52
5.	STEVE PODBORSKI, Canada	2:03.73
25.	Paul Boivin, Canada	2:06.25
28.	Chris Kent, Canada	2:06.63
33.	Felix Belczyk, Canada	2:07.27
37.	Gary Athans, Canada	2:07.45
38.	Robin McLeish, Canada	2:07.55

1983-84
World Cup Downhill Final Points Standing

1.	Urs Raeber, Switzerland	94
2.	Erwin Resch, Austria	91
3.	Bill Johnson, USA	87
5.	STEVE PODBORSKI, Canada	76
9.	Todd Brooker, Canada	64
21.	Gary Athans, Canada	17
30.	Paul Boivin, Canada	7

THE OLYMPIC GAMES: Sarajevo, Jugoslavia: 16 February, 1984

1.	Bill Johnson, USA	1:45.59
2.	Peter Mueller, Switzerland	1:45.86
3.	Anton Steiner, Austria	1:45.95
8.	STEVE PODBORSKI, Canada	1:46.59

9. Todd Brooker, Canada 1:46.64
26. Gary Athans, Canada 1:48.79

(Statistics courtesy of the National Alpine Ski Team/Canadian Ski Association.)